Good Governance and Human Development

S.N. Yadav
Indu Baghel

JNANADA PRAKASHAN (P&D)
NEW DELHI

Published by :
JNANADA PRAKASHAN (P&D)
4837/2, 24, Ansari Road, Daryaganj
New Delhi-110002
Phone : 011-23272047
Mobile : 9212137080

Assisted by :
TEXT BOOK PROMOTION SOCIETY OF INDIA
4837/2, 24, Ansari Road, Daryaganj
New Delhi-110002
Phone : 011-23272047
Mobile : 9212137080

Edition: 2022

Good Governance and Human Development

ISBN : 978-81-7139-252-0

Typesetting by :
Vardhman Computers
New Delhi-110017

Published by Mrs. S. Chowdhary for M/s. Jnanada Prakashan (P&D) Daryaganj, Ansari Road, New Delhi-110 002 and printed at Balaji Offset, Navin Shahdara, Delhi-110032.

Preface

Good governance is one of the most frequently used concepts in the Post-Cold War discourse on economic development and the form of government. This book exclusively deals with the concepts and characteristics of good governance and its overall impact on the contemporary economic, political and social order within the framework of sustainable human development.

The authors have made a comprehensive and critical study of the concept of governance employed in the contemporary social sciences literature. Essentially, governance stands for the process of decision-making and implemented. Broadly speaking, the notion of governance could be applied in various contexts, like corporate governance, national governance and local governance. In order to make the idea of good governance amply clear, the authors have simplified the characteristics of good governance in eight variables, like participation, rule of law, transparency, responsiveness, consensus-orientation, equity and inclusiveness, effectiveness and, efficiency and of course accountability.

Keeping in mind the broader framework of governance, the authors have paid particular attention to the problems of information and corruption and their overall impact on sustainable human development. Right to Information Act, 2005 is a major development in the direction of bringing transparency and accountability in the administration, particularly the bureaucracy. This book critically examines the current status and future prospects of the RTI in India.

Rampant corruption is one of the major hurdles in the path of economic growth and, indeed, the overall human development. In this context, it seems pertinent to point out that in Transparency International's 2008 Survey of the level of corruption in different countries, India ranks 85th out of 180 in Corruption Perception Index. The report remarkably points out that police, politics and lower judiciary are the worst dens of corruption in India.

In authors assessment, combating corruption should be the most urgent task before the government in order to have sustainable growth and development. Enactment and implementation of stringent anti-corruption measures are the prime need of the hour. The passage of the Lok Pal Bill, Corrupt Servants (Forfeiture of Property) Bill and, at the same time, ratification of the United Nations Convention against Corruption should form the top agenda of the Government of India's anti-corruption strategy.

The authors strongly feel that the publication of this book would generate wider policy debate which, in turn, could be instrumental in improving the quality of governance and sustainable human development. More significantly, this book is an important contribution to the literature on governance and human development.

S.N. Yadav

Indu Baghel

Acronyms

ADF	African Development Forum
AGR	Africa Governance Report
APIO	Assistant Public Information Officer
APRM	African Peer Review Mechanism
ARC	Administrative Reforms Commissions
BAT	British American Tobacco
BOD	Board of Director
CDP	City Data Programme
CSR	Corporate Social Responsibility
EMH	Efficient Market Hypothesis
FOI	Freedom of Information Act
FRBMA	The Fiscal Responsibility and Budget Maintenance Act
HDI	Human Development Index
ICESCR	International Covenant on Economic, Social and Cultural Rights
ICLEI	International Council for Local Environmental Initiatives
ICSA	Institute of Chartered Secretaries and Administrators
IDA	International Development Association

ISAR	International Standards of Accounting and Reporting
IULA	International Union of Local Authorities
LAC	Latin America and the Caribbean
MDF	Millennium Development Goals
MIF	Multilateral Investment Fund
NEPAD	New Partnership for Africa's Development
NGOs	Non-Governmental Organisations
PIO	Public Information Officer
RTI	Right to Information Act
SEBI	Security and Exchange Board of India
SMEs	Small and Medium Enterprises
STC	State Information Commission
UDHR	Universal Declaration of Human Rights
UMP	Urban Management Programme
UNCDP	The United Nations Committee for Development Planning
UNCED	United Nations Conference on Environment and Development
UNECA	United Nations Economic Commission for Africa
VAT	Value Added Tax

Contents

Chapter 1

Good Governance: A Conceptual Framework

Recently the terms "governance" and "good governance" are being increasingly used in the development literature. Bad governance is being increasingly regarded as one of the root causes of all evil within our societies. Major donors and international financial institutions, including the World Bank and IMF are increasingly basing their aid and loans on the condition that reforms that ensure "good governance" are undertaken. This study tries to explain, as simply as possible, what "governance" and "good governance" means.

GOVERNANCE

The concept of "governance" is not new. It is as old as human civilisation. Simply put "governance" means, the process of decision-making and also the process by which decisions are implemented or not. Governance can be used in several contexts, such as corporate governance, international governance, national governance and local governance.

Since governance is the process of decision-making and the process by which decisions are implemented, an analysis of governance focuses on the formal and informal actors involved in decision-making and implementing the decisions made and the formal and informal structures that have been set in place to arrive at and implement the decision.

Government is one of the actors in governance. Other actors involved in governance vary depending on the level of government that is under discussion. In rural areas, for example, other actors may include influential land lords, associations of peasant farmers, cooperatives, Non-Governmental Organisations (NGOs), research institutes, religious leaders, finance institutions political parties, the military etc. The situation in urban areas is much more complex. Figure 1 provides the interconnections between actors involved in urban governance. At the national level, in addition to the above actors, media, lobbyists, international donors, multi-national corporations, etc. may play a role in decision-making or in influencing the decision-making process.

All actors other than government and the military are grouped together as part of the "civil society." In some countries in addition to the civil society, organised crime syndicates also influence decision-making, particularly in urban areas and at the national level.

Similarly, formal government structures are one means by which decisions are arrived at and implemented. At the national level, informal decision-making structures, such as "kitchen cabinets" or informal advisors may exist. In urban areas, organised crime syndicates such as the "land Mafia" may influence decision-making. In some rural areas locally powerful families may make or influence decision-making. Such, informal decision-making is often the result of corrupt practices or leads to corrupt practices.

GOOD GOVERNANCE

Good governance has eight major characteristics. It is participatory, consensus oriented, accountable, transparent, responsive, effective and efficient, equitable and inclusive and follows the rule of law, It assures that corruption is minimised, the views of minorities are taken into account and that the voices of the most vulnerable in society are heard in decision-making. It is also responsive to the present and future needs of society.

Participation

Participation by both men and women is a key cornerstone of good governance. Participation could be either direct or through legitimate intermediate institutions or representatives. It is important to point out that representative democracy does not necessarily mean that the concerns of the most vulnerable in society would be taken into consideration in decision making. Participation needs to be informed and organised. This means freedom of association and expression on the one hand and an organised civil society on the other hand.

Rule of Law

Good governance requires fair legal frameworks that are enforced impartially. It also requires full protection of human rights, particularly those of minorities. Impartial enforcement of laws requires an independent judiciary and an impartial and incorruptible police force.

Transparency

Transparency means that decisions taken and their enforcement are done in a manner that follows rules and regulations. It also means that information is freely available and directly accessible to those who will be affected by such decisions and their enforcement. It also means that enough information is provided and that it is provided in easily understandable forms and media.

Responsiveness

Good governance requires that institutions and processes try to serve all stakeholders within a reasonable timeframe.

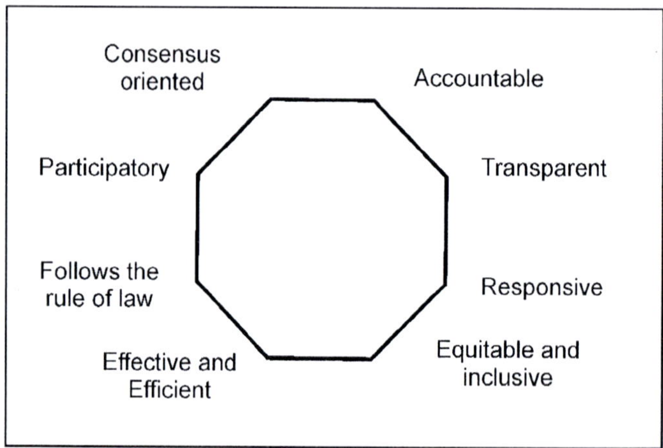

Characteristics of Good Governance

Consensus Oriented

There are several actors and as many view points in a given society. Good governance requires mediation of the different interests in society to reach a broad consensus in society on what is in the best interest of the whole community and how this can be achieved. It also requires a broad and long-term perspective on what is needed for sustainable human development and how to achieve the goals of such development. This can only result from an understanding of the historical, cultural and social contexts of a given society or community.

Equity and Inclusiveness

A society's well-being depends on ensuring that all its members feel that they have a stake in it and do not feel excluded from the mainstream of society. This requires all groups, but particularly the most vulnerable, have opportunities to improve or maintain their well being.

Effectiveness and Efficiency

Good governance means that processes and institutions produce results that meet the needs of society while making the best use of resources at their disposal. The concept of efficiency in the context of good governance also covers the sustainable use of natural resources and the protection of the environment.

Accountability

Accountability is a key requirement of good governance. Not only governmental institutions but also the private sector and civil society organisations must be accountable to the public and to their institutional stakeholders. Who is accountable to whom varies depending on whether decisions or actions taken are internal or external to an organisation or institution. In general, an organisation or an institution is accountable to those who will be affected by its decisions or actions. Accountability cannot be enforced without transparency and the rule of law.

From the above study, it is quite clear that good governance is an ideal which is difficult to achieve in its totality. Very few countries and societies have come close to achieving good governance in its totality. However, to ensure sustainable human development, actions must be taken to work towards this ideal with the aim of making it a reality.

Characteristics of Good Governance

Good governance as a concept has steadily entrenched itself in the political and development discourse. It has permeated all sectors and become part of the "common shared principles and virtues of different countries in the world. It has attained universality as an indicator of adherence to democracy and rule of law.

There is a danger, however, that good governance has become a catchword and that few bother to consider its implications. Good governance is given a broad definition that encompasses an array of issues in the socio-political and economic order of a country.

The United Nations Committee for Development Planning (UNCDP) in its report issued in 1992 entitled "Poverty Alleviation and Sustainable Development: Goals in Conflict?" identified the following as being part of the attributes of good governance:

1. Territorial and ethno-cultural representation, mechanisms for conflict resolution and for peaceful regime change and institutional renewal;
2. Checks on executive power, effective and informed legislatures, clear lines of accountability from political leaders down through the bureaucracy;
3. An open political system of law which encourages an active and vigilant civil society whose interests are represented within accountable government structures and which ensures that public offices are based on law and consent;
4. An impartial system of law, criminal justice and public order which upholds fundamental civil and political rights, protects personal security and provides a context of consistent, transparent rules for transactions that are necessary to modern economic and social development;
5. A professionally competent, capable and honest public service which operates within an accountable, rule governed framework and in which the principles of merit and the public interest are paramount;
6. The capacity to undertake sound fiscal planning, expenditure and economic management and system of financial accountability and evaluation of public-sector activities;
7. Attention not only to central government institutions and processes but also to the attributes and capacities of sub-national and local government authorities and to the issues of political devolution and administrative decentralisation.

It encompasses a broad agenda that includes effective government policies and administration, respect for the rule of law, protection of human rights and an effective civil society. However, it is imperative to point out that it is not confined only to political and social issues but also includes proper management of the economy as well as transparency and fair competition in business. In this broad definition of good governance sustainable development, especially in relation the utilisation of natural resources and environmental management, is also part of it.

Democracy and Good Governance

Good governance, to be effective and sustainable, must be anchored in a vigorous working democracy which respects the rule of law, a free press, energetic civil society organisations and effective and independent public bodies such as the Commission for Human Rights and Good governance, Prevention of Corruption Bureau and he Fair Trade Commission. The Commission is important in ensuring the promotion and protection of human rights, but also in ensuring both transparency and accountability on the part of the government. Good governance requires transparency and efficiency also in different government agencies.

At the political level, democratic practices, including transparency in policy making and administration, are important aspects of good governance. This is signified by a pluralistic political system that allows the existence of diversity in political and ideological opinions. No wonder that good governance is said to be more easily achieved and guaranteed in a multi-party system than in a mono-party system. It also means the holding of regular elections applying the principle of universal franchise. In order to qualify as democratic, elections must be free and fair.

Good governance deals with the nature and limits of state power. The doctrine of the separation of powers is, therefore, relevant in the establishment of whether or not a country has a political system that is responsive to good governance. The doctrine of the separation of powers is based on the acceptance that there are three main categories of government functions: legislative, executive, and judicial. Corresponding to these are the three main organs of government in a state - the Legislature, the Executive and the Judiciary. The doctrine insists that these three powers and functions of government in a free democracy must be kept separate and exercised by separate organs of the state.

Today, the doctrine should be taken to mean checks and balances based on a constitutional scheme. What is important today is not the separation of powers *strictu sensu,* but checks and balances. It is one of the functions of the Parliament to check the Executive. This is done by various means, including the authorisation of the budget, the scrutiny of government expenditure and the questioning of the government in parliament to account for its actions. It is the duty of the Judiciary to protect the constitution by seeing to it that the laws of the country are not contrary to the constitution.

The Judiciary stands between the citizens and the state as a balance against executive excesses or abuse of power, the transgression of constitutional or legal limitations by the Executive as well as the Legislature. This is why the Judiciary, as the custodian of the constitution, is empowered to declare an Act of Parliament as unconsti-tutional and therefore null and void. It also has the power of finding government action to be an infringement of the constitution. This has been brought about by the incorporation of fundamental freedoms and rights of the individual popularly known as the Bill of Rights in the constitution. This has resulted in the Constitution being supreme to the extent that powers of the judiciary extends to examining the validity of even an amendment to the constitution as it has been repeatedly held that no constitutional amendment can be sustained which violates the basic structure of the

Constitution. The structure of the constitution includes separation of powers.

Good Governance and Human Rights

Another equally important part of good governance is the promotion and protection of human rights. For this to be effective the rights and freedoms must be enshrined in the Constitution. This covers political and civil rights and they range from the right to life to freedom of expression. The courts of law should be independent to be able to enforce the rights of the individual vis-a-vis the state. The establishment of the Human Rights Commission is commendable and long overdue. However, there is a need to seize the opportunity, despite the inherent problems resulting from the Constitution and the Act, to advance further the protection and promotion of human rights in Tanzania.

Currently, the issue of good governance is widely regarded as one of the key ingredients for poverty reduction and sustainable development. It can be achieved in an enabling economic environment responsive to the basic needs of the people. It requires sound economic management and the sustainable use of resources as well as the promotion of economic and social rights.

ELEMENTS OF GOOD GOVERNANCE

Accountability

Accountability is imperative to make public officials answerable for government behaviour and responsive to the entity from which they derive their authority. This may be achieved differently in different countries or political structures, depending on the history, cultural milieu, and value systems involved. The mechanisms employed may vary from audit covenants, at one level, to broadly elected legislatures or more narrowly conceived consultative committees, at another.

Accountability also means establishing criteria to measure the performance of public officials, as well as oversight mechanisms to ensure that the standards are met. The litmus test is whether private actors in the economy have procedurally simple and swift recourse for redress of unfair actions or incompetence of the executive authority. Lack of accountability tends in time to reduce the state's credibility as an economic partner. It undermines the capacity of governments to sustain the long-term business confidence essential for growth-enhancing private sector investment. Looked at from this angle, accountability can help reduce sovereign risk.

The accountability of public sector institutions is facilitated by evaluation of their economic and financial performance. Economic accountability relates to the effectiveness of policy formulation and implementation, and efficiency in resource use. Financial accountability covers accounting systems for expenditure control, and internal and external audits.

Participation

The principle of participation derives from acceptance that people are at the heart of development. They are not only the ultimate beneficiaries of development, but are also the agents capacity, they act through groups or unions, chambers of commerce, nongovernmental [NGOs], political parties) and as individuals (e.g., through letters to newspaper editors, participating in radio and television talkshows, voting). Since development is both for and by people, they need to have access to the institutions that promote it (e.g., representative bureaucracies).

Participation is often related to accountability, but not necessarily so. In representative democracies, where citizens participate in government through the electoral process, public officials are, indeed, accountable ultimately to the electorate. This may not be the case, however, in other political systems (although accountability is still important). For all economies, though, the benefits of participatory approaches can be conferrable. These include improved performance and sustainability of policies, programmes, and projects, as well as enhanced capacity and skills of stakeholders.

At the grassroots level, participation implies that government structures are flexible enough to offer beneficiaries, and others affected, the opportunity to improve the design, and implementation of public programmes and projects. This increases "ownership" and enhances results. At a different level, the effectiveness of policies and institutions impinging on the economy as a whole may require the broad support and cooperation of major economic actors concerned. To the extent that the interface between public agencies and the private sector is conducive to the latter's participation in the economy, national economic performance (comprising the combined contributions of the public and private sectors) will be enhanced.

Participation in economic life by agents other than the state would cover not only the role of the private sector, but also the activities (growing in recent times) of NGOs. These elements of civil society offer an alternative means of channeling the energies of private citizens. They can be helpful in identifying people's interests, mobilising public opinion in support of these interests, and organising action accordingly. Being close to their constituents, NGOs can provide governments with a useful ally in enhancing participation at the community level and fostering a bottom-up" approach to economic and social development.

Predictability

Predictability refers to (i) the existence of laws, regulations, and policies to regulate society; and (ii) their fair and consistent application. The importance of predictability cannot be overstated since, without it, the orderly existence of citizens and institutions would be impossible. The rule of law encompasses both well-defined rights and duties, as well as mechanisms for enforcing them, and settling disputes in an impartial manner. It requires the state and its subsidiary agencies to be as much bound by, and answerable to, the legal system as are private individuals and enterprises.

The importance of rule-based systems for economic life is obvious. They are an essential component of the environment within which economic actors plan and take investment decisions. To the extent, therefore, that legal frameworks help ensure that (i) business risks can *be* assessed rationally, (ii) transaction costs are lowered, and (iii) governmental arbitrariness is minimised, they should prove conducive to risk taking, growth, and development. In the opposite scenario, the capricious application of rules generates uncertainty and inhibits the growth of private sector initiatives. Regulatory uncertainty also tends to raise the cost of capital by increasing the risk of investment.[1]

Besides legal and regulatory frameworks, consistency of public policy is also important. Government policies affect the investment climate directly, and economic actors require reasonable assurance about the future behaviour of key variables such as prices, the exchange rate, and employment levels. However, consistency does not mean rigidity. Governments do need to respond flexibly to changing circumstances and to make midcourse corrections, as necessary. Also, when governments change, the successor administration will, understandably, want public policy to reflect its priorities, rather than those of its predecessor. Barring such situations, though, consistency in the broad directions of government policy is valuable (with modifications being limited, as far as possible, to fine-tuning).

Predictability can be enhanced through appropriate institutional arrangements. For example, it has been argued that an autonomous central bank could lead to more predictable monetary and exchange rate policies. Many governments face the challenge of regulating money supply, while pursuing expansionary fiscal policies to encourage investment. In such situations, if monetary policy is too accommodating, inflationary pressures can put investor confidence at risk, thus defeating the very objective of the fiscal policy. In some countries, managing the fiscal deficit made more difficult by compulsions to bail out a politically manipulated banking sector. Granting greater autonomy to the central bank is one way that governments can signal investors that macroeconomic policy will be prudent and sound. Insulating economic ministries from political pressures can have similar benefits, but may be even more difficult to achieve.

Transparency

Transparency refers to the availability of information to the general public and clarity about government rules, regulations, and decisions. Thus, it both complements and reinforces predictability. The difficulty with ensuring transparency is that only the generator of information may know about it, and may limit access to it Hence, it may be useful to strengthen the citizens' right to information with' a degree of legal enforceability, For similar reasons, broadly restrictive laws that permit public officials to deny information to citizens (e.g., an Official Secrets Act) need to provide for independent review of claims that such denial is justified in the greater public interest.

Access to accurate and timely information about the economy and government policies can be vital for economic decision making by the private sector. On this basis of efficiency alone, such data should be freely and readily available to economic agents. While this is true across all areas of the economy, it is especially relevant in the case of those sectors that are intrinsically information intensive, such as the financial sector in general and capital markets in particular.

Transparency in government decision-making and public policy implementation reduces uncertainty and can help inhibit corruption among public officials. To this end, rules and procedures that are simple, straightforward, and easy to apply are preferable to those that provide discretionary powers to government officials or that are susceptible to different interpretations. However well-intentioned the latter type of rule might be in theory, its purpose can be vitiated in practice through error or otherwise.[2]

In practice, though, it may sometimes be necessary to place limits on the principle of transparency. In doing so, it may be helpful to distinguish information as a commodity from information as a process. For example, intellectual property rights may need to be protected in order to encourage innovation and invention; but decision making on the establishment of intellectual property and rights thereto (i.e., to whom they are granted and why) should be transparent.

REFERENCES

1. The Regulation of Private Monopoly in Developing Countries, Price Waterhouse, London, April 1994.
2. For example, a uniform tariff rate (where merchants know exactly what customs duty payment is required) is preferable, on this ground, to multiple tariff rates that offer customs officials discretion over the classification of.

Chapter 2

Governance Promotion Through Right to Information: The Indian Scenario

The Right to Information Act 2005 (Act No. 22/2005)[1] is a law enacted by the Parliament of India giving citizens of India access to records of the Central Government and State Governments.[2] The Act applies to all States and Union Territories of India, except the State of Jammu and Kashmir which is covered under a State-level law. Under the provisions of the Act, any citizen (including the citizens within J&K) may request information from a "public authority" (a body of Government or "instrumentality of State") which is required to reply expeditiously or within thirty days. The Act also requires every public authority to computerise their records for wide dissemination and to proactively publish certain categories of information so that the citizens need minimum recourse to request for information formally.

This law was passed by Parliament on 15 June 2005 and came fully into force on 13 October 2005.[3] Information disclosure in India was hitherto restricted by the Official Secrets Act 1923 and various other special laws which the new RTI Act now relaxes.

Background

Disclosure of Government Information in India is governed by a law enacted during the British/rule over large parts of what is now India, the Official Secrets Act of 1889 which was amended in 1923.[4] This law secures information related to security of the State, sovereignty of the country and friendly-relations with foreign states, and contains provisions which prohibit disclosure of nonclassified information.[5] Civil Service conduct rules and the Indian Evidence Act impose further restrictions on government officials' powers to disclose information to the public.[6]

In 1975, the Supreme Court delivered a landmark judgement[7] on the citizen's Right to Know.

State-level Laws

The RTI Laws were first successfully enacted by the state governments—Tamil Nadu (1997),[8] Goa (1997). Rajasthan (2000). Karnataka (2000), Delhi (2001), Maharashtra (2002), Madhya Pradesh (2003), Assam (2002) and Jammu and Kashmir (2004).

The Muharashtra and Delhi State level enactments are considered to have been the most widely used. The Delhi and J&K Right to Information Acts are still in force.

Freedom of Information Act (FOI)

Passage of a national level law, however, proved to be a difficult task. Given the experience of state governments in passing practicable legislation, the Central Government appointed a working group under H.D. Shourie and assigned it the task of drafting legislation. The Shourie draft, in an extremely diluted form, was the basis for the Freedom of Information Bill, 2000 which eventually became law under the freedom of Information Act. 2002. This Act was severely criticised for permitting too many exemptions, not only under the standard grounds of national security and sovereignty, but also for requests that would involve "disproportionate diversion of the resources of a public authority". There was no upper limit on the charges that could be levied. There were no penalties for not complying with a request for information, the FoI Act consequently, never came into effective force.

Enactment

The doomed FoI Act led to sustained pressure for a better National RTI enactment. The first draft of the Right to Information Bill was presented to Parliament on 22 December 2004. After intense debate, more than a hundred amendments to the draft Bill were made between December 2004 and 15 June 2005, when the hill finally passed. The Act came fully into effect on 13 October 2005.

Scope

The Act covers the whole of India except Jammu and Kashmir.[9] It is applicable to all constitutional authorities including the executive, legislature and judiciary; any institution or body established or constituted by an act of Parliament or a state legislature. It is also defined in the Act that bodies or authorities established or constituted by order or notification of appropriate government including bodies "owned, controlled or substantially financed" by government, or non-Government organisations "substantially financed, directly or indirectly by funds" provided by the government are also covered in the Act's ambit.[10]

Private bodies are not within the Act's ambit directly. However, information that can be accessed under any other law in force by a public authority can also be requested for. In a landmark decision of 30-Nov-2006 ('Sarhajit Roy versus DERC') the Central Information Commission also reaffirmed that privatised public utility companies continue to be within the RTI Act- their privatisation notwithstanding. The Act also explicitly overrides the Official Secrets Act and other laws in force on 15 June 2005 to the extent of any inconsistency.

Information

The Act specifies that citizens have a right to:

- request any information (as defined)
- lake copies of documents
- inspect documents, works and records
- take certified samples of materials of work.
- obtain information in form of printouts, diskettes, floppies, tapes, video cassettes or in any other electronic mode or through printouts.

Process

Under the Act, all authorities covered must appoint their Public Information Officer (PIO). Any person may submit a request to the PIO for information in writing. It is the PIO's obligation to provide information to citizens of India who request information under the Act. If the request pertains to another public authority (in whole or part) it is the PIO's responsibility to transfer/forward the concerned portions of the request to a PIO of the other within 5 days. In addition, every public authority is required to designate Assistant Public Information Officers (APIOs) to receive RTI requests and appeals for forwarding to the PIOs of their public authority. The citizen making the request is not obliged to disclose any information except his name and contact particulars.

The Act specifies time limits for replying to the request.

- If the request has been made to the PIO, the reply is to be given within 30 days of receipt.
- If the request has been made to an APIO, the reply is to be given within 35 days of receipt.
- If the PIO transfers the request to another public authority (better concerned with the information requested), the time allowed to reply is 30 days but computed from the day after it is received by the

PIO of the transferee authority

- Information concerning corruption and Human Rights violations by scheduled Security agencies (those listed in the Second Schedule to the Act) is to be provided within 45 days but with the prior approval of the Central Information Commission.
- However if life or liberty of any person is involved, the PIO is expected to reply within 48 hours.

Since the information is to be paid for, the reply of the PIO is necessarily limited to either denying the request (in whole or part) and/or providing a computation of "further fees". The time between the reply of 'the PIO and the time taken to deposit the further fees for information is excluded from the time allowed.

It information is not provided within this period, it is treated as deemed refusal. Refusal with or without reasons may he ground for appeal or complaint. Further, information not provided in the times prescribed is to he provided free of charge.

For Central Departments as of 2006, there is a fee of Rs. 10 for filing the request, Rs. 2 per page of information and Rs. 5 for each hour of inspection after the first hour. If the applicant is a Below Poverty Card holder then no See shall apply. Such BPL Card holders have to provide a copy of their BPL card along with their application to the Public Authority. States Government and High Courts fix their own rules.

Information Defined

In terms of the section 2 of the Act, information has been defined as any material in any form including records, documents, memos, e-mails, opinions, advices, press releases, circulars, orders, logbooks, contracts, reports, papers, samples, models, data material held in any electronic form and information relating to any private body which can be accessed by a public authority under any other law for the time being in force.

Right to Information

Under the Act (section 2 (j), right to information includes the right to:

- inspect works, documents, records.
- lake notes, extracts or certified copies of documents or records.
- take certified samples of material.
- obtain information in form of printouts, diskettes, floppies, tapes, video cassettes or in any other electronic mode or through printouts.

What is not open to disclosure?

The following is exempt from disclosure [section 8)]

- information disclosure of which would prejudicially affect the sovereignty and integrity of India, the security, "strategic, scientific or economic" interests of the State, relation with foreign State or lead to incitement of an offence;
- information which has been expressly forbidden to be published by any court of law or tribunal or the disclosure of which may constitute contempt of court;
- information, the disclosure of which would cause a breach of privilege of Parliament or the State Legislature;
- information including commercial confidence, trade secrets or intellectual property, the disclosure of which would harm the competitive position of a third party, unless the competent authority is satisfied that larger public interest warrants the disclosure of such information;
- information available to a person in his fiduciary relationship, unless the competent authority is

satisfied that the larger public interest warrants the disclosure of such information;

- information received in confidence from foreign Government;
- information, the disclosure of which would endanger the life or physical safety of any person or identify the source of information or assistance given in confidence for law enforcement or security purposes;
- information which would impede the process of investigation or apprehension or prosecution of offenders;
- cabinet papers including records of deliberations of the Council of Ministers, Secretaries and other officers;
- information which relates to personal information the disclosure of which has no relationship to an) public activity or interest, or which would cause unwarranted invasion of the privacy of the individual, but, it is also provided that the information which cannot be denied to the Parliament or a State Legislature shall not be denied by this exemption;
- Notwithstanding any of the exemptions listed above, a public authority may allow access to information, if public interest in disclosure outweighs the harm to the protected interests. (NB: This provision is qualified by the proviso to sub-section 11(1) of the Act which exempts disclosure of "trade or commercial secrets protected by law" under this clause when read along with K(l)(d))

Partial Disclosure

Section 10 of the Act allows those part(s) of the record which are not exempt from disclosure and which can reasonably be severed from every part that contains exempt information to be provided.

Exclusions

Central Intelligence and Security agencies specified in the Second Schedule like IB, RAW, Directorate of Revenue Intelligence. Central Economic Intelligence Bureau, Directorate of Enforcement, Narcotics Control Bureau. Aviation Research Centre, Special Frontier Force, BSF, CRPF, ITBP, CISF, NSG, Assam Riltes, Special Service Bureau, Special Branch (CID), Andaman and Nicobar, The Crime Branch-CID-CB. Dadra and Nagar Haveli and Special Branch, Lakshadweep Police. Agencies specified by the State Governments through a Notification will also be excluded. The exclusion, however, is not absolute and these organisations have an obligation to provide information pertaining to allegations of corruption and human rights violations. Further, information relating to allegations of human rights violation could be given but only with the approval of the Central or State Information Commission

Role of the Government

Section 26 of the Act enjoins the central government, as also the state governments of the Republic of India (excluding J&K), to initiate necessary steps to:

- Develop educational programmes for the public especially disadvantaged communities on RTI.
- Encourage Public Authorities to participate in the development and organisation of such programmes.
- Promote timely dissemination of accurate information to the public.
- Train officers and develop training materials.
- Compile and disseminate a User Guide for the public in the respective official language.
- Publish names, designation postal addresses and contact details of PIOs and other information such as notices regarding fees to be paid, remedies available in law if request is rejected etc.

Power to make rules

- The Central Government, State Governments and the Competent Authorities as defined in section 2(e) are vested with powers to make rules to carry out the provisions of the Right to Information Act, 2005. (section 27 & section 28)

Who has the power to deal with the difficulties while implementing this act?

- If any difficulty arises in giving effect to the provisions in the Act, the Central Government may, by Order published in the Official Gazette, make provisions necessary/expedient for removing the difficulty. (section 30)

Effects

. In the first year of National RTI 42.876 (not yet official) applications for information were filed to Central (i.e. Federal) public authorities. Of these 878 were disputed at the final appellate stage—the Central Information Commission at New Delhi. A few of these decisions have thereafter been mired in further legal controversy in the various High Courts of India. The first stay order against a final appellate decision of the Central Information Commission was granted on 3 May, 2006 by the High Court of Delhi in WP(C) 6833-35/2006 cited as "NDPL & Ors. versus Central Information Commission & Ors". The Government of India's purported intention in 2006 to amend the RTI Act was postponed after public disquiet.

ANNEXURE 1

THE RIGHT TO INFORMATION ACT, 2005 NO. 22 OF 2005

[15th June, 2005]

An Act to provide for setting out the practical regime of right to information for citizens to secure access to information under the control of public authorities, in order to promote transparency and accountability in the working of every public authority, the constitution of a Central Information Commission and State Information Commissions and for matters connected therewith or incidental thereto.

Whereas the Constitution of India has established democratic Republic;

And whereas democracy requires an informed citizenry and transparency of information which are vital to its functioning and also to contain corruption and to hold Governments and their instrumentalities accountable to the governed;

And whereas revelation of information in actual practice is likely to conflict with other public interests including efficient operations of the Governments, optimum use of limited fiscal resources and the preservation of confidentiality of sensitive information;

And whereas it is necessary to harmonise these conflicting interests while preserving the paramountcy of the democratic ideal;

Now, therefore, it is expedient to provide for furnishing certain information to citizens who desire to have it. Be it enacted by Parliament in the Fifty-sixth Year of the Republic of India as follows:

Chapter I

Preliminary

1. (1) This Act may be called the Right to Information Act, 2005.

   (2) It extends to the whole of India except the State of Jammu and Kashmir.

   (3) The provisions of sub-section (1) of section 4, sub-sections (1) and (2) of section 5, sections 12, 13, 15,16,

24, 27 and 28 shall come into force at once, and the remaining provisions of this Act shall come into force on the one hundred and twentieth day of its enactment.

2. In this Act, unless the context otherwise requires,—

(a) **"appropriate Government"** means in relation to a public authority which is established, constituted, owned, controlled or substantially financed by funds provided directly or indirectly—

(i) by the Central Government or the Union territory administration, the Central Government;

(ii) by the State Government, the State Government;

(b) **"Central Information Commission"** means the Central Information Commission constituted under sub-section (1) of section 12;

(c) **"Central Public Information Officer"** means the Central Public Information Officer designated under sub-section (1) and includes a Central Assistant Public Information Officer designated as such under sub-section (2) of section 5;

(d) **"Chief Information Commissioner" and "Information Commissioner"** mean the Chief Information Commissioner and Information Commissioner appointed under sub-section (3) of section 12;

(e) **"competent authority"** means—

(i) the Speaker in the case of the House of the People or the Legislative Assembly of a State or a Union territory having such Assembly and the Chairman in the case of the Council of States or Legislative Council of a State;

(ii) the Chief Justice of India in the case of the Supreme Court;

(iii) the Chief Justice of the High Court in the case of a High Court;

(iv) the President or the Governor, as the case may be, in the case of other authorities established or constituted by or under the Constitution;

(v) the administrator appointed under article 239 of the Constitution;

(f) **"information"** means any material in any form, including records, documents, memos, e-mails, opinions, advices, press releases, circulars, orders, logbooks, contracts, reports, papers, samples, models, data material held in any electronic form and information relating to any private body which can be accessed by a public authority under any other law for the time being in force;

(g) **"prescribed"** means prescribed by rules made under this Act by the appropriate Government or the competent authority, as the case may be;

(h) **"public authority"** means any authority or body or institution of self- government established or constituted—

(a) by or under the Constitution;

(b) by any other law made by Parliament;

(c) by any other law made by State Legislature;

(d) by notification issued or order made by the appropriate Government, and includes any—

(i) body owned, controlled or substantially financed;

(ii) non-Government organisation substantially financed, directly or indirectly by funds provided by the appropriate Government;

(i) **"record"** includes—

(a) any document, manuscript and file;

(b) any microfilm, microfiche and facsimile copy of a document;

(c) any reproduction of image or images embodied in such microfilm (whether enlarged or not); and

(d) any other material produced by a computer or any other device;

(j) **"right to information"** means the right to information accessible under this Act which is held by or under the control of any public authority and includes the right to—

(i) inspection of work, documents, records;

(ii) taking notes, extracts or certified copies of documents or records;

(iii) taking certified samples of material;

(iv) obtaining information in the form of diskettes, floppies, tapes, video cassettes or in any other electronic mode or through printouts where such information is stored in a computer or in any other device;

(k) **"State Information Commission (STC)"** means the State Information Commission constituted under sub-section (1) of section 15;

(l) **"State Chief Information Commissioner"** and "State Information Commissioner" mean the State Chief Information Commissioner and the State Information Commissioner appointed under sub-section (3) of section 15;

(m) **"State Public Information Officer"** means the State Public Information Officer designated under sub-section (1) and includes a State Assistant Public Information Officer designated as such under sub-section (2) of section 5;

(n) **"third party"** means a person other than the citizen making a request for information and includes a public authority.

Chapter II

Right to information and obligations of public authorities

3. Subject to the provisions of this Act, all citizens shall have the right to information.

4. (1) Every public authority shall—

(a) maintain all its records duly catalogued and indexed in a manner and the form which facilitates the right to information under this Act and ensure that all records that are appropriate to be computerised are, within a reasonable time and subject to availability of resources, computerised and connected through a network all over the country on different systems so that access to such records is facilitated;

(b) publish within one hundred and twenty days from the enactment of this Act,—

(i) the particulars of its organisation, functions and duties;

(ii) the powers and duties of its officers and employees;

(iii) the procedure followed in the decision making process, including channels of supervision and accountability;

(iv) the norms set by it for the discharge of its functions;

(v) the rules, regulations, instructions, manuals and records, held by it or under its control or used by its employees for discharging its functions;

(vi) a statement of the categories of documents that are held by it or under its control;

(vii) the particulars of-any arrangement that exists for consultation with, or representation by, the members of the public in relation to the formulation of its policy or implementation thereof;

(viii) a statement of the boards, councils, committees and other bodies consisting of two or more persons constituted as its part or for the purpose of its advice, and as to whether meetings of those boards, councils, committees and other bodies are open to the public, or the minutes of such meetings are accessible for public;

(ix) a directory of its officers and employees;

(x) the monthly remuneration received by each of its officers and employees, including the system of compensation as provided in its regulations;

(xi) the budget allocated to each of its agency, indicating the particulars of all plans, proposed expenditures and reports on disbursements made;

(xii) the manner of execution of subsidy programmes, including the amounts allocated and the details of beneficiaries of such programmes;

(xiii) particulars of recipients of concessions, permits or authorisations granted by it;

(xiv) details in respect of the information, available to or held by it, reduced in an electronic form;

(xv) the particulars of facilities available to citizens for obtaining information, including the working hours of a library or reading room, if maintained for public use;

(xvi) the names, designations and other particulars of the Public Information Officers;

(xvii) such other information as may be prescribed and thereafter update these publications every year;

(c) publish all relevant facts while formulating important policies or announcing the decisions which affect public;

(d) provide reasons for its administrative or quasi-judicial decisions to affected persons.

(2) It shall be a constant endeavour of every public authority to take steps in accordance with the requirements of clause (b) of sub-section (1) to provide as much information suo motu to the public at regular intervals through various means of communications, including internet, so that the public have minimum resort to the use of this Act to obtain information.

(3) For the purposes of sub-section (1), every information shall be disseminated widely and in such form and manner which is easily accessible to the public.

(4) All materials shall be disseminated taking into consideration the cost effectiveness, local language and

the most effective method of communication in that local area and the information should be easily accessible, to the extent possible in electronic format with the Central Public Information Officer or State Public Information Officer, as the case may be, available free or at such cost of the medium or the print cost price as may be prescribed.

Explanation.—For the purposes of sub-sections (3) and (4), "disseminated" means making known or communicated the information to the public through notice boards, newspapers, public announcements, media broadcasts, the internet or any other means, including inspection of offices of any public authority.

5. (1) Every public authority shall, within one hundred days of the enactment of this Act, designate as many officers as the Central Public Information Officers or State Public Information Officers, as the case may be, in all administrative units or offices under it as may be necessary to provide information to persons requesting for the information under this Act.

(2) Without prejudice to the provisions of sub-section (1), every public authority shall designate an officer, within one hundred days of the enactment of this Act, at each sub-divisional level or other sub-district level as a Central Assistant Public Information Officer or a State Assistant Public Information Officer, as the case may be, to receive the applications for information or appeals under this Act for forwarding the same forthwith to the Central Public Information Officer or the State Public Information Officer or senior officer specified under sub-section (1) of section 19 or the Central Information Commission or the State Information Commission, as the case may be:

Provided that where an application for information or appeal is given to a Central Assistant Public Information Officer or a State Assistant Public Information Officer, as the case may be, a period of five days shall be added in computing the period for response specified under sub-section (1) of section 7.

(3) Every Central Public Information Officer or State Public Information Officer, as the case may be, shall deal with requests from persons seeking information and render reasonable assistance to the persons seeking such information.

(4) The Central Public Information Officer or State Public Information Officer, as the case may be, may seek the assistance of any other officer as he or she considers it necessary for the proper discharge of his or her duties.

(5) Any officer, whose assistance has been sought under sub-section (4), shall render all assistance to the Central Public Information Officer or State Public Information Officer, as the case may be, seeking his or her assistance and for the purposes of any contravention of the provisions of this Act, such other officer shall be treated as a Central Public Information Officer or State Public Information Officer, as the case may be.

6. (1) A person, who desires to obtain any information under this Act, shall make a request in writing or through electronic means in English or Hindi or in the official language of the area in which the application is being made, accompanying such fee as may be prescribed, to—

(a) the Central Public Information Officer or State Public Information Officer, as the case may be, of the concerned public authority;

(b) the Central Assistant Public Information Officer or State Assistant Public Information Officer, as the case may be,

specifying the particulars of the information sought by him or her:

Provided that where such request cannot be made in writing, the Central Public Information Officer or State Public Information Officer, as the case may be, shall render all reasonable assistance to the person making the request orally to reduce the same in writing.

(2) An applicant making request for information shall not be required to give any reason for requesting the information or any other personal details except those that may be necessary for contacting him.

(3) Where an application is made to a public authority requesting for an information,—

(i) which is held by another public authority; or

(ii) the subject matter of which is more closely connected with the functions of another public authority,

the public authority, to which such application is made, shall transfer the application or such part of it as may be appropriate to that other public authority and inform the applicant immediately about such transfer:

Provided that the transfer of an application pursuant to this sub-section shall be made as soon as practicable but in no case later than five days from the date of receipt of the application.

7. (1) Subject to the proviso to sub-section (2) of section 5 or the proviso to sub-section (3) of section 6, the Central Public Information Officer or State Public Information Officer, as the case may be, on receipt of a request under section 6 shall, as expeditiously as possible, and in any case within thirty days of the receipt of the request, either provide the information on payment of such fee as may be prescribed or reject the request for any of the reasons specified in sections 8 and 9:

Provided that where the information sought for concerns the life or liberty of a person, the same shall be provided within forty-eight hours of the receipt of the request.

(2) If the Central Public Information Officer or State Public Information Officer, as the case may be, fails to give decision on the request for information within the period specified under subsection (1), the Central Public Information Officer or State Public Information Officer, as the case may be, shall be deemed to have refused the request.

(3) Where a decision is taken to provide the information on payment of any further fee representing the cost of providing the information, the Central Public Information Officer or State Public Information Officer, as the case may be, shall send an intimation to the person making the request, giving—

(a) the details of further fees representing the cost of providing the information as determined by him, together with the calculations made to arrive at the amount in accordance with fee prescribed under sub-section (1), requesting him to deposit that fees, and the period intervening between the despatch of the said intimation and payment of fees shall be excluded for the purpose of calculating the period of thirty days referred to in that sub-section;

(b) information concerning his or her right with respect to review the decision as to the amount of fees charged or the form of access provided, including the particulars of the appellate authority, time limit, process and any other forms.

(4) Where access to the record or a part thereof is required to be provided under this Act and the person to whom access is to be provided is sensorily disabled, the Central Public Information Officer or State Public Information Officer, as the case may be, shall provide assistance to enable access to the information, including providing such assistance as may be appropriate for the inspection.

(5) Where access to information is to be provided in the printed or in any electronic format, the applicant shall, subject to the provisions of sub-section (6), pay such fee as may be prescribed:

Provided that the fee prescribed under sub-section (1) of section 6 and sub-sections (1) and (5) of section 7 shall be reasonable and no such fee shall be charged from the persons who are of below poverty line as may be determined by the appropriate Government.

(6) Notwithstanding anything contained in sub-section (5), the person making request for the information shall be provided the information free of charge where a public authority fails to comply with the time limits specified in sub-section (1).

(7) Before taking any decision under sub-section (1), the Central Public Information Officer or State Public Information Officer, as the case may be, shall take into

consideration the representation made by a third party under section 11.

(8) Where a request has been rejected under sub-section (1), the Central Public Information Officer or State Public Information Officer, as the case may be, shall communicate to the person making the request,—

(i) the reasons for such rejection;

(ii) the period within which an appeal against such rejection may be preferred; and

(iii) the particulars of the appellate authority.

(9) An information shall ordinarily be provided in the form in which it is sought unless it would disproportionately divert the resources of the public authority or would be detrimental to the safety or preservation of the record in question.

8. (1) Notwithstanding anything contained in this Act, there shall be no obligation to give any citizen,—

(a) information, disclosure of which would prejudicially affect the sovereignty and integrity of India, the security, strategic, scientific or economic interests of the State, relation with foreign State or lead to incitement of an offence;

(b) information which has been expressly forbidden to be published by any court of law or tribunal or the disclosure of which may constitute contempt of court;

(c) information, the disclosure of which would cause a breach of privilege of Parliament or the State Legislature;

(d) information including commercial confidence, trade secrets or intellectual property, the disclosure of which would harm the competitive position of a third party, unless the competent authority is satisfied that larger public interest warrants the disclosure of such information; (e) information available to a person in his fiduciary relationship, unless the competent authority is satisfied that the larger public interest warrants the disclosure of such information;

(f) information received in confidence from foreign Government;

(g) information, the disclosure of which would endanger the life or physical safety of any person or identify the source of information or assistance given in confidence for law enforcement or security purposes;

(h) information which would impede the process of investigation or apprehension or prosecution of offenders;

(i) cabinet papers including records of deliberations of the Council of Ministers, Secretaries and other officers:

Provided that the decisions of Council of Ministers, the reasons thereof, and the material on the basis of which the decisions were taken shall be made public after the decision has been taken, and the matter is complete, or over:

Provided further that those matters which come under the exemptions specified in this section shall not be disclosed;

(j) information which relates to personal information the disclosure of which has no relationship to any public activity or interest, or which would cause unwarranted invasion of the privacy of the individual unless the Central Public Information Officer or the State Public Information Officer or the appellate authority, as the case may be, is satisfied that the larger public interest justifies the disclosure of such information:

Provided that the information which cannot be denied to the Parliament or a State Legislature shall not be denied to any person.

(2) Notwithstanding anything in the Official Secrets Act, 1923 nor any of the exemptions permissible in accordance with sub-section (1), a public authority may

allow access to information, if public interest in disclosure outweighs the harm to the protected interests.

(3) Subject to the provisions of clauses (a), (c) and (i) of sub-section (1), any information relating to any occurrence, event or matter which has taken place, occurred or happened twenty years before the date on which any request is made under secton 6 shall be provided to any person making a request under that section:

Provided that where any question arises as to the date from which the said period of twenty ' years has to be computed, the decision of the Central Government shall be final, subject to the usual appeals provided for in this Act.

9. Without prejudice to the provisions of section 8, a Central Public Information Officer or a State

Public Information Officer, as the case may be, may reject a request for information where such a request for providing access would involve an infringement of copyright subsisting in a person other than the State.

10. (1) Where a request for access to information is rejected on the ground that it is in relation to information which is exempt from disclosure, then, notwithstanding anything contained in this Act, access may be provided to that part of the record which does not contain any information which is exempt from disclosure under this Act and which can reasonably be severed from any part that contains exempt information.

(2) Where access is granted to a part of the record under sub-section (1), the Central Public Information Officer or State Public Information Officer, as the case may be, shall give a notice to the applicant, informing—

(a) that only part of the record requested, after severance of the record containing information which is exempt from disclosure, is being provided;

(b) the reasons for the decision, including any findings on any material question of fact, referring to the material on which those findings were based;

(c) the name and designation of the person giving the decision;

(d) the details of the fees calculated by him or her and the amount of fee which the applicant is required to deposit; and

(e) his or her rights with respect to review of the decision regarding non-disclosure of part of the information, the amount of fee charged or the form of access provided, including the particulars of the senior officer specified under sub-section (1) of section 19 or the Central Information Commission or the State Information Commission, as the case may be, time limit, process and any other form of access.

11. (1) Where a Central Public Information Officer or a State Public Information Officer, as the case may be, intends to disclose any information or record, or part thereof on a request made under this Act, which relates to or has been supplied by a third party and has been treated as confidential by that third party, the Central Public Information Officer or State Public Information Officer, as the case may be, shall, within five days from the receipt of the request, give a written notice to such third party of the request and of the fact that the Central Public Information Officer or State Public Information Officer, as the case may be, intends to disclose the information or record, or part thereof, and invite the third party to make a submission in writing or orally, regarding whether the information should be disclosed, and such submission of the third party shall be kept in view while taking a decision about disclosure of information:

Provided that except in the case of trade or commercial secrets protected by law, disclosure may be allowed if the public interest in disclosure outweighs in importance any possible harm or injury to the interests of such third party.

(2) Where a notice is served by the Central Public Information Officer or State Public Information Officer,

as the case may be, under sub-section (1) to a third party in respect of any information or record or part thereof, the third party shall, within ten days from the date of receipt of such notice, be given the opportunity to make representation against the proposed disclosure.

(3) Notwithstanding anything contained in section 7, the Central Public Information Officer or State Public Information Officer, as the case may be, shall, within forty days after receipt of the request under section 6, if the third party has been given an opportunity to make representation under sub-section (2), make a decision as to whether or not to disclose the information or record or part thereof and give in writing the notice of his decision to the third party.

(4) A notice given under sub-section (3) shall include a statement that the third party to whom the notice is given is entitled to prefer an appeal under section 19 against the decision.

Chapter III

The Central Information Commission

12. (1) The Central Government shall, by notification in the Official Gazette, constitute a body to be known as the Central Information Commission to exercise the powers conferred on, and to perform the functions assigned to, it under this Act.

(2) The Central Information Commission shall consist of—

(a) the Chief Information Commissioner; and

(b) such number of Central Information Commissioners, not exceeding ten, as may be deemed necessary.

(3) The Chief Information Commissioner and Information Commissioners shall be appointed by the President on the recommendation of a committee consisting of—

(i) the Prime Minister, who shall be the Chairperson of the committee;

(ii) the Leader of Opposition in the Lok Sabha; and

(iii) a Union Cabinet Minister to be nominated by the Prime Minister.

Explanation.—For the purposes of removal of doubts, it is hereby declared that where the Leader of Opposition in the House of the People has not been recognised as such, the Leader of the single largest group in opposition of the Government in the House of the People shall be deemed to be the Leader of Opposition.

(4) The general superintendence, direction and management of the affairs of the Central Information Commission shall vest in the Chief Information Commissioner who shall be assisted by the Information Commissioners and may exercise all such powers and do all such acts and things which may be exercised or done by the Central Information Commission autonomously without being subjected to directions by any other authority under this Act.

(5) The Chief Information Commissioner and Information Commissioners shall be persons of eminence in-public life with wide knowledge and experience in law, science and technology, social service, management, journalism, mass media or administration and governance.

(6) The Chief Information Commissioner or an Information Commissioner shall not be a Member of Parliament or Member of the Legislature of any State or Union territory, as the case may be, or hold any other office of profit or connected with any political party or carrying on any business or pursuing any profession.

(7) The headquarters of the Central Information Commission shall be at Delhi and the Central Information Commission may, with the previous approval of the Central Government, establish offices at other places in India.

13. (1) The Chief Information Commissioner shall hold office for a term of five years from the date on which he enters upon his office and shall not be eligible for reappointment:

Provided that no Chief Information Commissioner shall hold office as such after he has attained the age of sixty-five years.

(2) Every Information Commissioner shall hold office for a term of five years from the date on which he enters upon his office or till he attains the age of sixty-five years, whichever is earlier, and shall not be eligible for reappointment as such Information Commissioner:

Provided that every Information Commissioner shall, on vacating his office under this sub-section be eligible for appointment as the Chief Information Commissioner in the manner specified in sub-section (3) of section 12:

Provided further that where the Information Commissioner is appointed as the Chief Information Commissioner, his term of office shall not be more than five years in aggregate as the Information Commissioner and the Chief Information Commissioner.

(3) The Chief Information Commissioner or an Information Commissioner shall before he enters upon his office make and subscribe before the President or some other person appointed by him in that behalf, an oath or affirmation according to the form set out for the purpose in the First Schedule.

(4) The Chief Information Commissioner or an Information Commissioner may, at any time, by writing under his hand addressed to the President, resign from his office:

Provided that the Chief Information Commissioner or an Information Commissioner may be removed in the manner specified under section 14.

(5) The salaries and allowances payable to and other terms and conditions of service of—

(a) the Chief Information Commissioner shall be the same as that of the Chief Election Commissioner;

(b) an Information Commissioner shall be the same as that of an Election Commissioner:

Provided that if the Chief Information Commissioner or an Information Commissioner, at the time of his appointment is, in receipt of a pension, other than a disability or wound pension, in respect of any previous service under the Government of India or under the Government of a State, his salary in respect of the service as the Chief Information Commissioner or an Information Commissioner shall be reduced by the amount of that pension including any portion of pension which was commuted and pension equivalent of other forms of retirement benefits excluding pension equivalent of retirement gratuity:

Provided further that if the Chief Information Commissioner or an Information Commissioner if, at the time of his appointment is, in receipt of retirement benefits in respect of any previous service rendered in a Corporation established by or under any Central Act or State Act or a Government company owned or controlled by the Central Government or the State Government, his salary in respect of the service as the Chief Information Commissioner or an Information Commissioner shall be reduced by the amount of pension equivalent to the retirement benefits:

Provided also that the salaries, allowances and other conditions of service of the Chief Information Commissioner and the Information Commissioners shall not be varied to their disadvantage after their appointment.

(6) The Central Government shall provide the Chief Information Commissioner and the Information Commissioners with such officers and employees as may be necessary for the efficient performance of their functions under this Act, and the salaries and allowances payable to and the terms and conditions of service of the officers and other employees appointed for the purpose of this Act shall be such as may be prescribed.

14. (1) Subject to the provisions of sub-section (3), the Chief Information Commissioner or any Information

Commissioner shall be removed from his office only by order of the President on the ground of proved misbehaviour or incapacity after the Supreme Court, on a reference made to it by the President, has, on inquiry, reported that the Chief Information Commissioner or any Information Commissioner, as the case may be, ought on such ground be removed.

(2) The President may suspend from office, and if deem necessary prohibit also from attending the office during inquiry, the Chief Information Commissioner or Information Commissioner in respect of whom a reference has been made to the Supreme Court under sub-section (1) until the President has passed orders on receipt of the report of the Supreme Court on such reference.

(3) Notwithstanding anything contained in sub-section (1), the President may by order remove from office the Chief Information Commissioner or any Information Commissioner if the Chief Information Commissioner or a Information Commissioner, as the case may be,—

(a) is adjudged an insolvent; or

(b) has been convicted of an offence which, in the opinion of the President, involves moral turpitude: or

(c) engages during his term of office in any paid employment outside the duties of his office; or

(d) is, in the opinion of the President, unfit to continue in office by reason of infirmity of mind or body; or

(e) has acquired such financial or other interest as is likely to affect prejudicially his functions as the Chief Information Commissioner or a Information Commissioner.

(4) If the Chief Information Commissioner or a Information Commissioner in any way, concerned or interested in any contract or agreement made by or on behalf of the Government of India or participates in any way in the profit thereof or in any benefit or emolument arising there from otherwise than as a member and in common

with the other members of an incorporated company, he shall, for the purposes of sub-section (1), be deemed to be guilty of misbehaviour.

Chapter IV

The State Information Commission

15. (1) Every State Government shall, by notification in the Official Gazette, constitute a body to be known as the......... (name of the State) Information Commission to exercise the powers conferred on, and to perform the functions assigned to, it under this Act.

(2) The State Information Commission shall consist of—

(a) the State Chief Information Commissioner, and

(b) such number of State Information Commissioners, not exceeding ten, as may be deemed necessary.

(3) The State Chief Information Commissioner and the State Information Commissioners shall be appointed by the Governor on the recommendation of a committee consisting of—

(i) the Chief Minister, who shall be the Chairperson of the committee;

(ii) the Leader of Opposition in the Legislative Assembly; and

(iii) a Cabinet Ministrer to be nominated by the Chief Minister.

Explanation.—For the purposes of removal of doubts, it is hereby declared that where the Leader of Opposition in the Legislative Assembly has not been recognised as such, the Leader of the single largest group in opposition of the Government in the Legislative Assembly shall be deemed to be the Leader of Opposition.

(4) The general superintendence, direction and management of the affairs of the State Information Commission shall vest in the State Chief Information Commissioner who shall be assisted by the State Information Commissioners and may exercise all such powers and

do all such acts and things which may be exercised or done by the State Information Commission autonomously without being subjected to directions by any other authority under this Act.

(5) The State Chief Information Commissioner and the State Information Commissioners shall be persons of eminence in public life with wide knowledge and experience in law, science and technology, social service, management, journalism, mass media or administration and governance.

(6) The State Chief Information Commissioner or a State Information Commissioner shall not be a Member of Parliament or Member of the Legislature of any State or Union territory, as the case may be, or hold any other office of profit or connected with any political party or carrying on any business or pursuing any profession.

(7) The headquarters of the State Information Commission shall be at such place in the State as the State Government may, by notification in the Official Gazette, specify and the State Information Commission may, with the previous approval of the State Government, establish offices at other places in the State.

16. (1) The State Chief Information Commissioner shall hold office for a term of five years from the date on which he enters upon his office and shall not be eligible for reappointment:

Provided that no State Chief Information Commissioner shall hold office as such after he has attained the age of sixty-five years.

(2) Every State Information Commissioner shall hold office for a term of five years from the date on which he enters upon his office or till he attains the age of sixty-five years, whichever is earlier, and shall not be eligible for reappointment as such State Information Commissioner:

Provided that every State Information Commissioner shall, on vacating his office under this sub-section, be eligible for appointment as the State Chief Information

Commissioner in the manner specified in sub-section (3) of section 15:

Provided further that where the State Information Commissioner is appointed as the State Chief Information Commissioner, his term of office shall not be more than five years in aggregate as the State Information Commissioner and the State Chief Information Commissioner.

(3) The State Chief Information Commissioner or a State Information Commissioner, shall before ' he enters upon his office make and subscribe before the Governor or some other person appointed by him in that behalf, an oath or affirmation according to the form set out for the purpose in the First Schedule.

(4) The State Chief Information Commissioner or a State Information Commissioner may, at any time, by writing under his hand addressed to the Governor, resign from his office:

Provided that the State Chief Information Commissioner or a State Information Commissioner may be removed in the manner specified under section 17.

(5) The salaries and allowances payable to and other terms and conditions of service of—

(a) the State Chief Information Commissioner shall be the same as that of an Election Commissioner;

(b) the State Information Commissioner shall be the same as that of the Chief Secretary to the State Government:

Provided that if the State Chief Information Commissioner or a State Information Commissioner, at the time of his appointment is, in receipt of a pension, other than a disability or wound pension, in respect of any previous service under the Government of India or under the Government of a State, his salary in respect of the service as the State Chief Information Commissioner or a State Information Commissioner shall be reduced by the amount of that pension including any portion of pension which was commuted and pension equivalent of other forms of retirement benefits excluding pension equivalent of retirement gratuity:

Provided further that where the State Chief Information Commissioner or a State Information Commissioner if, at the time of his appointment is, in receipt of retirement benefits in respect of any previous service rendered in a Corporation established by or under any Central Act or State Act or a Government company owned or controlled by the Central Government or the State Government, his salary in respect of the service as the State Chief Information Commissioner or the State Information Commissioner shall be reduced by the amount of pension equivalent to the retirement benefits:

Provided also that the salaries, allowances and other conditions of service of the State Chief Information Commissioner and the State Information Commissioners shall not be varied to their disadvantage after their appointment.

(6) The State Government shall provide the State Chief Information Commissioner and the State Information Commissioners with such officers and employees as may be necessary for the efficient performance of their functions under this Act, and the salaries and allowances payable to and the terms and conditions of service of the officers and other employees appointed for the purpose of this Act shall be such as may be prescribed.

17. (1) Subject to the provisions of sub-section (3), the State Chief Information Commissioner or a State Information Commissioner shall be removed from his office only by order of the Governor on the ground of proved misbehaviour or incapacity after the Supreme Court, on a reference made to it by the Governor, has on inquiry, reported that the State Chief Information

Commissioner or a State Information Commissioner, as the case may be, ought on such ground be removed.

(2) The Governor may suspend from office, and if deem necessary prohibit also from attending the office during inquiry, the State Chief Information Commissioner or a State Information Commissioner in respect of whom a reference has been made to the Supreme Court under sub-section (1) until the Governor has passed orders on receipt of the report of the Supreme Court on such reference.

(3) Notwithstanding anything contained in sub-section (1), the Governor may by order remove from office the State Chief Information Commissioner or a State Information Commissioner if a State Chief Information Commissioner or a State Information Commissioner, as the case may be,—

(a) is adjudged an insolvent; or

(b) has been convicted of an offence which, in the opinion of the Governor, involves moral turpitude; or

(c) engages during his term of office in any paid employment outside the duties of his office; or

(d) is, in the opinion of the Governor, unfit to continue in office by reason of infirmity of mind or body; or

(e) has acquired such financial or other interest as is likely to affect prejudicially his functions as the State Chief Information Commissioner or a State Information Commissioner.

(4) If the State Chief Information Commissioner or a State Information Commissioner in any way, concerned or interested in any contract or agreement made by or on behalf of the Government of the State or participates in any way in the profit thereof or in any benefit or emoluments arising there from otherwise than as a member and in common with the other members of an incorporated company, he shall, for the purposes of sub-section (1), be deemed to be guilty of misbehaviour.

Chapter V

Powers and Functions of the Information Commissions, appeal and penalties

18. (1) Subject to the provisions of this Act, it shall be the duty of the Central Information Commission or State Information Commission, as the case may be, to receive and inquire into a complaint from any person,—

(a) who has been unable to submit a request to a Central Public Information Officer or State Public Information Officer, as the case may be, either by reason that no such officer has been appointed under this Act, or because the Central Assistant Public Information Officer or State Assistant Public Information Officer, as the case may be, has refused to accept his or her application for information or appeal under this Act for forwarding the same to the Central Public Information Officer or State Public Information Officer or senior officer specified in subsection (1) of section 19 or the Central Information Commission or the State Information Commission, as the case may be;

(b) who has been refused access to any information requested under this Act;

(c) who has not been given a response to a request for information or access to information within the time limit specified under this Act;

(d) who has been required to pay an amount of fee which he or she considers unreasonable;

(e) who believes that he or she has been given incomplete, misleading or false information under this Act; and

(f) in respect of any other matter relating to requesting or obtaining access to records under this Act.

(2) Where the Central Information Commission or State Information Commission, as the case may be is satisfied that there are reasonable grounds to inquire into the matter, it may initiate an inquiry in respect thereof.

(3) The Central Information Commission or State Information Commission, as the case may be, shall, while inquiring into any matter under this section, have the same powers as are vested in a civil court while trying a suit under the Code of Civil Procedure, 1908, in respect of the following matters, namely:—

(a) summoning and enforcing the attendance of persons and compel them to give oral or written evidence on oath and to produce the documents or things;

(b) requiring the discovery and inspection of documents;

(c) receiving evidence on affidavit;

(d) requisitioning any public record or copies thereof from any court or office;

(e) issuing summons for examination of witnesses or documents; and

(f) any other matter which may be prescribed.

(4) Notwithstanding anything inconsistent contained in any other Act of Parliament or State Legislature, as the case may be, the Central Information Commission or the State Information Commission, as the case may be, may, during the inquiry of any complaint under this Act, examine any record to which this Act applies which is under the control of the public authority, and no such record may be withheld from it on any grounds.

19. (1) Any person who, does not receive a decision within the time specified in sub-section (1) or clause (a) of sub-section (3) of section 7, or is aggrieved by a decision of the Central Public Information Officer or State Public Information Officer, as the case may be, may within thirty days from the expiry of such period or from the receipt of such a decision prefer an appeal to such officer who is senior in rank to the Central Public Information Officer or State Public Information Officer as the case may be, in each public authority:

Provided that such officer may admit the appeal after the expiry of the period of thirty days if he or she is satisfied that the appellant was prevented by sufficient cause from filing the appeal in time.

(2) Where an appeal is preferred against an order made by a Central Public Information Officer or a State Public Information Officer, as the case may be, under section 11 to disclose third party information, the appeal by the concerned third party shall be made within thirty days from the date of the order,

(3) A second appeal against the decision under sub-section (1) shall lie within ninety days from the date on which the decision should have been made or was actually received, with the Central Information Commission or the State Information Commission:

Provided that the Central Information Commission or the State Information Commission, as the case may be, may admit the appeal after the expiry of the period of ninety days if it is satisfied that the appellant was prevented by sufficient cause from filing the appeal in time.

(4) If the decision of the Central Public Information Officer or State Public Information Officer, as the case may be, against which an appeal is preferred relates to information of a third party, the Central Information Commission or State Information Commission, as the case may be, shall give a reasonable opportunity of being heard to that third party.

(5) In any appeal proceedings, the onus to prove that a denial of a request was justified shall be on the Central Public Information Officer or State Public Information Officer, as the case may be, who denied the request.

(6) An appeal under sub-section (1) or sub-section (2) shall be disposed of within thirty days of the receipt of the appeal or within such extended period not exceeding a total of forty-five days from the date of filing thereof, as the case may be, for reasons to be recorded in writing.

(7) The decision of the Central Information Commission or State Information Commission, as the case may be, shall be binding.

(8) In its decision, the Central Information Commission or State Information Commission, as the case may be, has the power to—

(a) require the public authority to take any such steps as may be necessary to secure compliance with the provisions of this Act, including—

   (i) by providing access to information, if so requested, in a particular form;

   (ii) by appointing a Central Public Information Officer or State Public Information Officer, as the case may be;

   (iii) by publishing certain information or categories of information;

   (iv) by making necessary changes to its practices in relation to the maintenance, management and destruction of records;

   (v) by enhancing the provision of training on the right to information for its officials;

   (vi) by providing it with an annual report in compliance with clause (b) of sub-section (1) of section 4;

(b) require the public authority to compensate the complainant for any loss or other detriment suffered;

(c) impose any of the penalties provided under this Act;

(d) reject the application.

(9) The Central Information Commission or State Information Commission, as the case may be, shall give notice of its decision, including any right of appeal, to the complainant and the public authority.

(10) The Central Information Commission or State Information Commission, as the case may be, shall decide the appeal in accordance with such procedure as may be prescribed.

20. (1) Where the Central Information Commission or the State Information Commission, as the case may be, at the time of deciding any complaint or appeal is of the opinion that the Central Public Information Officer or

the State Public Information Officer, as the case may be, has, without any reasonable cause, refused to receive an application for information or has not 'furnished information within the time specified under sub-section (1) of section 7 or malafidely denied the request for information or knowingly given incorrect, incomplete or misleading information or destroyed information which was the subject of the request or obstructed in any manner in furnishing the information, it shall impose a penalty of two hundred and fifty rupees each day till application is received or information is furnished, so however, the total amount of such penalty shall not exceed twenty-five thousand rupees:

Provided that the Central Public Information Officer or the State Public Information Officer, as the case may be, shall be given a reasonable opportunity of being heard before any penalty is imposed on him:

Provided further that the burden of proving that he acted reasonably and diligently shall be on the Central Public Information Officer or the State Public Information Officer, as the case may be.

(2) Where the Central Information Commission or the State Information Commission, as the case may be, at the time of deciding any complaint or appeal is of the opinion that the Central Public Information Officer or the State Public Information Officer, as the case may be, has, without any reasonable cause and persistently, failed to receive an application for information or has not furnished information within the time specified under sub-section (1) of section 7 or malafidely denied the request for information or knowingly given incorrect, incomplete or misleading information or destroyed information which was the subject of the request or obstructed in any manner in furnishing the information, it shall recommend for disciplinary action against the Central Public Information Officer or the State Public Information Officer, as the case may be, under the service rules applicable to him.

Chapter VI

Miscellaneous

21. No suit, prosecution or other legal proceeding shall lie against any person for anything which is in good faith done or intended to be done under this Act or any rule made thereunder.

22. The provisions of this Act shall have effect notwithstanding anything inconsistent therewith contained in the Official Secrets Act, 1923, and any other law for the time being in force or in any instrument having effect by virtue of any law other than this Act.

23. No court shall entertain any suit, application or other proceeding in respect of any order made under this Act and no such order shall be called in question otherwise than by way of an appeal under this Act.

24. (1) Nothing contained in this Act shall apply to the intelligence and security organisations specified in the Second Schedule, being organisations established by the Central Government or any information furnished by such organisations to that Government:

Provided that the information pertaining to the allegations of corruption and human rights violations shall not be excluded under this sub-section:

Provided further that in the case of information sought for is in respect of allegations of violation of human rights, the information shall only be provided after the approval of the Central Information Commission, and notwithstanding anything contained in section 7, such information shall be provided within 45 days from the date of the receipt of request.

(2) The Central Government may, by notification in the Official Gazette, amend the Schedule by including therein any other intelligence or security organisation established by that Government or omitting therefrom any organisation already specified therein and on the publication of such notification, such organisation shall be deemed to be included in or, as the case may be, omitted from the Schedule.

(3) Every notification issued under sub-section (2) shall be laid before each House of Parliament.

(4) Nothing contained in this Act shall apply to such intelligence and security organisation being organisations established by the State Government, as that Government may, from time to time, by notification in the Official Gazette, specify:

Provided that the information pertaining to the allegations of corruption and human rights violations shall not be excluded under this sub-section:

Provided further that in the case of information sought for is in respect of allegations of violation of human rights, the information shall only be provided after the approval of the State Information Commission and, notwithstanding anything contained in section 7, such information shall be provided within forty-five days from the date of the receipt of request.

(5) Every notification issued under sub-section (4) shall be laid before the State Legislature.

25. (1) The Central Information Commission or State Information Commission, as the case may be, shall, as soon as practicable after the end of each year, prepare a report on the implementation of the provisions of this Act during that year and forward a copy thereof to the appropriate Government.

(2) Each Ministry or Department shall, in relation to the public authorities within their jurisdiction, collect and provide such information to the Central Information Commission or State Information Commission, as the case may be, as is required to prepare the report under this section and comply with the requirements concerning the furnishing of that information and keeping of records for the purposes of this section.

(3) Each report shall state in respect of the year to which the report relates,—

(a) the number of requests made to each public authority;

(b) the number of decisions where applicants were not entitled to access to the documents pursuant to the requests, the provisions of this Act under which these decisions were made and the number of times such provisions were invoked;

(c) the number of appeals referred to the Central Information Commission or State Information Commission, as the case may be, for review, the nature of the appeals and the outcome of the appeals;

(d) particulars of any disciplinary action taken against any officer in respect of the administration of this Act;

(e) the amount of charges collected by each public authority under this Act;

(f) any facts which indicate an effort by the public authorities to administer and implement the spirit and intention of this Act;

(g) recommendations for reform, including recommendations in respect of the particular public authorities, for the development, improvement, modernisation, reform or amendment to this Act or other legislation or common law or any other matter relevant for operationalising the right to access information.

(4) The Central Government or the State Government, as the case may be, may, as soon as practicable after the end of each year, cause a copy of the report of the Central Information Commission or the State Information Commission, as the case may be, referred to in subsection (1) to be laid before each House of Parliament or, as the case may be, before each House of the State Legislature, where there are two Houses, and where there is one House of the State Legislature before that House.

(5) If it appears to the Central Information Commission or State Information Commission, as the case may be, that the practice of a public authority in relation to the

exercise of its functions under this Act does not conform with the provisions or spirit of this Act, it may give to the authority a recommendation specifying the steps which ought in its opinion to be taken for promoting such conformity.

26. (1) The appropriate Government may, to the extent of availability of financial and other resources,—

(a) develop and organise educational programmes to advance the understanding of the public, in particular of disadvantaged communities as to how to exercise the rights contemplated under this Act;

(b) encourage public authorities to participate in the development and organisation of programmes referred to in clause (a) and to undertake such programmes themselves;

(c) promote timely and effective dissemination of accurate information by public authorities about their activities; and

(d) train Central Public Information Officers or State Public Information Officers, as the case may be, of public authorities and produce relevant training materials for use by the public authorities themselves.

(2) The appropriate Government shall, within eighteen months from the commencement of this Act, compile in its official language a guide containing such information, in an easily comprehensible form and manner, as may reasonably be required by a person who wishes to; exercise any right specified in this Act.

(3) The appropriate Government shall, if necessary, update and publish the guidelines referred to in sub-section (2) at regular intervals which shall, in particular and without prejudice to the generality of sub-section (2), include—

(a) the objects of this Act;

(b) the postal and street address, the phone and fax number and, if available, electronic mail address of the Central Public Information Officer or State

Public Information Officer, as the case may be, of every public authority appointed under sub-section (1) of section 5;

(c) the manner and the form in which request for access to an information shall be made to a Central Public Information Officer or State Public Information Officer, as the case may be;

(d) the assistance available from and the duties of the Central Public Information Officer or State Public Information Officer, as the case may be, of a public authority under this Act;

(e) the assistance available from the Central Information Commission or State Information Commission, as the case may be;

(f) all remedies in law available regarding an act or failure to act in respect of a right or duty conferred or imposed by this Act including the manner of filing an appeal to the Commission;

(g) the provisions providing for the voluntary disclosure of categories of records in accordance with section 4;

(h) the notices regarding fees to be paid in relation to requests for access to an information; and

(i) any additional regulations or circulars made or issued in relation to obtaining access to an information in accordance with this Act.

(4) The appropriate Government must, if necessary, update and publish the guidelines at regular intervals.

27. (1) The appropriate Government may, by notification in the Official Gazette, make rules to carry out the provisions of this Act.

(2) In particular, and without prejudice to the generality of the foregoing power, such rules may provide for all or any of the following matters, namely:—

(a) the cost of the medium or print cost price of the materials to be disseminated under sub-section (4) of section 4';

(b) the fee payable under sub-section (1) of section 6;

(c) the fee payable under sub-sections (1) and (5) of section 7;

(d) the salaries and allowances payable to and the terms and conditions of service of the officers and other employees under sub-section (6) of section 13 and sub-section (6) of section 16;

(e) the procedure to be adopted by the Central Information Commission or State Information Commission, as the case may be, in deciding the appeals under sub-section (10) of section 19; and

(f) any other matter which is required to be, or may be, prescribed.

28. (1) The competent authority may, by notification in the Official Gazette, make rules to carry out the provisions of this Act.

(2) In particular, and without prejudice to the generality of the foregoing power, such rules may provide for all or any of the following matters, namely:—

(i) the cost of the medium or print cost price of the materials to be disseminated under sub-section (4) of section 4;

(ii) the fee payable under sub-section (1) of section 6;

(iii) the fee payable under sub-section (1) of section 7; and

(iv) any other matter which is required to be, or may be, prescribed.

29. (1) Every rule made by the Central Government under this Act shall be laid, as soon as may be after it is made, before each House of Parliament, while it is in session, for a total period of thirty days which may be comprised in one session or in two or more successive sessions, and if, before the expiry of the session immediately following the session or the successive sessions aforesaid, both Houses agree in making any modification in the rule or both Houses agree that the rule should not be made, the rule shall thereafter have effect only

in such modified form or be of no effect, as the case may be; so, however, that any such modification or annulment shall be without prejudice to the validity of anything previously done under that rule.

(2) Every rule made under this Act by a State Government shall be laid, as soon as may be after it is notified, before the State Legislature.

30. (1) If any difficulty arises in giving effect to the provisions of this Act, the Central Government may, by order published in the Official Gazette, make such provisions not inconsistent with the provisions of this Act as appear to it to be necessary or expedient for removal of the difficulty;

Provided that no such order shall be made after the expiry of a period of two years from the date of the commencement of this Act.

(2) Every order made under this section shall, as soon as may be after it is made, be laid before each House of Parliament.

31. The Freedom of Information Act, 2002 is hereby repealed.

THE FIRST SCHEDULE

[See sections 13(3) and 16(J)]

Form of Oath or Affirmation to be made by the Chief Information Commissioner/the Information Commissioner/the State Chief Information Commissioner/ the State Information Commissioner

"I,................ having been appointed Chief Information Commissioner/Information Commissioner/State Chief Information Commissioner/State Information Commissioner swear ill the name of God solemnly affirm that I will bear true faith and allegiance to the Constitution of India as by law established, that I will uphold the sovereignty and integrity of India, that I will duly and faithfully and to the best of my ability, knowledge and judgment perform the duties of my office without fear or favour, affection or ill-will and that I will uphold the Constitution and the laws."

THE SECOND SCHEDULE

(See section 24)

Intelligence and Security Organisation Established by the Central Government

1. Intelligence Bureau.
2. Research and Analysis Wing of the Cabinet Secretariat.
3. Directorate of Revenue Intelligence.
4. Central Economic Intelligence Bureau.
5. Directorate of Enforcement.
6. Narcotics Control Bureau.
7. Aviation Research Centre.
8. Special Frontier Force.
9. Border Security Force.
10. Central Reserve Police Force.
11 Indo-Tibetan Border Police.
12. Central Industrial Security Force.
13. National Security Guards.
14. Assam Rifles.
15. Special Service Bureau.
16. Special Branch (CID), Andaman and Nicobar.
17. The Crime Branch-C.I.D.- CB, Dadra and Nagar Haveli.

REFERENCES

1. Right to Information Act, 2005" (http://persmin.nic.in/RTI/WelcomeRTI.htm)". Ministry of Personnel, Public Grievances and Pensions (2005-12-10).
2. The details of the RTI Act, 2005 is attached as a Annexure at the end of the chapter.
3. The effective date is often incorrectly referred to as 12 October 2005. The Act actually came to force on the midnight between the 12th and 13th, which means that it came into effect from the 13th onwards.
4. "The Official Secrets Act, 1923" (http://www.mdialawinfo.com/ India (1923).

5. World Report: Libraries and Intellectual Freedom (India) (http://www.it1a.org/ta International Federation of Library Association and Institutions (1999-06-07).
6. Kumar, Ann (1999-06-07). "Right to Information— Background and Perspective (http://www.infochangeindia. org/ Righttinfolbp.
7. State of U.P. v. Raj Narain, AIR 1975 SC 865 http:// judis.nic.in/supremecourt/.
8. Tamil Nadu Right to Information Act No. 24 of 1997 (http:// www.tn.gov.in/acts-rules/right2info.htm)". Government of Tamil Nadu (1998-05-06).
9. Under Article 370 (http://lawmin.nic.in/) of the Indian Constitution, laws passed by the Parliament are not automatically applicable to the state of Jammu and Kashmir, unless endorsed by the state's legislature.
10. "Right to Information Act. 2005. Obligations and Responsibilities (http://www.rti.gov.in/rti_slides)". Government of India

Chapter 3

Transparency and Good Governance: The Case Study of India

India Corruption Study 2007 by the Transparency International India and Centre for Media Studies is unique. Unlike earlier annual surveys of CMS, this one for 2007 is focused on BPL households, mostly in rural India. The coverage of this study includes all parts of the country except some outlying islands. The study, like the earlier ones, is based on CMS PEE model where the scope is not limited to perceptions about corruption in general, but perception in specific context of a service and, more importantly, actual experience of paying bribe by BPL households in availing one or more of the 11 selected public services. Depending on the frequency of interaction, the eleven services are divided broadly into "basic services" (PDS). Hospital, School Education (up to class XII). Electricity and Water Supply Services) and "need based services" (Land Records Registration. Housing, Forest. NREGS, Banking and Police Service (traffic, and crime). The study does not include operational irregularities in the system and any corruption that does not involve citizens, directly.

The survey covered 22.728 randomly selected BPL households across the States. The fieldwork was conducted between November 2007 and January 2008. The concepts and methodology for the study were finalized after extensive consultations with experts and those familiar with the services covered. The CMS methodology for the study involved household level sample survey, exit interviews at service delivery outlets, discussions with the concerned "service providers" in each case and observations on display of information is the service delivery points, etc. Large-scale surveys, spread across States of varying performance and services, of distinct and different characteristics, will not have same reliability when one "looks at the data from a micro level of an individual State or service.

Experienced investigators and researchers conducted the fieldwork after pilot testing of instruments and Held orientation. The fieldwork was independently validated by sub-sample checks. About 150 experienced investigators and a dozen senior researchers of CMS who were engaged for quality control of the field data carried on the fieldwork for the study. The preliminary findings were further put through a series of extended consultations with about 35 outside experts whose advice was brought to hear on the analysis presented.

The perceptions about corruption in the specific context of the 11 services include whether corruption increased or declined in the last one year and whether presence of any redressal mechanism was noticed. Similarly, experience of corruption includes actual bribe paid or use of a "contact" in availing a public service, in the previous one year in this process, the study also brings out die percentage of BPL households who could not avail the particular service as they could not either pay bribe or they had no "contact". Together, these three types indicate the total size of BPL households caught in the trap of corruption white trying to avail the service. Overall, more than 40 per cent of the BPL households, who approached Police, Land and Housing Services in the previous one year, either (actually) paid bribe or had to use a contact. On the other hand, a higher percentage of people paid bribe in the case of "need based services" than in (the case of) "basic services". Another interesting finding is that there is not much difference in the extent of corruption that BPL households experience in urban and rural areas.

TABLE 1
Services Covered

Basic Services:

Public Distribution System (PDS)

Hospital

School Education (up to class XII)

Electricity

Water supply

Need Based Services:

National Rural Employment Guarantee Scheme (NREGS)

Land Records/ Registration

Forest

Housing

Banking

Police

TII-CMS India Corruption Study-2007

An Overview

The Gap: This TII-CMS India Corruption Study 2007 brings out that one out of every three BPL households had paid bribe in availing one or more of the 11 public services covered in the previous year. The study brings out the wide gap between (levels of) perception and experience of BPL households about corruption. This gap, however, is relatively narrow in the case of some "need based services" like Land (Registration), Housing/plots. Forest and Police in comparison to "basic services" (like PDS, Hospital, School Education).

TABLE 2
Per cent of BPL Households interact

Basic Services:	
PDS	88
Hospital	80
School Education (up to class XII)	39
Electricity	52
Water Supply	14
Need Based:	
NREGS	24
Land Records registration	18
Forest	15
Housing	14
Banking	38
Police	10

TII-CMS India Corruption Study-2007

Access to Service: At the national level, about two-thirds of BPL households possess a "BPL Card". In Delhi, West Bengal and in most of the North-Eastern States, more than half of households, with income of BPL, did not have a card for one or the other reason including because they could not pay bribe or they did not have a "contact" to influence. Their frequent migration could also be a reason for not having a card. More than half of eligible households in the North-Eastern States did not have a BPL card. As could be seen from the table, 10 per cent of BPL households contacted/visited/used Police Service in the year against about 88 and 80 per cent-in the case of PDS and Hospital Service, respectively. The extent of the interaction percentage depends on how many BPL households were in need of these services during the year.

Most BPL households, especially in rural areas), do not require to interact more often with the services like Housing. Land. Electricity, Water and School Education. Those who applied or registered in the earlier years for these services, need not interact with the department every year. If someone already had electricity or water connection, they need not interact with the department for that service. That is how percentage of BPL households who interacted with the service in the previous one year varies distinctly from State-to-State and service-to-service. For example, in services like. Police or Land Registration the percentage who interacted would be much lower than in the case of services like Hospital or PDS services.

Perception about Corruption: Perception about corruption was a mixed one. Corruption as perceived by users of the service, is relatively high (two-thirds or more) in Police, Land and Housing services. In these services, the percentage of those who think corruption has increased in the previous one year is also high. These services are monopolistic in the nature, with more scope for discretionary decision making and also because the money involved in these transactions is higher. More households acknowledged that corruption had declined in the last one year in the case of School Education and Banking services. But, over 40 per cent of BPL households had "no idea" of any decline in corruption in the specific context of most of the services covered in this study.

More than half of users of Banking Services, School Education, Water and Forest perceived that corruption had remained at "same level" or increased than the percentage of those who thought it had decreased during the year. In the case of Police service, a higher percentage (54 per cent) of users thought that corruption had increased. Percentage who thought that corruption had declined in the last one year, is less than half in all the services.

Both perception and experience of corruption among BPL households are relatively more in the case of "need based services" like Police, Land Registration/ transfer and Housing as compared to "basic services" like PDS. School

Education and Hospital services. Also, relatively more among BPL households' respondents think that corruption has either declined or remained same in the case of "basic services" than in the case of "need based services".

TABLE 3

Levels of Overall Corruption in States (involving BPL households) (in Per cent)

Services	Corruption	Level of Corruption		
	Exists	Come down	Same	Increased
PDS	54	22	46	32
Hospital	46	24	51	25
School Education (up to 12th class)	28	37	46	18
Electricity	44	22	49	29
Water Supply	42	25	50	25
NREGS	47	22	46	31
Land Records Registration	69	12	43	45
Forest	36	24	57	18
Housing	70	14	41	45
Banking	27	40	43	17
Police	78	7	39	54

TII-CMS India Corruption Study-2007

Any Improvement in Redressal: Despite various kind of measures taken to improve the delivery of services, like computerisation, e-governance, use of Citizen Charter. RTI Act, Social Audit, etc., such measures have not made much difference on users' grievances perhaps because the benefit is yet to be realised by BPL households. In the case of services like School Education, Electricity. Water Supply and Banking, however, relatively more (20 per cent or more households) had acknowledged existence of one or other "grievance redressal" mechanism (this phenomena of "redressal" was explained to respondents during the interview in local language). In fact, more than half of BPL households using the services in the year found redressal practice same as earlier. Although, some households see that redressal had improved, a much higher percentage of the BPL households thought that redressal situation had not changed over the previous year.

TABLE 4

Perceptions on Grievance Redresal

Per cent

Service	**Improved**	**Same**	**Deteriorated**
PDS	21	52	27
Hospital	23	55	21
School Education (up to class XII)	33	53	14
Electricity	21	58	21
Water Supply	22	60	18
NREGS	19	57	27
Land Records Registration	12	54	34
Forest	20	64	15
Housing	13	51	36
Banking	37	50	13
Police	7	54	39

TII-CMS India Corruption Study-2007

Use of "a contact": If they cannot pay bribe to avail a public service like PDS. NREGS or Housing, even though it is a targeted programmes aimed at BPL households, a "contact" would enable them to access the same. This "contact" could be a "middle man" or a functionary including an elected representative. This survey, brings out that the percentage of BPL households who avail service using a "contact" vary from State to State - between 25-44 per cent in the case of housing and between 13-41 per cent in the case of Police Service. Even in the case of NREGS, the per cent of BPL households who used a contact in the previous year range from 12-26 per cent depending on the State. Such a reliance on a "contact" was observed in the case of basic as well as need based services. In fact, in some States (like Bihar and Assam) a "contact" was used by a higher per cent of BPL households to avail most of these public services.

TABLE 5

Perceptions on Grievance Redresal

Per cent

Service	**Experience**		
	Paid Bribe	**Used a Contact**	**Did not take the service because asked for bribe**
PDS	5.9	4.1	1.8
Hospital	9.3	5.8	1.8
School Education (up to class XII)	3.4	4.4	2.3
Electricity	9.7	4.6	1.8
Water Supply	8.7	5.9	3.8
NREGS	7.5	7.5	4.4
Land Records Registration	32.1	9.7	4.0
Forest	10.8	4.0	2.0
Housing	19.5	11.6	12.5
Banking	4.5	3.7	2.5
Police	48.3	16.1	4.5

TII-CMS India Corruption Study-2007

To avail Land and Housing related services, a higher per cent used a "contact" than in the case of other services. Even in the ease of NREGS, 7 per cent across various States relied on a contact—may be a local representative, in lad, more than 10 per cent in some States like Bihar, Chhattisgarh, Madhya Pradesh. Jharkhand, Rajasthan. Meghalaya and Arunachal Pradesh used one or the other "contact' 10 avail NKEGS. The percentage of those who availed the service using a "contact" was significantly lower than the percentage who used the service by paying bribe. In other services, a much higher per cent of BPL households paid bribe to avail the service in the previous one year.

Non-Availability of Services: The TII-CMS India Corruption Study 2007 brings out that the percentage of BPL households who could not avail basic services that a citizen is entitled to because they could not pay bribe or they had no contact to influence. In fact, in the case of services like housing plots, land registration and NREGS, as high as a quarter of BPL households in some States could not avail the service (or that reason despite their eligibility and effort.

The percentage of BPL households who could not avail the services as they could not either pay bribe or had no "contact" to influence, is more in the case of housing, police. Land and NREGS than in the other seven services. In the ease of Housing, this percentage is as high as 12 per cent.

But, in States like Uttar Pradesh, Gujarat, Arunachal Pradesh, Sikkim and Karnataka, the percentage of those who could not avail housing or house plots is 20 per cent or more. In States like Madhya Pradesh and Rajasthan it is 15 per cent who could not avail housing services as they could not pay bribe.

Paid Bribe: Overall, among those who interacted with the service providers, the who paid bribe was as high as 48 per cent in the case of Police, 32 per cent in the case of Land Registration and 22 per cent in the case of Housing (all need based services). Whereas, in the ease of basic services like PDS (70). School Education (3.4). Hospital Services (10.2) and Electricity (9.7) the per cent of BPL households who paid bribe in the previous year was anywhere between 3 and 10 per cent. In fact, in some States like Andhra Pradesh, Karnataka and Tamil Nadu, about half of the BPL households paid bribe for land, housing services and to get drinking water. In Delhi 9 per cent of BPL households had to pay bribe to avail PDS. In Assam, 48 per cent paid bribe to avail Hospital services.

Who were the recipient of the bribe?: In two-thirds of the instances, bribe was paid to an official staff in the concerned service. In fact in the case of police most often the bribe was paid directly to the concerned functionary. In 20 per cent of the instances, it was a "middlemen" 10 from in the was paid. Bribe is paid even to "local public representative". In fact, in the case of NREGS. 25 per cent of BPL households who availed the service in the last one year paid bribe to a local "public representative".

TABLE 6

Recipient of Bribes (in per cent)

Services	**Experience**		
	Official staff	**Middle-men**	**Local representative (elected or otherwise)**
Basic Services:			
PDS	74	19	7
Hospital	90	11	1
School Education	86	12	1
Electricity	81	18	1
Water Supply	81	18	1
Need Based Services:			
NREGS	55	20	25
Land Records	82	17	2
Forest	91	10	0
Housing	64	23	11
Banking	73	22	4
Police	92	8	1

TII-CMS India Corruption Study-2007

TABLE 7
Major Purposes for Paying Bribe

Basic Services	**Purposes of paying (in that order)**
PDS	New card, for monthly quota, change address, change shop, addition, license to sell
Hospital	For bed, out patient, diagnostic service, medicine, ANC/PNC, operation, certificate, blood
School Education (up to class XII)	New admission, certificates, attendance/ promotion, scholarship, hostel seat
Electricity	New connection, meter repair, bill related, meter installation, bill adjustment agriculture connection, ensure better supply
Water Supply	Installation maintenance of hand pump regularisation of unauthorised connection, meter installation, repair of pipe, irrigation water, supply of water tanker
Need Based Services:	
NREGS	Registration / to get selected, issuance of job card, wage payment
Land Records/Registration	Income certificate, obtaining land record, sale/purchase deed, mutation, land survey, caste certificate, properly tax
Forest	To pick fuel wood for cutting trees, for saplings, to collect forest produce, forest land for farming, for grazing
Police	For filing complaint and FIR as an accused, remove name as witness, passport verification, verification for job, character certificate, violation of traffic laws
Housing	Allotment of plot/house, release of house loan, toilet construction, ownership transfer
Banking	To take loan, open new A/c, pension, withdrawal, deferment of loan installment

TII-CMS India Corruption Study 2007

Not surprising, when asked who is "more responsible" for corruption in general 44 per cent of BPL households mentioned "official/functionary", against 29 per cent who mentioned "politician" as being responsible.

Purpose for Paying Bribe: One-third or more of BPL households paid bribe in the ease of basic services only "to get into the very service" like getting a new ration card, new connection, new installation or an admission in school. In fact, in the case of need based services, hall or more of BPL households either paid bribe for obtaining a certificate record, to get registered as eligible, to get an allotment, to get bank loan or to file complaint in the police station.

Only 25 per cent of BPL households in the study were from urban areas. No significant difference is (bund between urban and rural households in the pattern of their responses, even in the case of services like PDS, school education and water.

Frequent Visits: Corruption is more likely where and when the number of visits a citizen has to make to get a particular service is more, In fact, the number of visits one has to make is an indirect indicator for "seeking bribe" in service. Such a phenomena also adds to perceptions about the service as a corrupt one. For a BPL. household, for example, repeat visits that a citizen has to make to avail a public service, needs to the minimised, if it cannot be altogether be avoided. This survey identifies specific purposes for which BPL households visited the service providers three times or ore.

For getting a new ration card 62 per cent of BPL households who had applied for it had to visit the Rationing office three or more times. Even to open a new account in local bank or post office, half of them visited three or more limes in the last one year. Also for getting selected to get the job card in NREGS. 56 per cent of BPL households had to visit three or more times.

Causes of Corruption: In the delivery of basic services, it is procedures that were pointed out as the cause of corruption and for their need to be simplified. In the case of need-based services, it is more counseling and sensitising of the staff and transparency in the processes that needs lo be addressee) seriously. Establishment of accountability with an internal system of concurrent monitoring is a *sine qua nun* for improving efficiency and curtailing corruption. Such measures could eliminate the compulsions for paying bribe by citizens. Only then middlemen menace could be minimised or eliminated. Because middlemen often work in league with internal functionaries. Citizens" felt that "absence and non-availability of staff' reinforces the environment for "bribe seeking". Similarly, the discretionary powers of the functionaries at the service delivery point, the more the scope for corruption as in Police, Forest and Housing services. On the other hand in a service which is otherwise perceived as relatively efficient as in the case of Banking Service (also at post offices) 48 per cent of BPL households feel that procedures are cumbersome and are the cause, of corruption.

Estimation of Bribe: Based on the incidence of bribe paid by sample BPL households, an estimate is made for the total amount paid as bribe by BPL households in the country during the last one year, in the eleven services. This exercise had taken into account the estimate of BPL households by the Planning Commission (Year 2004-05). More than a couple of States have had questioned the Planning Commission's estimate of BPL households. For example, in the case of Orissa, while the State Government puts the figure of BPL households at 4.2 million, the Planning Commission figure was 3.5 million. Since allocation of houses to poor under Indira Awas Yojana, as well as most other targeted programmes is based on the estimates of Planning Commission, the estimate made in this study for the bribe paid by BPL households in the previous year was done using Planning Commission's figures.

The total bribe amount involved in a year in BPL households availing the eleven services covered in this study is estimated as Rs. 8.K30 million. This could only be a conservative estimate and more an indicative one. The money involved in these estimates appear petty as in the case of NREGS. School Education and PDS, but most of it was paid directly to that functionaries. But the overall perception and "damage effect" of this petty corruption is much greater' and calls for serious consideration of the Government to come up with schemes which would bring down corruption to "zero level".

TABLE 8

Specific Service Requiring Repeat Visits

Service-some examples for which 3 or more visits were reported	**Rounded per cent of Users of the Service**
As in-patient for getting bed	29
Electricity bill related	37
To obtain land records	23
For filing a complaint with police	46
Bill payment of water	45
Plot/House allotment	69
For getting selected/job card in NREG	56
To open new A/c in Bank/Post Office	51
For new ration card	62

TII-CMS India Corruption Study-2007

Services Ranking: School Education (up to class XII and Government schools) among II services studied stands last in the ranking that is the lowest in the level of corruption. But, when one looks at this service individually, it is also entrenched with some corruption involving BPL households. Thai Police service stood number one currohorates the general impression. But, that Land Records Registration in House Plot winch are specially tailored fur BPL households, stand at two and three in ranking should be a matter of concern. While the level and extent of corruption in Police service was high in all States, as if it is universal—but the of other services shows variations across the states. Given the nature of need based services which are monopolistic or involve asset creation or volume, these services ranked high on corruption as compared to basic services.

TABLE 9
Factors Faced in Availing Public Services

in percentage

Services	Procedural	No forms	Absence of staff	Corrupt staff	Middle man
PDS	37	3	18	38	4
Hospital	38	4	26	31	2
School Education (up to class XII)	35	7	21	33	3
Electricity	40	3	18	35	4
Water Supply	36	5	23	31	5
NREGS	33	7	10	37	13
Land Records Registration	27	4	11	51	6
Forest	28	2	11	53	5
Housing	24	3	9	50	14
Banking	48	6	13	28	4
Police	17	2	4	73	4

TII-CMS India Corruption Study-2007

TABLE 10
Services Ranked

Services	Rank
PDS	450
Hospital	870
School Education (up to class XII)	120
Electricity	1,050
Water Supply	240
NREGS	70

TABLE 10 *contd...*

Services	Rank
Land Records Registration	1,240
Forest	240
Housing	1,570
Banking	830
Police	2,150
Total for 11 services covered in the survey	8,830

TII-CMS India Corruption Study-2007

TABLE 11

Services Ranked

Services	Rank
Police	1
Land Records/Registration	2
Housing	3
Water Supply	4
NREGS	5
Forest	6
Electricity	7
Health	8
PDS	9
Banking	10
School Education (up to 12th class)	11

TII-CMS India Corruption Study-2007

Levels of Corruption in States: This TII-CMS India Corruption Study 2007 as in the case of one for 2005, brought out that corruption involving citizens including BPL households is all pervasive across the States and public services. No State or service is anywhere near "zero corruption" level. Nevertheless, taking the degree of variation from State-to-State and service, the States are grouped into four levels to explain the extent level of corruption based on a weightage scheme - Moderate. High,

TABLE 12

Levels of Overall Corruption in State (involving BPL households)

(arranged in alphabetical order)

States by size	**Levels of Corruption**			
	Alarming	**Very High**	**High**	**Moderate**
Big	Assan	Karnalaka	Chhallisgarh	Andhra Pradesh
	Bihar	Rajasthan	Delhi	Haryana
Jammu & Kashmir	Tamil Nadu	Gujarat	Himahal Pradesh	
	Madhya Pradesh		Jharkhand	Maharashta
	Uttar-Pradesh		Kerala	Punjab
			Orissa	Uttarakhand
				West Bengal
Small Uts	Goa	Meghalaya	Arunahal Pradesh	Chandigarh
	Nagland	Sikkim	Manipur	Mizoram
				Pondicherry
				Tripura

Very High and Alarming. This grouping and positioning of States is limited to interaction of BPL households in availing the eleven services covered in this study.

The service specific reports, covering the eleven services, present the relative position of States in the context of that service. Within each category, the States are arranged alphabetically. Considering significant difference between bigger and smaller States of North-East and others like Pondicherry. Chandigarh and Goa, the grouping is arranged separately for "Big" or "Small" ones.

The above grouping reflects relative position of States in the context of all the eleven services. "Moderate" level of corruption does not mean that corruption is tolerable. Nevertheless, for better understanding the States are grouped based on the level of corruption in the context of the particular service. "Very high" and "high" level indicates that corruption level concerning BPL household is extensive both with respect to perception and experience in that year. Moderate level also indicates that the services are either not within the reach or access of the BPL households or that the extent of corruption level is relatively low. But, the States under "alarming" group calls for serious introspection, restructuring and even repositioning of certain services meant for BPL households.

It is not that high corruption exists in all the services of a State or the position of services in all the States was alarming. In fact, in no State corruption involving BPL households in all the 11 services was "very high" or "alarming". In some services, corruption was moderate but it was very high in the same State in other services. State would be better served if it focuses and seriously review services where corruption level was "high", "very high" and "alarming". By doing this both extent of perception and experience of corruption could be brought down and the gap between the two could be narrowed.

In Himachal Pradesh, the level of corruption is "moderate" in all the 11 services studied whereas in the case Madhya Pradesh and Assam, corruption level in all the 11 services was high or very high or alarming. For example, in Delhi and West Bengal, corruption level was moderate in most services surveyed.

Among smaller States of North-east and UTs, most of the 11 services in Nagaland and Goa had high or very high or alarming level of corruption. Whereas it was moderate in Chandigarh and Tripura.

RIGHT TO INFORMATION ACT

This TII-CMS India Corruption Study 2007 looked into the extent RTI Act has come into play or has become a potential tool in the hands of economically vulnerable sections of people of the country. In fact, that would be a good measure of success of the RTI Act. This study brings out that, in about half a dozen States more than 10 per cent of BPL households knew about RTI Act at the end of the second year since the Act was implemented. Considering the overall levels across the population, this finding is not a disappointing one.

Overall awareness about RTI Act among BPL households is much more (6 per cent) despite the Act being only two years old as compared to Citizens' Charter (2.5 per cent), which has been in vogue for more than five years. Going by this, awareness level among other sections of society should be much higher. Both in terms of awareness about the RTI Act and the extent BPL households availed the Act by actually applying for information under it is not bad considering that Government or any of the 11 services studied hardly made any special effort locally to promote the Act as a potent weapon in the hands of poor or as a tool for improving the delivery of the services.

In fact, this survey brings out that it is the news media and campaigns by civil society organisations that are mostly responsible for such a level of awareness. Since the study is based on a sample of 2 to 5 districts in each State whereas the civil society campaigns were more often confined to one or oilier locations within a State, the finding here may not be reflective of the State as a whole.

TABLE 13

Awareness about RTI Act among BPL households

State	BPL household (%)	State	BPL household (%)
Andhra Pradesh	13.0	Maharashtra	6.9
Arunachal Pradesh	4.5	Manipur	13.0
Assam	10.3	Meghalaya	0.6
Bihar	1.4	Mizoram	12.0
Chhattisgarh	4.1	Nagaland	14.1
Delhi	5.0	Orissa	3.8
Goa	1.2	Pondicherry	8.0
Gujarat	4.4	Punjab	2.7
Haryana	2.7	Rajasthan	5.7
Himachal Pradesh	2.9	Sikkim	2.7
Jammu & Kashmir	4.5	Tamil Nadu	6.7
Jharkhand	5.0	Tripura	0.5
Karnataka	12.8	Uttar Pradesh	1.4
Kerala	10.7	Uttarakhand	8.4
Madhya Pradesh	4.9	West Bengal	1.4

More than 10 per cent of BPL households know about RTI Ad in Andhra Pradesh. Assam. Karnataka and kerala. In States like Gujarat, Andhra Pradesh, Chhattisgarh. West Bengal. Kerala and Rajasthan. BPL household used RTI Act mostly for information on PDS, Hospital Service. School Education, NREGS and Banking Service.

TABLE 14

Percentage Applied Under RTI Act

State	BPL household	State	BPL household
Andhra Pradesh	1.0	Mizoram	0.2
Arunachal Pradesh	0.2	Madhya Pradesh	0.3
Assam	0.2	Nagaland	0.4
Bihar	0.1	Orissa	0.4
Chhattisgarh	0.8	Pondicherry	0.2
Delhi	0.1	Punjab	0.3
Gujarat	1.5	Rajasthan	0.6
Haryana	0.3	Sikkim	0.2
Karnataka	0.4	Tamil Nadu	0.2
Kerala	0.6	Uttarakhand	0.1
Maharashtra	0.1	West Bengal	0.8

This study reminds the potential of Citizens' Charters if they are formulated in consultation with all the stakeholders and displayed at delivery outlets of concerned public services. Tins is notwithstanding the measures taken towards e-governance schemes in the pipeline. This will further strengthen the scope of RTI Act.

SERVICE PROVIDERS PERSPECTIVE AND THE TYPES

- Service providers" perspective across States and services could be summed up into different types, as follows:
- "Yes, we are ready lo help, but we hardly gel any complaints". These providers knew the problem of reach and reliability of the service, but keep wailing for an occasion.
- "Yes we promptly attend" to the problems brought to our notice hut there are too many problems / deficiencies.

- "We are short of to do am tiling more our work load has increased so much.
- "We are ready to serve, but public do not cooperate".
- "Not in our hand, procedures are from above...."
- "No differentiation between performer and non-performer", no motivation to do more better and to take initiatives, locally.
- "We are operating with outdated facilities, support and rules"
- "We are operating work load often driven by political pressures"
- "Stall hardly acts any training to cope with increasing demands and expectations"
- We hardly ret any guidance from above outside for correctives"
- "Out priorities is not only BPL... households..."
- "Catering BPL households is more complex, difficult and requires special efforts".

Broadly, service providers responses across basic and need based services fall into three typologies: (1) defenders, of what they are doing; (2) passive executives who think things will take their own course, and (3) reactive executives who responds positively, but only individually appealed. The training or orientation should be to see that some "proactive" outlook functionaries are provided the opportunity, particularly while interacting with BPL households.

SUGGESTIONS

Based on the findings TII-CMS India Corruption Study 2007 and CMS's earlier studies in this series, the following general suggestion could be made. Together these facilitate initiatives towards "zero-corruption" both in the case of basic and need based services.

A Four Prounged Strategy Needed

The findings of this study calls for the following four-pronged efforts:

1. Simplification: Urgently required are simplification of procedures and even eliminating certain formalities for BPL households; more visible and interactive redressal practices: curbing discretionary options with individuals at service delivery points; and accountability by giving identities of functionaries'

2. Streamline Information Flows: Improved information now for a more transparent and trust-based transactions and customised service orientation with the help of IT tools, e-governance initiatives and better organised front ends of service delivery points are required. Also, priorities and concerns of e-governance projects should keep in view the special needs of vulnerable sections of households.

3. From End Staff Need Special Concern: Reorienting staff to serve BPL and vulnerable households with special attention and on a priority basis is required. Their sensitivity to special needs of BPL households need to he improved with periodic workshops and training programmes and special arrangements in the operations.

4. Civil society Activism is Better Bet: Finally, civil society activism has 16 come more in to play. It should be possible with RTI Act, Citizens' Charters, Social Audit and on-line services. This study has shown that social activism can make difference in favour of the poor. There is ample scope for a collaborative course.

Very Scope of "BPL" Household Needs a Relook

Proof of claims of "inclusive growth", "good governance", "social justice", etc., depend how well BPL households are being reached and served. The very concept of "BPL households" needs to be reviewed in the light of recent report on 'Social Security for Unorganised Workers' and the State Governments' race to change threshold level for BPL eligibility for "'subsidised services". The more the widening in the criteria of BPL, the more likelihood of the "poorest of the poor" or "hardcore BPL households" being deprived. A task force can come up with State specific and service specific changes and suggestions in this regard to make sure that poorest of the poor are not further deprived.

Need to he Understand and Seriously Address "Perception"

The gap between "perception" about corruption in basic public services and "experience" of paying bribe or using a contact for availing those services, need to be taken more seriously. Actual corruption in the context of the basic services is lower than the extent of perception. Nevertheless, repositioning public confidence and demonstrating improvement in the system by making it more responsive to needs, should be a priority concern. However, without addressing perception related phenomena, actual level of corruption cannot be brought down.

"The gap" cannot he addressed without cooperation of mass media. Despite some decline in the experience of corruption involving citizens in availing Mink' public services recently, perception levels have not come down but somewhat increased as if is in proportion to portrayal of corruption in general and in the electronic media, more specifically. It is important to understand that while media itself has become a new source of redressal for citizens, if is also keeping corruption in public eye but to the extent that people becoming immune or treating corruption as a non-issue. This phenomenon is more to do with repetitive coverage and hyping. But this trend needs to he studied seriously, transparently and with voluntary cooperation from the broadcasters.

Proactive Use of Local Media

In the context of BPL households. FM radio in urban and local TV channels in the rural areas could play a special role. Those responsible for the contents of news media in particular should lie sensitised about the very character and structure of corruption and its implication to different sections of people and best ways and strategies in which the media could pay a role in the war against corruption, particularly in areas involving citizens and in their use of public utilities.

Corrective Potential of Social Audit

Social Audit of Hoi only targeted programmes but of other services like Banking services. Hospital and School Education services should become an ongoing exercise at least once a year. Social Audit with civil society groups but in a collaborative spirit would help in ensuring that BPL households are not disadvantaged. "Community audit" in the case of basic services and social audit in the case of need based services once 2 or 3 years is likely lo help narrow the gap between perception and experience.

RTI Campaigns among BPL Communities

This TII-CMS India Corruption Study 2007 brings out that once the potential of RTI Act, is understood BPL. households will not lag behind; in fact they are likely to make use of the service even more. That is the time when one could say that RTI Act has done what is UK-hiding reducing corruption. There is urgency for civil society groups, the news media and local academics to come together and organize campaigns among BPL communities on RTI Act.

Include Unique Needs of BPL Users

The visible effect of IT and E-governance will not be evident unless special efforts are made aiming in BPL communities. The so-called "digital divide" even in urban areas could be because BPL and such other communities are two or three years behind in getting the benefits. This study indicates that computerisation of land records as a priority programme of E-governance had not helped BPL households much perhaps their unique requirements were not as much a focus. Computerisation of information or service alone may not be effective unless it is given in the public domain.

E-governance Schemes Specially Address BPL Needs

Although it is obvious that the first advantage of IT and e-governance would always be taken by those, who are better educated, better exposed, and economically better off there -is need to make some special effort to reduce lead time and hasten the process so that the disadvamaged people realize the benefits, parallely. With broadband reaching rural and far off locals and at reduced cost it should be possible to make available the benefits of e-governance parallely to the poor.

Redesign Front End Offices of Public Services

It is better that "front end" of most Government services/departments involved in serving citizens in large numbers and cutting across socio-economic backgrounds, are redesigned professionally in such a way that there is provision for display of pertinent information, helpdesk and equipped with modem communication facilities.

Universalize "BPL Card"

The size of BPL households is not fixed in the case of both basic and need based public services. It fluctuates often. Migratory character of the poorest calls for a "universal BPL card"—a card which provides access and entitlement anywhere, at least in the concerned State (similar to bank ATM cards).

Special Schemes to Ensure Service to BPL

BPL households require special service delivery facility to the "senior citizens". Repeat visits need to be avoided as it obviously imply that BPL households are not getting the priority that is promised. The fact that functionaries themselves are the direct recipients of bribe from the poor in most cases, need to be viewed far more seriously.

Encourage Users' Feedback

BPL households/communities should be encouraged with special benefit schemes so that they could be more organised, more active and articulate in giving their feedback. The fact that hardly a few lake time lo write their feedback is something that need to be taken up to encourage them to do so as often. Panchayats have to be entrusted with responsibilities so that the reach, access and reliability of targeted programmes to BPL households become better and redressal is not ignored or delayed.

Redressal System Should not be Limited to "Written Complaints"

Mechanism and practice of redressal of grievance requires much higher level of attention, sensitivity and follow up particularly in the context of BPL households. Criteria of having to have "written complaints" and their number should not be viewed as good enough in the context of BPL households. Scope for discretionary decision making need lo be minimised at the delivery end both in the case of basic and need based services 'and made more responsible or accountable.

Constant Supervision and Active Follow-up

Issues of staff attitudes and mindset cannot be moderated without constant feedback, guidance or supervision and training. Frequently changing procedures and formalities specific to various section of people as in the case of BPL households, need to be familiarised. In his regard, local management schools and such other independent academic bodies could play a role by organising workshops, sensitivity and training programmes, for the staff of basic public services at the grassroots.

One-Third Compulsions for Bribe can be Avoided by Rerouting Responsibilities

This study has identified the core functions, which cause most corruption in the case of each of the 11 services. If the processes involved in these specific functions are attended by revamping and by way of computerisation and keeping them in public domain compulsions for paying bribe could be avoided or minimised. In fact, by sorting out the very procedures and formalities for availing the service, the very scope for paying bribe by citizens could be eliminated in one-third to half of the cases depending on the service mid and the State in context. Establishing identity /entitlement procedures and formalities case need to be and responsibilities could be shifted. In the case of, for example land records, banks could directly obtain on-line or otherwise the references or particulars instead of making BPL households run around.

Achievement Claims Less Significant if Access not Assured

This study brings out that "performance achievements" or "target achievement" claims of Governments, even in the case of individual services, does not mean much for BPL households unless special emphasis is given to BPL households at the service delivery points. Some effort to validate such claims is needed periodically.

Special Drives/Camps to Reach Out to BPL Communities

While efforts are being made to expand the reach, there must be ways to see that no BPL household is deprived of the basic services, for whatever reasons. Special efforts should be made to reach households by way of specific drives, camps or campaigns.

Reduce Compulsions for Frequent Visits

More specifically, the nee for repeal visits should be curbed which is possible to some extent by re-looking into procedural complexities and improving grievance redressal mechanism and, at the same time. curtailing discretionary powers of individual functionaries.

Competitive Politics Should Spare Targeted Schemes

An important finding of TII-CMS India Corruption Study 2007 is that "competitive politics", of late, are affecting directly and indirectly, the very noble objectives of most targeted programmes aimed at the poor. They are adding to the problem of access to the service and the extent of corruption. This is one of the concerns of service providers themselves and also of course of BPL households. There are too many case examples that have come lo the notice of CMS field researchers. The case narrated from Assam on housing service is not an isolated example.

In fact, in more than a couple of States it was found that party leaders openly threatened BPL, ST, SC households to withdraw benefits of one or other targeted programme, if they did not vote for their respective local party. (Tins. includes NREGS. BPL cards, housing. Rs. 2/ kg rice, pension, *patta* for land, housing loam and bank loans). As long as "discretionary powers" of individuals at the service delivery point and certain confusion as to the responsibilities and accountabilities are not addressed, political interference is going to be a major source for corruption affecting the poor more.

Chapter 4

Corruption, Development and Governance: A Comparative Study of China and Indonesia

The question of whether corruption is antithetical to economic development has been extensively researched and debated since the 1960s. This has occurred largely in connection with law and economic reform efforts directed by governmental development agencies and non-governmental organisations in Western[1] countries toward developing countries in Africa, Asia and Latin America. More recently, interest in this question has been rejuvenated by China's dramatic economic growth (especially as contrasted with other states in political and economic transition), despite widespread corruption in that country.

While nearly all participants in the debate appear to agree that corruption ultimately is antithetical to long-term economic development, the extent to which it positively or negatively affects economic development in the short term depends upon highly contextual factors. In different countries and regions of the world, factors of local culture and history, the nature of the state, the type of corruption and actors involved, and the political responses and motivations to curtail corruption all inform the answer to this question.

Two countries are considered in this chapter: Indonesia and China. These countries were chosen for discussion because both are rife with corruption, especially in public administration and, although both are in Asia, they represent very different cultures and political systems from each other. It is suggested in this study that corruption in Indonesia is a significant deterrent to economic development and is a problem which needs to be addressed more vigorously and eliminated by the Indonesian government. Corruption in Indonesia not only siphons-off and reallocates resources in a non-productive manner, it also discourages much-needed direct foreign investment. Paradoxically, corruption in China appears to be a useful State tool that actually encourages economic development in the short term, while creating less optimistic long-term prospects. Due, in part, to the nature of China's political system, corruption appears to advance economic development by slowing political reform while still allowing less disruptive market reforms. Accordingly, an analysis of corruption as it affects economic development in Indonesia and in China illustrates that the extent to which corruption is antithetical to economic development ultimately depends upon context.

WHAT IS CORRUPTION? DEFINITIONS AND CONCEPTS

Corruption evades definition. As has been said of beauty and obscenity, ironically, one could also say that corruption "lies in the eye of the beholder," and that, while we may not be able to define it, we "know it when we see it."[2] Moralists, for example, define corruption according to simple (and simplistic) terms of right and wrong action, akin to stealing or lying. This moralist definition often supposes that there is a universal moral code, usually a Western moral code or some idealised version of it. Moralists also may purport to incorporate prevailing local cultural norms which are likely to change from time to time.

On the other hand, some scholars avoid moral absolutes in defining corruption. They see such morality-based definitions as hypocritical.[3] To them, definitions based on some supposed universal moral code are seen as ethnocentric, failing to take into account local cultures and norms. These scholars instead rely on more objective terms usually derived from economic or legal principles. They define corruption in terms of "the market" and diversion or (mis)allocation of scarce resources, or in terms of illegal practices which violate specific legal codes or administrative regulations.

Scholars further break down the concept of corruption into various subcategories according to the greater public interest or even public opinion. These scholars use a "litmus test" by which corruption is characterised (much like acceptable "white" lies versus unacceptable lies) as black, white or gray, according to whether the lie directly and immediately benefits the public as well as the corrupt actors.[4] Thus, for example, a public official diverting public funds from an intended project is seen as less corrupt (white or gray corruption) if his action will benefit his constituency even if his noblesse is tainted by what he skims for himself. Still other scholars break down corruption into further typologies, such as quasi-corruption, pre-corruption, integrative corruption and disintegrative corruption, in an effort to "provide some systematic method of approaching so complex a phenomenon."[5]

Each of these definitions and categories has its weaknesses. The problems with morality-based definitions have been summarised above. Legal codes often lag behind societal norms and may not be in sync with what is considered as corrupt conduct. Economic principles are somewhat subjective, generally free-market based, and tend to assume that there are vaguely different standards applicable to public officials in comparison with private business persons.[6] Definitions based upon concepts of public interest and public opinion are not only based upon highly transient judgments, but public interests and opinions are also extremely diverse and difficult to ferret out effectively. Moreover, even the best efforts to "eliminate moralising rhetoric and stick to the more rational language of economic advantage or defense of a presumptively neutral and locally adopted rule of law," may still suffer from "moral opprobrium" which unavoidably colors the discourse regarding corruption.

Corruption in the context of Indonesia and China is even more difficult to define because attempts at definition risk further extending the express or implied issue of morality into a debate over Western values versus Asian values. Asian culture has been traditionally characterised by Western (Orientalist) writers as essentially "defective to the point of being immoral and corrupt...."[7] Asian legal culture, for example, may be demonised in the West as "immature, primitive, backward, subjective and irrational," in contrast to Western laws which are seen as "developed, modern and advanced, objective and rational." At the same time, some Asian leaders-especially Dr. Mahathir of Malaysia and Lee Kuan Yew of Singapore—have fallen back on a sort of "reverse Orientalism" in deflecting Western attempts to define and combat corruption in Asia. They argue that Asia has its own unique, and uniform, way of doing things and that Western attempts at reform are a neo-colonialist form of cultural imperialism. This "Asian values" debate is beyond the scope of this article, but it is noted that any definition of corruption, especially as it pertains to Asia, is susceptible to criticism as being heavily biased in favor of Western ideology.

Probably the most widely accepted definition of corruption often relied upon when discussing corruption in Asia, is the World Bank definition of corruption as "the abuse of public office for private gain."[8] That definition, while limited to the public administration arena (as opposed to corruption purely in the private sector), is useful to the following analysis of corruption in Indonesia and China. While it implicitly conceptualises corruption in somewhat normative terms, essentially a violation of formal or legal norms,[9] the World Bank definition does not imply any negative economic consequences of corruption. This is an especially important factor when considering the premise of this article that corruption in China may have some positive short-term effects on the Chinese economy, despite negative long-term effects. In practical terms, moreover, that definition extends over those areas of public corruption most frequently encountered in both Indonesia and China: bribery, extortion, patronage, nepotism, theft of state assets, and diversion of state revenues. It is the World Bank definition, therefore, which underlies the discussions in this article.

THE CULTURE OF CORRUPTION: CHINA AND INDONESIA—A COMPARATIVE PERSPECTIVE

In the 1960s, in conjunction with the law and development[10] movement, it generally was accepted that corruption was "a usual and expected part of the national maturation process" in developing countries.[11] Certain "corrupt" practices were attributed to the immature development of the rule of law in those countries. In fact, characterising those practices as corrupt was seen as a West-centric imposition of Western values on indigenous practices (such as gift-giving or payment of tribute to authority figures). Conduct that might be "viewed as corruption in the West would be interpreted differently within the customs of emerging economies."[12] It was suggested that in developing countries there was simply "a gap between law (as imposed by western and alien standards) and accepted informal social norms (sanctioned by prevailing social ethics)," into which slipped the "folklore," "climate," or "way of life" of corruption."[13]

More recent scholars, however, assert that "the theoretical tenet that corruption is a dependant variable of development is false."[14] It generally is agreed today that corruption exists in all countries and in all societies, at all stages of economic and political development.[15] Even in the United States, for example, "common wisdom... indicates that corruption has now become part of the national lifestyle."[16] It is said to be "endemic to United States politics, businesses, and social institutions."[17]

Corruption is very different, however, in each country wherein it occurs. There are wide variations from one country to the next, both as to the degree to which it prevails and the nature of corrupt activity. As such, any analysis of corruption and its effects in different countries must examine the particular context of corruption in each country. Depending on the country involved, factors might include the local culture and history, nature of the state, type of corruption, actors involved, and political responses and motivation to curtail corruption (or not). These factors collectively form the culture of corruption in a given country. Significantly, the term "culture of corruption" is not used in this article in the same ethnocentric and apologetic sense it appeared in the law and development movement, especially as an effort to deflect criticisms of that movement's failures.[18] Rather, it is used in the sense that local context is an important factor in discussing corruption.

Culture of Corruption in Indonesia

With respect to Indonesia, it has long been said that there is a "culture of corruption."[19] In fact, with a diverse population of more than 240 million people[20] spread over an archipelagic state of 17,508 islands,[21] corruption may be Indonesia's predominant cultural common-denominator. The reasons for such widespread corruption are difficult to ascertain and somewhat controversial (particularly when so-called "Asian values" are invoked). Indonesia's political history, including recent efforts to accomplish greater government decentralisation, may be the most important factor in shaping the current culture of corruption. Other contributing factors may include a certain sense of resignation or acquiescence by the average person in Indonesia (even in the midst of widespread calls to eradicate corruption). Further, there has been a lack of "staying power" by outside donor organisations, intermittently "ramping-up" their insistence for anti-corruption reforms, only to later lose momentum and interest.

Following centuries of Dutch colonialism, subsequent Japanese occupation during World War II, and a brief attempt after the war by the Dutch to regain control (prevented largely through intervention by the United States and Great Britain through the United Nations), Indonesia finally emerged as a "democracy" slightly more than fifty years ago. The country's first constitution (drafted in 1945) established a very basic framework of fundamental government institutions necessary for an effective legislature, executive, and judiciary.[22]

Despite a "thin" rule of law,[23] however, that gave the appearance of democracy, Indonesia passed through a prolonged period of authoritarian rule that: "implicitly—sometimes explicitly -rejected the universalism of human rights as an innately Western concept that was alien to East Asia...[,] asserted the irrelevance of separation of powers[;] and elevated the state to a position of almost unchecked authority."[24] Only after the fall of Soeharto's "New Order" in 1998 (which spanned 32 years), did Indonesia finally commence "a formal constitutional transition from authoritarianism to a liberal representative democratic system, with a new institutional framework that would allow separation of powers," in essence favoring a "historically weak, but now politically irresistible, Anglo-American 'thick' interpretation of rule of law."[25]

As suggested above, these political transitions from colonialism to authoritarianism to real democracy, coupled in turn with greater decentralisation of the government, were protracted catalysts for the pervasive culture of corruption in Indonesia today. It has been observed that "[colonisation distorts relationships, destroys or petrifies institutions, and corrupts men and women, both colonizers and colonised."[26] The authoritarian governments which replaced the colonial government, in turn, were firmly autocratic and the state operated virtually as a family enterprise for the benefit of the.president, his family and friends. The Soeharto government, for example, was so corrupt that doing business in Indonesia necessarily involved a "complex web of corrupt deals and political payoffs," generally tied to Soeharto's family and cronies.[27] Thus, corrupt practices and a sense that the state (and the bureaucratic machinery) was above the law not only continued, but became even more firmly entrenched in the wake of colonialism as relationships and institutions were further distorted.

Finally, with the end of the New Order and its authoritarian rule, Indonesia underwent a transition from an autocracy to a real democracy. The social and political disruption as Indonesia began reworking its fundamental institutions, however, continued to provide a fertile climate for corruption. Indeed, it has been observed generally that such transitional periods of "political modernisation... [are] usually accompanied by increases in corruption."[28]

Decentralisation of the government as part of this political transition has also exacerbated widespread corruption. Over the past decade, Indonesia has moved somewhat haphazardly from the highly-centralised autocratic regime of Soeharto, through a period in the late 1990s of politically motivated (popularly mandated, and not always peaceful) demands for greater administrative and political autonomy at the regional level, and ultimately to a more carefully crafted decentralisation of governmental, especially fiscal authority to the provincial and local governments.[29] While this decentralisation may be good for local fiscal autonomy and relieves the unnecessary burdens on the central government as it inefficiently has tried to administer programmes across such a widely dispersed population, it also has created decentralised opportunities for corruption that previously did not exist at the provincial and local level in Indonesia. As provincial and local governments administer more programs and control more government funds and expenditures, local bureaucrats also now have opportunities for diversion of funds and "rent-seeking"[30] activities: primarily bribery and collection of excess "administrative" fees in connection with the performance of official duties.

Indeed, most of the corruption in Indonesia is in the nature of rent-seeking activities by government officials. Very low government salaries which encourage rent-seeking, together with a broad cultural "expectation that if anyone provides a service, there will some payment for it,"[31] combine to foster the culture of corruption. As one American schoter has observed, "[i]n a sense, the ordinary functions of government have been quietly "privatised" in what we would think of as perverse ways."[32] And, where the top strata of the state and its bureaucracy set an example of corruption, corruption becomes part of the national culture. An editorial in the *Jakarta Post* recently explained.

> [i]n a hierarchical society, such as Indonesia's... norms and values are defined by those at the apex of the societal structure. If the public perceives their leaders as being able to get away with "murder", than the only logical conclusion is that such behaviour is acceptable.[33]

This has also been characterised as the "leader-follower spillover effect" of corruption: "left to itself, corruption will grow, 'spilling over' and affecting increasing portions of a given organisation or society."[34] As Niccolo Machiavelli cautioned a half-millennium ago, "what the prince does the many will also soon do - for in their eyes the prince is ever in view."

Ironically, in the midst of this culture of corruption, the call for an end to "corruption, collusion, and nepotism" - *korupsi, kolusi dan nepotisme* ("KKN") - has been a rallying cry throughout Indonesia for many years. The press devotes significant attention to the subject and there are frequent articles in the newspapers regarding corruption and efforts to combat it in Indonesia. Even the World Bank has moved beyond its earlier euphemistic reference to bureaucratic corruption in Indonesia as "common local practices," and now expressly addresses the need to combat Indonesia's corruption.[35] Yet, there is also an air of resignation about corruption,[36] which may be a product of its sheer magnitude in Indonesia.

Corruption in Indonesia has long been "rampant throughout all levels of Indonesian society." As noted, in a decision in 2005 by the Indonesian Constitutional Court *(Makhama Konstitusi),* corruption in Indonesia involves "almost all elements and strata in the three branches of the government - the executive, the legislative and judiciary, which colluded - directly or indirectly - to protect themselves, rather than checking one another in a complex democratic system of checks and balances."[37] It has been observed that in Indonesia "[c]orruption colors every regime. Like an old tree, its strong roots spread everywhere. From the Old Order to the New Order to the Reform Order, corruption has continued.... In this republic, corruption is the child of every regime."[38] As pointed out above in this study, the Soeharto government was so corrupt that doing business in Indonesia generally involved corrupt payments to Soeharto's family and cronies. Likewise, subsequent presidents have been characterised by the Indonesian press as all having "waxed lyrically about eradicating corruption and launched high profile anticorruption campaigns," yet until now they have "left office under a cloud of suspicion of having facilitated, if not directly participated in, the misappropriation of state funds."[39]

In fact, the Indonesian press is not optimistic about current President Susilo Bambang Yudhoyono's pledge to combat corruption either. It has been observed by the press that the "President inherited the same corrupt system that had been built up over decades,"[40] and that "with the lack of political will, corrupt legal system, inconsistency in law enforcement and a penchant for the good life, the possibility of success for the government's anticorruption programme is in fact slim."[41] Even with some dramatic successes in combating corruption, the opinion in Indonesia remains that "we have been in this situation before - high profile case, big headlines, severe punishment, reprieve and back to business as usual."[42] The culture of corruption in Indonesia persists despite reform efforts.

Culture of Corruption in China

A relatively recent article by Chinese economist Shuntian Yao eloquently summarises that:

> Some people hold the view that China's corruption problems have their root deep in the Chinese culture. They argue that the Chinese people, as well as most of their counterparts in Asian countries, have a long tradition of placing personal connections above the law, and that this is the real source of corruption. They conclude that, no matter what political system China chooses, the corruption problem can never be avoided. Many CCP officials and business bigwigs agree with this view, although they do not admit it in public. I have had discussions with several friends who are either CCP officials or very successful businessmen; all of them privately supported this view [sic]. They even argued that corruption was not too bad, and that if you could take advantage of it, it could work for you very efficiently, and that, after all, you had to accept it if you wanted to survive in China.[43]

Yao disputes the "culture-root view," however, as it applies to China. He maintains that the political system in combination with the legal system in China is the true root of corruption. To support this hypothesis, Yao. draws on historical examples of the early Han and Tang Dynasties as periods with rule of law and no serious corruption. In contrast, Yao suggests, "the darkest periods in China's history are all related to a corrupt political system and to the illegal behaviours of a tiny group of bigwigs or aristocrats who were protected by a fatuous and self-indulgent ruler." According to Yao, rather than a cultural phenomenon, corruption in China is merely a consequence of the faulty political system compounded by the faulty legal system.

It is suggested in this study that, although Yao and other scholars do not to admit it, there is indeed a culture of corruption in China. It is shaped, in part, by the political and legal systems, as well as by the economic systems, that Yao indicates are the sole cause of corruption. In addition to the factors mentioned previously in this article, as generally coalescing into a culture of corruption in a given country, certain historical and sociopolitical factors found in China also combine to define and color the prevailing culture of corruption in that country. These include a centuries-old Confucian sense of strict hierarchy and order, and a tradition of tributary payments to government officials. They also include the long-standing traditions of *guanxi,* "whereby 'personal connections' among government officials and firm managers control the allocation of resources.... [a] response, rooted in Chinese culture, to an underdeveloped system of property rights and contract law."[44] Finally, the Chinese culture of corruption is also shaped by contemporary popular attitudes, the Communist nature and interventionist stance of the state, and the state's response to corruption.[45]

No one disputes that China is currently in a "dark period" of extensive and pervasive corruption, a "cancer of the Chinese society."[46] Prominent journalists in China decry that "[corruption in China's system reaches every level and can't be solved"[47] and even ponder whether some aspects of corruption in China are "one hundred times worse even than that of Indonesia under Suharto's ruling."[48] It is reported by the media that "[corruption has long been rife in Chinese society, where government and party officials control access to business licenses and a host of other vital permits."[49] In that context, corruption "takes the form of rules, edicts and certificates, all requiring extra fees rather than blunt requests for money."[50]

Significantly, the Chinese culture of corruption appears to be cultivated and used surreptitiously by the Communist Party and the government to achieve their social, political and economic ends. Although the Chinese Communist Party Central Committee issued a 36-page policy paper in 2004 calling corruption "a life and death struggle" for the Party,[51] such statements appear to be, at best, mere window-dressing. For example, it has been observed that the Party has an incentive to allow corruption as an alternative to Western-style compensation and that the government may only selectively enforce laws that prohibit corrupt practices. Consistent with long-standing propaganda that "every Communist Party member is a selfless 'public servant of the people,'" corruption allows the government to pay low salaries, but with the recognition that higher compensation will be earned through rent-seeking schemes by public officials.[52] In some ways, payment of bribes and administrative "facilitation" fees is analogous to, and perhaps more effectively and fairly administered than, performance-based bonuses paid in the West. Chengze Simon Fan and Herschel I. Grossman argue:

Corruption, whether in the form of *tanwu shouhui* or *nuoyong gongkuan,* mitigates the problem of measuring and monitoring economic performance because local officials who make the largest economic contribution are likely to be able to extract the largest fees or nepotistic favors or to have the most valuable property to appropriate. Also the compensation that local officials obtain through corruption, particularly in the form of bribery, is paid by local firms, which have the best information on the performance of local officials.[53]

In addition, although Western-style explicitly-paid higher salaries and bonuses based on economic performance might benefit many public officials, there are also many Chinese officials who do not have any direct economic role and, therefore, would be bypassed by such rewards. As has been observed:

An explicit system of material incentives and rewards for economic performance would undermine the political and social standing of those government officials and Party members who are not involved in economic activities. Because the Communist Party, like any political organisation, is a potentially fragile coalition, jealousy and discontent, especially in the army, would threaten to destabilize and to undermine its cohesiveness.

Thus, rent-seeking and other corrupt activities by public officials become a compensation scheme that may, at least in the short run, benefit the Communist Party and the government despite their public pronouncements to the contrary. This phenomenon contributes significantly to the culture of corruption in China.

Notwithstanding the beneficial use of corruption as an incentive programme for public officials, however, the Communist Party and the government do have an incentive to selectively prosecute some officials for corruption. When reports of major corruption crack-downs are published, it reflects well on the Communist Party both in China and abroad. In addition, selective prosecution of corruption furthers strong internal cohesiveness and absolute power by the Party and supports the Party's hierarchical structure.

Where every official knows that another especially a higher-ranking official could successfully charge him with corruption, "lack of exposure is in effect special treatment for which the official gratefully exchanges his political support." Public officials whose loyalty to the Party is questioned or who become too greedy can be reigned in. High-profile prosecutions do occur and the media does periodically tout the successes of government anti-corruption campaigns - such as a China News Service report that Beijing recovered as much as 700 million yuan (US$84 million) in the first year of the government's campaign against corruption.[54] Finally, as discussed in the last section of this article, corruption needs to be tightly controlled, even if it is not fully discouraged by the Party. Ultimately, corruption is highly inefficient and disruptive to China's economy and causes quantifiable economic loss despite the country's growing economy.

Significantly, it is the manner in which the Chinese government has co-opted the culture of corruption in that country that distinguishes it from Indonesia and other countries that also experience a strong culture of corruption. In China and Indonesia alike, the governments insist that they are fighting corruption and trumpet their high-profile successes. The public and the press in both countries vociferously decry the state of corruption in public administration; but only in Indonesia does it appear that the government actually has an incentive to eliminate corruption.

Despite modest GDP growth in Indonesia, corruption significantly suppresses business investments and overall economic development. By contrast, China may benefit in the short-term from corruption. The following suggests that, although corruption in China poses a substantial cost to the economy in terms of inefficiencies and actual yuan lost, Chinese economic growth paradoxically continues to outpace every other economy in Asia.[55]

CORRUPTION AS ANTITHETICAL TO ECONOMIC DEVELOPMENT: CHINA AND INDONESIA—A COMPARATIVE PERSPECTIVE

Most people would agree that, as an ethical matter, most forms of corruption are undesirable. Moreover, as is noted in the discussions above, there is widespread lip service paid to the eradication of corruption. But, the question of whether fighting corruption should be a "true priority or merely a rhetorical one" remains hotly debated.[56] A great deal of ambiguity remains with respect to whether corruption is good, bad, or irrelevant for economic development,[57] especially in countries like China that simultaneously have a vigorous economy and yet an entrenched culture of corruption.

Many scholars promoting "rule of law" as a development strategy enthusiastically embrace anti-corruption measures. Rather than a purely economics-based approach, these scholars look at the inter-relationships of investment, economic growth, and the strength of public institutions. They advocate the elimination of corruption "to avoid squandered resources, to promote security and predictability, to inspire confidence, eliminate price distortions and promote an efficient distribution of resources,"[58] albeit in the interests of encouraging development. They further insist that "corruption somehow drains resources from the system as a whole—its costs are costs of transactions, not costs of the product or service purchased."[59] If those transaction costs are removed, they believe, the whole economy improves. There is some ambiguity in their research, however, as to the separate effects of corruption vis-a-vis other factors contributing to poor quality public institutions.[60]

Still other scholars, economists as well as non-economists, argue that corruption is actually beneficial to poor quality institutions. Corruption is viewed as the grease that makes the otherwise rigid machinery of government function smoothly. According to this "functionalist"[61] view, corruption promotes certain efficiencies. For example, in the case of competitive bidding for government contracts, where the highest bidder in *bribes* is awarded the contract, a certain "allocation efficiency is maintained, as only the lowest-cost firm can afford the largest bribe."[62] In addition, according to the functionalists, corruption also encourages bureaucrats to work harder, acting as a sort of piece rate for government work. Moreover, it supposedly permits entrepreneurs to circumvent or at least navigate efficiently through an otherwise slow-moving and burdensome regulatory framework.

The so-called "speed money" paid to expedite administrative action or to reduce delay in public administration, has been demonstrated (using complex Nash equilibrium game theory) to actually reduce inefficiencies in public administration by speeding up the overall queue for services, thus minimising waiting costs for everyone in the queue.[63] This is especially true in those countries with excessive bureaucratic regulations and discretion.[64] Samuel Huntington has succinctly captured the essence of this argument, colorfully asserting that "[i]n terms of economic growth the only thing worse than a society with a rigid, over-centralised, dishonest bureaucracy is one with a rigid, over-centralised, *honest* bureaucracy."[65]

The flip side of the functionalist coin is "post-functionalism," an approach that began in the 1970s in an attempt to rebut functionalism.[66] Warning that "academia, state and society must rouse themselves from the autonarcotic effects of the 'functional corruption' myth,"[67] post-functionalists argue that corruption has dysfunctional consequences for the economy and society generally. They maintain that "corruption wastes revenues and resources that might be utilised elsewhere, erodes the trust and loyalty granted to political leaders by their followers, and solidifies inequities in the apportionment of goods in favor of certain strata of society."[68] In their view, corruption also stifles innovation, entrepreneurship, and both domestic and foreign productive investment. It also encourages even more excessive and discretionary regulation.[69] As for the "grease the machinery" argument, it has been observed that corrupt officials actually may be incentivised to "cause more administrative delays in order to attract more bribes."[70] Such deliberate delays may also occur where public officials have no ability to speed up the process in any event, and they are instead bribed to slow down the process with respect to a payer's competitors.[71] Finally, the post-functionalists point to research which indicates that even where corruption has some short-term benefits to the economy, it still leads ultimately to dysfunction. In a number of countries studied, corruption has led to smuggling, black market economies, mass starvation, imposition of martial law, and the complete disintegration of economy and society, in general.[72] Moreover, corruption feeds upon itself, "blocking organisational change and societal reform... [and as reform consequently] becomes increasingly onerous to achieve, more corruption is fostered as a remedy to existing corruption."[73]

It is suggested in this study that both the functionalist and the post-functionalist positions have merit, depending upon the specific country under consideration. As the following discussions indicate, corruption in Indonesia appears to be a deterrent to more than modest economic growth and development. In China, on the other hand, credible research indicates that economic development continues to race forward, even though corruption's inherent inefficiencies and misallocation of resources is costing the economy heavily and likely will be quite harmful in the long term.

Economic Impact of Corruption in Indonesia

Despite the wide-spread culture of corruption in Indonesia, there has been relatively little research quantifying the economic impact. It is widely asserted that the "crony capitalism" and overall corruption of the Soeharto regime - thirty-two years of a dysfunctional "black state"[74] - was a root cause of Indonesia's economic crisis in the late 1990s.[75] Moreover, the media has not been shy about proclaiming the dire economic consequences of corruption in Indonesia more recently. Headlines exclaim, "Investors desert Indonesia as rot of corruption sets in."[76] It is reported that "millions of Indonesians face poverty as investors continue to desert the country largely because of rampant corruption and collapsing infrastructure,"[77] and that "problems with regional autonomy and increasing demands for bribes are further slowing Indonesia's exports in a highly competitive regional market."[78] The media declares that "the President must decide whether corruption eradication is part of economic recovery, the improvement of public services, the efficiency of the state budget or just about improving Indonesia's rank in the Corruption Perception Index survey by [Transparency International]. Each option has its consequences and requirements."[79] Moreover, in a recent survey, *Doing Business in Indonesia 2005,* the World Bank reportedly "confirmed that Indonesia is not attractive for foreign investors. To invest in Indonesia requires more time, more complex procedures and much more money, all because of corruption."[80]

Yet, while it generally is accepted that corruption is hurting the Indonesian economy, there is little empirical data specifically examining its effects. As such, this article looks at several key factors of corruption present in Indonesia that are regarded as hindering economic development. It is suggested that these factors, consistent with anecdotal evidence reported in the press and by several surveys conducted by the World Bank and organisations such as Transparency International, are in fact crippling the Indonesian economy.

Possibly the most significant factor antithetical to economic development in Indonesia is what has been characterised as a "shadow system"[81] or extralegal administrative system parallel to the official public administration. This shadow system was established especially during the thirty-two years of Soeharto's New Order rule, and while not as all-encompassing as it was during that regime, vestiges of it remain. Business people still complain, for example, of corruption in the courts and the instability and unpredictability that this injects into business transactions.[82] The law is largely irrelevant in the face of powerful connections or money.[83] As a prominent scholar on Indonesia has observed, in the wake of Scenario's systematic co-option of all formal administrative institutions in Indonesia, "there is really nothing left to work with... there's corruption everywhere"[84]. Even today:

> The result is a highly developed legal formalism (hard law) and public rhetoric; seemingly impenetrable and secretive politics; state sanctioned "corruption" and legal informality in practice (soft law norms); and apparent irrelevance and absurdity in the practice of law by reason of it being the interface between the two systems.[85]

Apart from the political and legal consequences of such a shadow system, such pervasive corruption is also socially and economically parasitic and exploitive:

> It is not a self-sufficient or stand alone system but depends on co-existing economic and social systems, for example, on the agricultural economy; on markets or state enterprises; on the self-employed; on small and medium enterprises; on the informal or black economy operating outside, or on the contestable margins of, the law.[86]

Corruption in Indonesia "interpenetrates these and other systems and lives off them." It fails to produce any tangible socio-economic benefits and it is a highly inefficient use of resources. As one scholar notes, corruption in Indonesia "comprises essentially non-productive behaviours or behaviours excessively costly to the host. It does not, in economists' terms, use resources efficiently nor give people the incentive to engage in productive activities."

Significantly, it is likely that administrative corruption in Indonesia also undermines the country's macroeconomic stability by siphoning off government revenues and encouraging excessive government spending. As noted in a World Bank report on corruption and economic development:

> This can happen through corruption in tax and customs departments, through debt incurred when the scrutiny of finance ministries and central banks is bypassed, through contracts that are awarded to high-cost bidders or without competitive tendering, and through the general erosion of expenditure control. Excessive debt may be incurred thorough "white elephant" investment projects that owe their origin, in part, to bribes. Macroeconomic stability may also be threatened by debt guarantees and other off-budget contingent liabilities agreed to in corrupt transactions without public scrutiny. It may also be threatened by fraud in financial institutions, leading to loss of confidence by savers, investors, and foreign exchange markets.[87]

In similar fashion, the diverting of public resources for personal use (such as construction materials intended for public works used on private homes or even misappropriated and sold by public officials) also disrupts economic stability and growth in favor of nonproductive resource allocations.[88]

Perhaps, the greatest effect of corruption on the Indonesian economy is both foreign and domestic investors' reluctance to invest in Indonesia. In much the same way that weeds crowd healthy plants out of a garden, widespread bribery and related rent-seeking by public officials "imply declining profitability on productive investments relative to rent-seeking investments, thus tending to crowd out the former." Exacerbating this effect, in fact, increased rent-seeking makes further rent-seeking less costly relative to the cost of productive investment. Moreover, as rent-seeking increases, entrepreneurial investment is particularly hard-hit. Compared to existing and static businesses, new or expanding businesses often are more at the mercy of public officials who issue licenses and permits. The costs of paying bribes to these officials, for example, can undermine the ability to predict start-up or expansion costs, essential for attracting or accurately allocating capital investment and can disproportionately increase those costs.[89] Innovators and entrepreneurs may decide not even to enter the market because of moral compunctions over paying bribes, as well as a fear of getting caught.[90] This decline in competitiveness and diversity in the market also negatively affects the economic development overall.[91]

The economic cost of corruption and a reluctance to invest has been the subject of a number of important studies focused on developing countries. International Monetary Fund economist Paolo Maoro, for example, found that "the negative association between corruption and investment, as well as growth, is significant."[92] In one study, Maoro argues that "if a given country were to improve its corruption "grade" from 6 out of 10 to 8 out of 10, its investment-GDP ratio would rise by almost 4 percentage points and its annual growth of GDP per capita would rise by almost half a percentage point."[93]

A similar study by another IMF economist, Shang-Jin Wei, examined the effects of taxation and corruption on international direct investment from fourteen source countries to forty-five host countries. He concluded that an increase in corruption level in a host country would decrease foreign direct investment. Illustrating his conclusion, We points out that an increase in the corruption level of a relatively low-corruption country such as Singapore to that of a high corruption country such as Mexico "would have the same negative effect on inward FDI as raising the tax rate by eighteen to fifty percentage points, depending on the specification."[94] While limited attention has been paid to how these factors specifically affect Indonesia's economy, the considerable prevalence of rent-seeking by public officials in Indonesia[95] indicates that these factors would adversely affect the economy in that country.

Economic Impact of Corruption in China

It is interesting that much of the recent impetus for quantitative analysis and the collection of empirical evidence on the effects of corruption on economic development has been propelled by the apparent success of the Chinese economy despite significant corruption. As Shang-Jin Wei points out at the beginning of his study, he was motivated to conduct his research because "China has rampant corruption according to various newspaper accounts as well as surveys of business executives. Yet, for every year in the last four, China has been the largest developing host of international investment. Even its FDI flow-to-GDP ratio has been among the highest among developing countries."[96] While the effects of corruption in other developing economies, such as Indonesia's, appear to be directly and immediately antithetical to economic development and growth, China appears on the surface to present a paradox.

Contemporary conventional wisdom—especially as promulgated by scholars at the World Bank and others promoting good governance and its virtual doppel-ganger, anti-corruption efforts—insists that:

> countries with stable government, predictable methods of changing laws, secure property rights and a strong judiciary enjoy higher rates of investment and growth than countries lacking such institutions. Indeed, a number of multiple-country empirical studies have shown that rule of law and enforceable property rights are positively correlated with growth."[97]

In addition, there is significant empirical evidence to suggest that corruption negatively correlates with economic development, such as the case of Indonesia. Yet, in China, despite an apparent lack of rule of law and at least tacitly state-sanctioned (albeit somewhat controlled) administrative corruption, a present-day economic miracle appears to be continuing unabated. The reasons for this are complex.

However, recent studies do indicate that corruption is negatively affecting economic development in China, despite the current growth.

Unlike other developing countries, China presents a unique set of circumstances. Much of the economic growth is "attributed to cultural factors, a distinct form of 'Chinese capitalism,' a *guanxi*-based rule of relationships, clientelism and corporatism. Importantly, "what they all share in common is an emphasis on relationships as a substitute for rule of law." However, corruption itself is also a significant factor fueling economic growth. As discussed previously in this article, it is suggested that the Chinese Communist Party uses corruption as a form of "bonus" or "incentive" programme to encourage greater economic performance by public officials." Thus, public officials who work hard and contribute the most economically may also get the most back in bribes and "facilitation" fees. Public officials also are incentivised to undertake local development projects, and to attract both domestic and foreign investment in those projects, by the opportunity to benefit from corrupt payments they will receive.[98] While misallocation of scarce resources and an incoherent distribution according to competing local interests, rather than fundamental market principles, may distort the economy in the long-run,[99] corruption does push the economy forward in the short run.

Partly as a result of enthusiastic economic development efforts by local officials who stand to gain from increased rent-seeking opportunities, and partly due to a "lemming effect" by foreign investors, much of the economic growth in China is attributed to foreign investors who are flocking to invest there, despite the rampant corruption. In the past, many foreign investors lacked sufficient information with which to make a well-reasoned and informed decision about investing in China. They invested despite the risks and difficulties involved in navigating a corrupt and unpredictable landscape.[100] But, it has also been observed that ignorance, more recently, may not be the only excuse:

> Eyes dazed by the (fictive) promise of a market of 1.3 billion captive consumers, foreign investors have been willing to discount or ignore the considerable risks of doing business in China... [Some of these] decisions have been driven not by any long term strategic plan but rather by organisational politics and dynamics. Even senior management of major multinational companies at times appears to have been swept up in the hype over the Pac-Rim century, and rushed to enter China simply because others were doing so... In other cases, lower level management saw China as a good place to advance their careers and aggressively pursued projects.

In addition to increased foreign investment, much of the economic growth in China is attributed to other factors unique to China. These clearly include short-term phenomena. Government programs promoting the "reallocation of labor from low to high productivity sectors, in particular from agriculture to manufacturing and services," for example, figure prominently in promoting economic development. Such short-term phenomena appear largely unaffected by corruption, although long-term productivity within each sector could suffer.

The nature of the state and the nature of corruption in China are also important factors contributing to the proportionately more limited impact of corruption in China than in other countries. For example, building on a well-established institutional legacy, the Chinese state remains strong and well-disciplined as it progresses with economic reforms. The reforms are gradual and accomplished through existing state institutions controlled by the Communist Party.[101] Moreover, the "Chinese regime has not only preserved old mechanisms [for discipline] but also created new ones to deal with the prevention, discovery, and control of corruption." As such, it is able to effectively "limit the nature and impact of corruption."

The nature of Chinese corruption itself is also an important factor mitigating the negative effects of corruption on economic development. It is significant that most of the corruption in China is in the form of rent-seeking and "profit-sharing",[102] rather than outright theft of public money. The potential positive short-term effects on the economy from rent-seeking, such as incentives for local economic development efforts, have been discussed above. Profit-sharing also is regarded as a type of corruption which "may be the least harmful and could even lead to good social results." With respect to the development of township and village enterprises, for example, it has been observed that exchanging profit shares for commercial privileges granted by local officials actually has helped the growth of those local enterprises. Further, it has been observed that money derived from profit-sharing and to a lesser extent from rent-seeking is more likely to be reinvested in a country's economy than is money derived from other types of corruption. Although there is a lack of conclusive empirical evidence in this respect, reinvestment of corrupt money in the Chinese economy may serve to lessen capital losses incurred through corruption.

Despite the apparently more controlled and limited impact of corruption in China, particularly as compared with countries such as Indonesia, corruption is still seen as causing "prodigious economic losses for the country and its people."[103] The reduced economic output and inefficiencies that result from corruption in China are draining the Chinese economy.[104] One of the first studies estimating total economic losses resulting from Chinese corruption over the period 1995-1998 indicated that is was 13.2-16.8 per cent ofGDP. A further study based on official statistics examined ten specific areas of "systematic economic losses caused by corruption" in China. It was estimated that for the period 1999-2001, the total economic losses "amounted to an annual average of 14.5-14.9 per cent of GDP." Moreover, the author of both studies, Professor Angang Hu of Tsinghua University, acknowledged that, "in reality, the forms of corruption are more than those listed, and the real losses are far beyond that... It is still an unknown economic 'black hole.'" As he summarises:

> China's GDP accounts for over 10 per cent of the world's total, ranking second only after the United States. Up to the end of 2001, the GDP of China was approximately eight times of that of 1978 (7.9 times), which is one of the great wonders in human history (to create capital at the fastest speed).

However, as a result of the large amount of economic losses and illegal capital transfer, which is caused by prevalent and systematic corruption... the increase was much less than eightfold."

Whereas corruption has not fully prevented economic development from occurring in China, the inefficiencies and nonproductive transfers of resources it creates, combined with lost investment opportunities, appear to be significantly hurting the Chinese economy. Indeed, as reflected by Professor Hu's studies, "[i]t is not exaggerating to say that, China may very well be the country with the most enormous economic losses in the world caused by corruption.

Conclusion

The degree to which corruption is antithetical to economic development continues to be researched and debated, particularly as the unprecedented growth of China's economy continues relatively unabated. It appears that virtually everyone agrees that corruption ultimately leads to institutional and administrative dysfunction and that it is antithetical to economic development in the long run. There is a great deal of debate, however, regarding whether it can benefit economic development in the short run. In considering the consequences of corruption in Indonesia and in China, it is apparent that whether—and the extent to which—corruption is antithetical to long-term and short-term economic development depends significantly upon contextual factors. These include the culture, political history, nature of the state and the corruption occurring, and the response by the state to administrative corruption. These also include less rational factors, such as those presently driving foreign investment in China despite rampant corruption.

In Indonesia, despite modest growth, corruption is holding back the economy and frightening away foreign investment. The government has no choice but to act aggressively to eliminate corruption. It is clearly antithetical to economic development in that country. In China, on the other hand, the economy is still hurtling forward despite corruption. The state appears less eager to completely eliminate corruption, but instead it appears to be harnessing it in some positive ways. Corruption is very costly to the Chinese economy, however, especially considering estimated losses between 13.2 and 16.8 per cent of GDP over a two to three year period. Although the position of China's public officials to less than vigorously combat corruption is consistent with the wisdom that "Thou shalt not muzzle the ox when he treadeth out the corn,"[105] there will eventually come a point at which China must stem its economic losses as a result of corruption. Despite China's enormous economic success, corruption is ultimately antithetical to the country's future economic development.

REFERENCES

1. In this study, the terms "West" and "Western" are used in their contemporary, non-geographic sense as encompassing the Americas and Western Europe, as well as countries such as Australia and New Zealand which are geographically far from Western Europe and the U.S. but culturally still very "Western."
2. *Jacobellis v. Ohio,* 378 U.S. 184, 197 (1964). U.S. Supreme Court Justice Potter Stewart is oft-quoted for his statement

in *Jacobellis* regarding what is obscene: "I shall not today attempt further to define the kinds of material I understand to be embraced.... [b]ut I know it when I see it...." *Ibid.*

3. We apply different standards and definitions to ourselves, for example, when we buy tickets to a sold-out game from a scalper, or when we tip a *maitre d'* in order to jump the queue in a crowded restaurant.

4. Simcha B. Werner, *New Directions in the Study of Administrative Corruption,* Vol. 43 No. 2 Pub. Admin. R. 146, 147 (1983).

5. Kate Gillespie & Gwenn Okruhlik, *The Political Dimensions of Corruption Cleanups: A Framework for Analysis,* V. 24 No. 1 Comp. Pol. 77, 79 (1991).

6. David Kennedy, *The International Anti-Corruption Campaign,* 14 Conn. J. Int'L L. 455,455 (1999). Kennedy also notes that a further dimension to this double-standard is a First World vs. Third World bias. Practices characterised as corrupt when conducted by government officials in the Third World may be no different than the accepted private practices of First World individuals and corporations. *Ibid.* at 458.

7. Tim Lindsey, *History Always Repeats? Corruption, Culture and "Asian Values," in* Corruption in Asia: Rethinking The Governance Paradigm 1, 1 (Tim Lindsey & Howard Dick, eds., 2002).

8. World Bank, Corruption and Economic Development, Helping Countries Combat Corruption: The Role Of The World Bank 8 (1997), http://wwwl.worldbank.org/publicsector/anticorrupt/corruptn/corrptn.pdf. Although a useful definition, there may be some conduct that falls outside the scope of this definition but which nevertheless would generally be considered corrupt. An abuse of public office, for example, might fall outside the scope of this definition if the abuse does not actually benefit the public official and instead benefits the public. Returning to an earlier example in this article, one can further question whether corruption exists when a public official fraudulently diverts funds from an intended project in another jurisdiction to benefit his own constituency. Morality and law-based definitions of corruption, and most

economics-based definitions, would deem such action as corrupt.

9. Howard Dick, *Corruption and Good Governance: The New Frontier of Social Engineering, in* Corruption in Asia: Rethinking the Governance Paradigm 71, 72 (Tim Lindsey & Howard Dick, eds., 2002).

10. The so-called law and development movement was largely spearheaded by U.S. law professors, sponsored by the U.S. government (USAID) and the Ford Foundation, who saw it as a way to stabilize various developing countries' economic and political systems; the experiment was first introduced in Africa, with resounding failure, and later in various forms in Asia and Latin America over a period of about ten years.

11. Werner, *supra* note 4, at 147.

12. Daniel Kaufman, *Corruption: The Facts,* 107 Foreign Pol'y 114, 115(1997).

13. Werner, *supra* note 4, at 148 (internal comments added).

14. *Ibid.* at 148; *see also* Kaufman, *supra* note 16, at 114 ("In more recent times a revisionist view has held that corruption may not be inconsistent with development and at times may even foster it.").

15. Werner, supra note 4, at 148; Isaac Ehrlich & Francis T. Lui, Bureaucratic Corruption and Endogenous Economic Growth, 107(S6) J. Pol. Econ.s 270, S271 (Dec. 1999); Nora M. Rubin, Notes and Comments; A Convergence of 1996 and 1997 Global Efforts to Curb Corruption and Bribery in International Business Transactions: The Legal Implications of the OECD Recommendations and Convention for the United States, Germany, and Switzerland, 14 AM. U. INT'L L. REV. 257, 265-66 (1998); but see Peter W. Schroth, American Law in a Time of Global Interdependence: U.S. National Reports to the XVIth International Congress of Comparative Law: Section V, The United States and the International Bribery Conventions, 50 AM. J. COMP. L. 593, 619 (Fall 2002) ("There is a silly conventional wisdom that corruption is everywhere, only in different forms.").

16. Werner, *supra note* 4, at 148.

17. *Ibid.* According to a relatively recent World Bank study, "perceived corruption" may have "risen slightly during the

1990s in Western Europe and North America, but still, as of 1999, [it was indexed] at less than half of any other region and about one-third of the level in sub-Saharan Africa." Schroth, *supra* note 19, at 622, note 141 (citing Lederman, Loayza & Reis Scares, *Accountability and Corruption: Political Institutions Matter,* World Bank Working Paper No. 2708 (2001)).

18. Lindsey, supra note 7, at 1.

19. Gary Goodpaster, *Ref lections on Corruption in Indonesia, in* Corruption in Asia: Rethinking the Governance Paradigm 87, 87 (Tim Lindsey & Howard Dick, eds., 2002) ("Indonesia's first vice-president, Mohammad Hatta, said this a long time ago, but it is often repeated....").

20. United States Central Intelligence Agency, The World Factbook, http://www.cia.gov/cia/publications/factbook/geos/id.html (last visited Sept. 10, 2006).

21. Republik Indonesia Portal Nasional, Posisi Gegrafis, http://www.indonesia.go.id/navigasiDetail.php7n avld=l&content=0 (last visited Sept. 10,2006).

22. The 1945 Constitution of the Republic of Indonesia, especially Articles 2-17, 19-22E, and 24-25.

23. A "thin" rule of law is characterised by certain procedures and fundamental institutions. This is in contrast to a "thick rule" of law, which is more substantive, tends to emphasize the importance of law, and may even include notions of "morality related to economic governance... regime type... and human rights." Erik G. Jensen, *The Rule of Law and Judicial Reform, in* Beyond Common Knowledge 336, 339 (Erik G. Jensen & Thomas C. Heller, eds., 2003).

24. Tim Lindsey, *Indonesia: Devaluing Asian Values, Rewriting Rule of Law, in* Asian Discourses of Rule of Law 286, 286 (Randall Peerenboom, ed., 2004).

25. *Ibid.*

26. George J. Aditjondro, Liberating Our Colonial Mindset (Aug. 16, 1995), http://www.hartfordhwp.com/archives/ 54b/034.html (last visited Sept. 9, 2006) (paraphrasing Albert Memmi, the Colonizer and the colonised 217 (Earthscan Publications 1990) (1957)).

27. Jared Levinson, *Indonesia's Odyssey: A Nation's Long, Perilous Journey to the Rule of Law and Democracy,* 18 Ariz. J. Int'l & Comp. L. 103, 112 (2001). Even Soeharto's late wife, Siti, "was known as 'Madame Ten Percent', reflecting her share of all public contracts." *Ibid.*
28. Andrei Shieifer & Robert W. Vishny, *Corruption,* Vol. 108 No. 3 Q.J.Econ. 599, 610 (1993).
29. The most significant steps toward decentralisation have been accomplished by Law Number 18/1997; Law Number 22/1999; Law Number 25/1999; Law Number 34/2000 (amending Law Number 18/1997); and, late in 2004, the enactment of Law Number 32/2004 and Law Number 33/2004, which replaced Law Number 22/1999 and Law Number 25/1999, respectively, regarding the authority of the central government (Undang-undang Nomor 18 Tahun 1997, Undang-undang Nomor 22 Tahun 1999, Undang-undang Nomor 25 Tahun 1999, Undang-undang Nomor 34 Tahun 2000, Undang-undang Nomor 32 Tahun 2004, and Undang-undang Nomor 33 Tahun 2004, respectively).
30. David Kennedy, the Dark Sides of Virtue: Reassessing International Humanitarianism 165 (2004). "Rent-seeking" is frequently used in literature to refer to "using power to extract a higher price than what would be possible in an arm's length or freely competitive bargain." *Ibid.*
31. Goodpaster, *supra* note 23, at 92.
32. *Ibid.*
33. Editorial, *Rooting Out Corruption,* Jakarta Post (Indonesia), Apr. 13 2005, *available at* http://www.anti korupsi.org/eng/mod.php?mod=publisher&op=viewarticle&artid=429.
34. Werner, *supra* note 4, at 149. This theory appears to be adapted from basic principles of group dynamics.
35. Dick, *supra* note 13, at 71.
36. Levinson, *supra* note 31, at 121. Levinson recounts a meeting of business people in Jakarta for a World Bank survey, after which one business person "sadly" told him with respect to the meeting, "Nothing will come of it."
37. Ardimas Sasdi, *Govt Must Not Waver in its Battle Against Corruption,* Jakarta Post (Indonesia), March 16, 2005,

available at http://www.antikorupsi.org/eng/mod.php?mod= publisher&op=viewarticle&artid=4 16. As reported by Sasdi, the Constitutional Court ruled on February 17, 2005 that the Corruption Eradication Commission ("KPK"), lacks authority to address graft cases that arose before its establishment in 2003. *Ibid.*

38. Levinson, *supra* note 31, 'at 113-14 (citing Editorial, *Corruption, The Child of Every Regime,* Media Indonesia (Indonesia), Feb. 23, 2001).

39. Editorial, *supra* note 33.

40. J. Danang Widoyoko, *Awaiting the results of SBY antigraft campaign,* JAKARTA POST (Indonesia), Oct. 20, 2005, *available at* http://www.antikorupsi.org/eng/mod.php?mod=publisher &op=viewarticle&artid=4 52.

41. Sasdi, *supra* note 44.

42. Editorial, *supra* note 37.

43. Shuntian Yao, Privilege and Corruption: The Problems of China's Socialist Market Economy - New Perspectives on Transition Economics: *Asia,* Vol. 61 No. 1am J. of Econ. & Soc. 279 (Jan. 2002).

44. C. Simon Fan & Herschel I. Grossman, *Incentives and Corruption in Chinese Economic Reform* 3 (Mar. 2000), http:/ /www.anti-corr.ru/archive/Incentives%20and%20corruption% 20in%20Chinese%20Economic %20Refor m.pdf (internal citations omitted) (last visited Sept. 10,2 006).

45. Martin Stuart-fox, A Short History of China and Southeast Asia: Tribute, Trade and Influence 11-14, 20-22 (2003). The evolution and nature of Chinese culture itself and the impact of Confucianism on present-day issues facing China (a controversial and complex issue in itself) is well beyond the scope of this article. A good discussion of China's cultural history, including the Confucian emphasis on hierarchy and order, and the tributary system that historically existed both within the Middle Kingdom and with its neighbors, is provided generally in Martin Stuart-Fox's *A Short History of China and Southeast Asia: Tribute, Trade and Influence.* As noted above, other factors include popular local culture and history, the nature of the state, type of corruption, actors

involved, and political responses and motivation to curtail corruption (or not).

46. Yao, *supra* note 50.

47. Wang Fang & Wang Zhen, *Corruption Fuels China's "Overheated" Economy,* The Epoch Times (P.R.C.),J un, 17, 2004, www.theepochtimes.com/news/4-6-17/21997.html (last visited Sept. 10, 2006).

48. Hu Ping, *On Corruption with "Chinese Characteristics",* Association for Asian Research, Sept. 30, 2002, hUp:// www.asianresearch.org/articles/939.html (last visited Sept. 10, 2006).

49. Mary Hennock, *China's gráft: Tough talk, old message,* BBC News Online, Sept. 24, 2004, http://news.bbc.co.uk/2/hi/asia-pacific/3693714.stm (last visited Sept. 10, 2006).

50. *Ibid.*

51. *China Leaders Warn of Corruption,* BBC News Online, Sept. 27, 2004, http://news.bbc.co.uk/2/hi/asia-pacific/3692530;stm (last visited Sept. 10, 2006).

52. Chengze Simon Fan & Herschel I. Grossman, *Entrepreneurial Graft in China,* Providence J., May 3, 2001, at B5, *available at* http://www.econ. brown. edu/fac/Herschel_Grossman/ papers/pdfs/chinaop.pdf.

53. *Ibid.*

54. 700 *Million Yuan Recovered in One-year Campaign Against Corruption: Report,* People's Daily (Oct. 31, 2001) (P.R.C.), http://english/200110/31/eng20011031_83587.html (last visited Sept. 10, 2006).

55. J.A.-Mund, N. Brandt & S. Hansakul, China-India Chartbook: China & India: A visual essay, Deutsche Bank Research Global Risk Analysis 24 (Oct. 10, 2005), http:// www.dbresearch.com/PROD/DBR_INTERNET_DE-PROD/ PROD0000000000192108.PDF(last visited Sept. 10, 2006); People's Daily, *ADB Revises Down East Asia's Economic Growth for 2005* (August 9, 2005) (P.R.C.), http:// english.people.com.cn/200508/09/eng20050809_201228.html.

56. Kaufman, *supra note* 16,at 115.

57. *Ibid.*

58. Kennedy, *supra* note 34, at 163.

59. *Ibid.*

60. World Bank Report, *supra* note 12, at 15.

61. Also referred to as "revisionist", functionalism was largely a response arising in the 1960s to the moralist view. *See generally* Gillespie & Okruhlik, *supra* note 5, at 78. Function is the ultimate consideration; the end justifies the means. Functionalists have also characterised as "positive functions" the corrupt political machines and systems of patronage controlled by powerful political bosses, smuggling, black-marketing, usury, and even slavery and war, arguing that they fulfill "positive functions which are at the time not adequately fulfilled by other existing patterns and structures." Edward Van Roy, *On the Theory of Corruption,* Vol. 19 No. 1 Econ. Dev. & Cultural Change 86, 89 (1970).

62. Pranab Bardhan, *Corruption and Development: A Review of Issues,* 35 J. Econ. Literature 1320, 1322 (1997). It is irrelevant to allocation efficiency that an excess payment is going to the corrupt official instead of the public treasury.

63. *Ibid.* 1323.

64. Paolo Mauro, *Corruption and Growth,* Vol. 110 No. 3, *Q. J. Econ.* 681 (1995).

65. Samuel P. Huntington, *Political Order in Changing Societies,* 69 (1-968) (emphasis added).

66. Werner, *supra* note 4, at 147.

67. *Ibid.*

68. Gillespie & Okruhlik, *supra* note 5, at 79.

69. Kaufman, *supra* note 16, at 116; Werner, *supra* note 4, at 149; Bardhan, *supra* note 76, at 1327-328.

70. Bardhan, *supra note 76,* at 1323 (citing a study conducted in India).

71. Kaufman, *supra* note 16, at 117. Kaufman cites an example in India where a "high-level civil servant who had been bribed could not process an approval any faster given the multiple bureaucrats involved in the process, yet [who] willingly offered his services to slow the approval process for rival companies."

72. Werner, *supra* note 4, at 148-49. It is interesting that functionalists counter-argue that corruption actually helps prevent violence and lawlessness in some circumstances. For example, functionalists argue that those who corrupt the police are more likely to identify with them and less prone to violence against them. *Ibid.* at 148. Similarly, others suggest that corruption may be an alternative to violence and point to periods in history, some quite recent, when groups who "had been killing each other to obtain power.... substituted a system of patronage, bribery, and corruption for the previous method of bloodletting." Bardhan, *supra* note 76, at 1328-329.
73. Werner, *supra* note 4, at 149.
74. Lindsey, *supra* note 8, at 15.
75. Levinson, *supra* note 31, at 111.
76. Matthew Moore, *Investors Desert Indonesia as Root of Corruption Sets In,* Sydney Morning Herald (Australia), Jan. 17, 2003, http://www.smh.com.au/articles/2003/01/16/1042520724884.html?oneclick=true (last visited Sept. 10, 2006).
77. *Ibid.*
78. Mudrajad Kuncoro, *Bribes, Regulatory Constraints, and Boosting Indonesian Exports,* Jakarta Post (Indonesia), Dec. 5, 2004, *available at* http://antikorupsi.org/eng/mod.php?mod=publisher&op=vie'warticle&art id=247.
79. Widoyoko, *supra* note 47.
80. *Ibid.*
81. Lindsey, *supra* note 8, at 15.
82. Levinson, *supra* note 31, at 114.
83. *Ibdi.* at 115.
84. *Ibid.* at 118 (quoting Professor Daniel Lev).
85. Lindsey, *supra* note 8, at 15 (internal citations omitted).
86. Goodpaster supra note 23, at 90.
87. World Bank, *supra* note 12, at 18.
88. Bardhan, *supra* note 76, at 1328.

89. World Bank, *supra* note 12, at 18.

90. This may be particularly true not only for domestic investors, but especially for U.S. investors who are subject to U.S. law prohibiting payment of bribes to foreign officials and other foreign corrupt practices. *But see,* Rubin, *supra* note 19, at 268 (citing a study that implies that American investors "indulge in bribery practices to compete, and risk prosecution under United States law.").

91. Susan Rose-Ackerman, *The Role of the World Bank in Controlling Corruption,* Law & Pol'y Int'l Bus. 93, 97-98 (1997).

92. Maoro, *supra* note 64, at 683.

93. Paolo Maoro, *The Effects of Corruption on Growth, Investment, and Government Expenditure: A Cross-Country Analysis, in* Corruption and the Global Economy 83, 91 (Kimberly Ann Elliott, ed., 1997). *See also,* Maoro, *supra* note 64, at 683.

94. Shang-Jin Wei, *How Taxing is Corruption on International Investors?,* Vol. 82 No. 1 Rev. Econ. & Statistics 1, 8, *available at* http://www.nber.org/~wei/data/wei2000a/wei2000a.pdf.

95. Goodpaster, *supra* note 19, at 92-99.

96. Wei, *supra* note 94, at 1.

97. Randall Peerenboom, *Seek Truth from Facts: An Empirical Study of Enforcement of Arbitral Awards in the PRC,* 49 am. J. Comp. L. 249, 309 (2001).

98. Excessive debt, of course, is a concern as "white elephant" projects are undertaken solely for the benefit of corrupt officials.

99. Concerns have been expressed in the press that the economy is expanding too quickly as a result of these projects, resulting in "a massive depletion of the nation's assets" and *ad hoc* development and resource distribution. *See* Fang & Zhen, *supra* note 59.

100. Peerenboom, *supra* note 115, at 310-12.

101. Yan Sun, Reform, State, and Corruption: Is Corruption Less Destructive in China Than in Russia? Vol. 32 No. 1 Comp. Pol.i, 5-6 (1999).

102. Profit-sharing occurs where "nonstate actors pay government officials to induce favorable policies concerning, for example, capital for investment, land for expansion, and export quotas." *Ibid.* at 12.

103. Angang Hu, *Public Exposure of Economic Losses Resulting from Corruption,* 4 China & World Econ. 44, 44 (2002).

104. Charles Wolf, Jr., Et Al., Fault lines in China's Economic Terrain 32-33 (2003), *available at* http://www.rand.org/pubs/monograph_reports/MR1686/MR 1686.pref.pdf

105. Werner, *supra* not 4, at 150 (citing the late Israeli Prime Minister, Levi Eshkol, who once quoted *Deuteronomy* passage 25:4 when asked about corruption.)

Chapter 5

Corporate Governance: Issues and Perspectives

Corporate governance is the set of processes. customs, policies, laws and institutions affecting the way a corporation is directed, administered or controlled. Corporate governance also includes the relationships among the many stakeholders involved and the goals for which the corporation is governed. The principal stakeholders are the shareholders, management and the board of directors. Other stakeholders include employees, suppliers, customers, banks and other lenders, regulators, the environment and the community at large.

Corporate governance is a multi-faceted subject.[1] An important theme of corporate governance is to ensure the accountability of certain individuals in an organisation through mechanisms that try to reduce or eliminate the principal-agent problem. A related but separate thread of discussions locus on the impact of a corporate governance system in economic efficiency, with a strong emphasis on shareholders welfare. There are yet other aspects to the corporate governance subject, such as the stakeholder view and the corporate governance models around the world.

There has been renewed interest in the corporate governance practices of modern corporations since 2001. particularly due to the high-profile collapses of a number of large U.S. firms such as Enron Corporation and Worldcom. In 2002 the US federal government passed the Sarbanes-Oxley Act. Intending to restore public confidence in corporate governance.

DEFINITION OF CORPORATE GOVERNANCE

In "A Board Culture of Corporate Governance" business author Gabrielle O'Donovan defines corporate governance as 'an internal system encompassing policies, processes and people, which serves the needs of shareholders and other stakeholders, by directing and controlling management activities with good business savvy. objectivity and integrity. Sound corporate governance is reliant on external marketplace commitment and legislation, plus a healthy board culture which safeguards policies and processes'.

O'Donovan goes on to say that 'the perceived quality of a company's corporate governance can influence its share price as well as the cost of raising capital. Quality is determined by the financial markets, legislation and other external market forces plus the international organisational environment; how policies and processes are implemented and how people are led. External forces are, to a large extent, outside the circle of control of any board. The internal environment is quite a different matter, and offers companies the opportunity to differentiate from competitors through their board culture. To date, too much of corporate governance debate has centred on legislative policy, to deter fraudulent activities and transparency policy which misleads executives to treat the symptoms and not the cause.[2]

It is a system of structuring, operating and controlling a company with a view to achieve long term strategic goals to' satisfy shareholders, creditors, employees, customers and suppliers, and complying with the legal and regulatory requirements, apart from meeting environmental and local community needs.

Report of Security and Exchange Board of India (SEBI) committee on Corporate Governance defines corporate governance as the acceptance by management of the inalienable rights of shareholders as the true owners of the corporation and of their own role as trustees on behalf of the shareholders. It is about commitment to values, about ethical business conduct and about making a distinction between personal and corporate funds in the management of a company." The definition is drawn from the Gandhian principle of trusteeship and the Directive Principles of the Indian Constitution. Corporate Governance is viewed as ethics and a moral duty.

HISTORY

In the 19th century, state corporation laws enhanced the rights of corporate boards to govern without unanimous consent of shareholders in exchange for statutory benefits like appraisal rights, to make corporate governance more efficient. Since that time, and because most large publicly traded, corporations in the US are incorporated under corporate administration friendly Delaware law and because the US's wealth has been increasingly securitised into various corporate entities and institutions', the rights of individual owners and shareholders have become increasingly derivative and dissipated. The concerns of shareholders over administration pay and stock losses periodically has led to more frequent calls for corporate governance reforms.

In the 20th century, in the immediate aftermath of the Wall Street Crash of 1929, legal scholars such as Adolf Augustus Berle. Edwin Dodd, and Gardiner C. Means pondered on the changing role of the modern corporation in society. Berle and Means' monograph "The Modern Corporation and Private Property" (1932. Macmillan) continues to have a profound influence on the conception of corporate governance in scholarly debates today.

From the Chicago school of economics, Ronald Coase's "The Nature of the Firm" (1937) introduced the notion of transaction costs into the understanding of why firms are founded and how they continue to behave. Fifly years later. Eugene Fama and Michael Jensen's "The Separation of Ownership and Control" (1983, *Journal of Law and Economics*) firmly established agency theory as a way of understanding corporate governance: the firm is seen as a series of contracts. Agency theory's dominance was highlighted in a 1989 article by Kathleen Eisenhardt (Academy of Management Review).

US expansion after World War II through the emergence of multinational corporations saw the establishment of the managerial class. Accordingly, the following Harvard Business School management professors published influential monographs studying their prominence: Myles Mace (entrepreneurship). Alfred D. Chandler. Jr. (business history). Jay Lorsch (organisational behaviour) and Elizabeth Maelver (organisational behaviour). According to Lorsch and Maclver "many large corporations have dominant control over business affairs without sufficient accountability or monitoring by their board of directors."

Since the late 1970's. corporate governance has been the subject of significant debate in the U.S. and around the globe. Bold. broad efforts to reform corporate governance have been driven, in part, by the needs and desires of shareowners to exercise their rights of corporate ownership and to increase the value of their shares and. therefore, wealth. Over the past three decades, corporate directors' duties have expanded greatly beyond their traditional legal responsibility of duty of loyalty to the corporation and its shareowners.[3]

In the first half of the 1990s, the issue of corporate governance in the U.S. received considerable press attention due to the wave of CEO dismissals (e.g.: IBM, Kodak,

Honeywell) by their boards. Calpers led a wave of *institutional* shareholder activism (something only very rarely seen before), as a way of ensuring that corporate value would not be destroyed by the now traditionally cozy relationships between the CEO and the board of directors (e.g., by the unrestrained issuance of stock options, not infrequently back dated).

In 1997, the East Asian Financial Crisis saw the economies of Thailand, Indonesia, South Korea, Malaysia and The Philippines severely affected by the exit of foreign capital after property assets collapsed. The lack of corporate governance mechanisms in these countries highlighted the weaknesses of the institutions in their economies.

In the early 2000s, the massive bankruptcies (and criminal malfeasance) of Enron and Woridcom. as well as lesser corporate debacles, such as Adelphia Communications, AOL. Arthur Andersen, Global Crossing. Tyco. and. more recently, Fannie Mae and Freddie Mac, led to increased shareholder and governmental interest in corporate governance. This culminated in the passage of the Sarbanes-Oxiey Act of 2002.[4] But. since then. the stock market has greatly recovered, and shareholder zeal has waned accordingly.

Impact of Corporate Governance

The positive effect of good corporate governance on different stakeholders ultimately is a strengthened economy, and hence good corporate governance is a tool for socio-economic development.[5] After East Asian economies collapsed in the late 20th century, the World Bank's president warned those countries, that for sustainable development, corporate governance has to be good. Economic health of a nation depends substantially on how sound and ethical businesses are.

Role of Institutional Investors

Many years ago, worldwide, buyers and sellers of corporation stocks were *individual* investors, such as wealthy businessmen or families, who often had a vested, personal and emotional interest in the corporations whose shares they owned. Over time, markets have become largely *institutionalised:* buyers and sellers are largely institutions (e.g., pension funds, insurance companies, mutual funds, hedge funds, investor groups, and banks).

The rise of the institutional investor has brought with it some increase of professional diligence which has tended to improve regulation of the stock market (but not necessarily in the interest of the small investor or even of the nave institutions, of which there are many). Note that this process occurred simultaneously with the direct growth of individuals investing *indirectly* in the market (for example individuals have twice as much money in mutual funds as they do in bank accounts). However this growth occurred primarily by way of individuals turning over their funds to 'professionals' to manage, such as in mutual funds. In this way, the majority of investment now is described as "institutional investment" even though the vast majority of the funds are for the benefit of individual investors. Programme trading, the hallmark of institutional trading, is averaging over 60 per cent a day in 2007.

Unfortunately, there has been a concurrent lapse in the oversight of large corporations, which are now almost all owned by large institutions, 'the Board of Directors of large corporations used to be chosen by the principal shareholders, who usually had an emotional as well as monetary investment in the company (think Ford), and the Board diligently kept an eye on the company and its principal executives (they usually hired and fired the President, or Chief executive officer—CEO).

Nowadays, if the owning institutions don't like what the President/CEO is doing and they feel that firing them will likely be costly (think "golden handshake") and/or time consuming, they will simply sell out their interest. The Board is now mostly *chosen* by the President/CEO, and may be made up primarily of their friends and associates, such as officers of the corporation or business colleagues. Since the (institutional) shareholders rarely object, the President/CEO generally takes the Chair of the Board position for his herself (which makes it much more difficult for the institutional owners to "fire" him/her). Occasionally, hut rarely, institutional investors support shareholder resolutions on such matters as executive pay and anti-takeover measures.

Finally, the largest pools of invested money (such as the mutual fund 'Vanguard 500', or the' largest investment management firm for corporations. State Street Corp.) are designed simply to invest in a very large number of different companies with sufficient liquidity, based on the idea that this strategy will largely eliminate individual company financial or other risk and, therefore, these investors have even less interest in a particular company's governance.

Since the marked rise in the use of Internet transactions from the 1990s, both individual and professional stock investors around the world have emerged as a potential new kind of major (short term) force in the direct or indirect ownership of corporations and in the markets: the casual participant. Even as the purchase of individual shares in any one corporation by individual investors diminishes, the sale of derivatives (e.g., exchange-traded funds (ETFs), Stock market index options[6] has soared. So, the interests of most investors are now increasingly rarely tied lo the fortunes of individual corporations.

But, the ownership of stocks in markets around the world varies; for example, the majority of the shares in the Japanese market are held by financial companies and industrial corporations (there is a large and deliberate amount of cross-holding among Japanese keiretsu corporations and within S. Korean chaebol 'groups')[7], whereas stock in the USA or the UK and Europe are much more broadly owned, often still by large individual investors.

PARTIES TO CORPORATE GOVERNANCE

Parties involved in corporate governance include the regulatory body, e.g. the Chief Executive Officer, the hoard of directors, management and shareholders. Other stakeholders who take part include suppliers, employees, creditors, customers and the community at large.

In corporations, the shareholder delegates decision rights to the manager to act in the principal's best interests. This separation of ownership from control implies a loss of effective control by shareholders over managerial decisions. Partly as a result of this separation between the two parties, a system of corporate governance controls is implemented to assist in aligning the incentives of managers with those of shareholders. With the significant increase in equity holdings of investors, there has been an opportunity for a reversal of the separation of ownership and control problems because ownership is not so diffuse.

A board of directors often plays a key role in corporate governance. It is their responsibility to endorse the organisation's strategy, develop directional policy, appoint, supervise and remunerate senior executives and to ensure accountability of the organisation to its owners and authorities.

The Company Secretary, known as a Corporate Secretary in the US and often referred to as a Chartered Secretary if qualified by the Institute of Chartered Secretaries and Administrators (ICSA), is a high ranking professional who is trained to uphold the highest standards of corporate governance, effective operations, compliance and administration.

All parties to corporate governance have an interest, whether direct or indirect, in the effective performance of the organisation. Directors, workers and management receive salaries, benefits and reputation, while shareholders receive capital return. Customers receive goods and services; suppliers receive compensation for their goods or services. In return these individuals provide value in the form of natural, human social and other-forms of capital.

A key factor in an individual's decision to participate in an organisation e.g. through providing financial capital and trust that they will receive a fair share of the organisational returns. If some parties are receiving more than their fair return then participants may choose to not continue participating leading to organisational collapse.

PRINCIPLES

Key dements of good corporate governance principles include honesty, trust and integrity, openness, performance orientation, responsibility and accountability, mutual respect, and commitment to the organisation.

Of importance is how directors and management develop a model of governance that aligns the values of the corporate participants and then evaluate this model periodically for its effectiveness. In particular, senior executives should conduct themselves honestly and ethically, especially concerning actual or apparent conflicts of interest, and disclosure in financial reports.

Commonly accepted principles of corporate governance include:

- Rights and equitable treatment of shareholders: Organisations should respect the rights of shareholders and help shareholders to exercise those rights. They can help shareholders exercise their rights by effectively communicating information that is understandable and accessible and encouraging shareholders to participate in general meetings.

- Interests of other stakeholders: Organisations should recognize that they have legal and other obligations to all legitimate stakeholders.
- Role und responsibilities of the board: The board needs a range of skills and understanding to be able to deal with various business issues and have the ability to review and challenge management performance. It needs to be of sufficient size and have an appropriate level of commitment to fulfill its responsibilities and duties. There are issues about the appropriate mix of executive and non-executive directors. The key roles of chairperson and CEO should not be held by the same person.
- Integrity and ethical behaviour: Ethical and responsible decision making is not only important for public relations, but it is also a necessary element in risk management and avoiding lawsuits. Organisations should develop a code of conduct for their directors and executives that promotes ethical and responsible decision making. It is important to understand, though, that reliance by a company on the integrity and ethics of individuals is bound to eventual failure. Because of this may organisations establish Compliance and Ethics Programmes to minimize the risk that the firm steps outside of ethical and legal boundaries.
- Disclosure and transparency: Organisations should clarify and make publicly known the roles und responsibilities of board and management to provide shareholders with a level of accountability. They should also implement procedures to independently verify and safeguard the integrity of the company's

financial reporting. Disclosure of material matters concerning the organisation should be timely and balanced to ensure that all investors have access to clear. Factual information.

Issues involving corporate governance principles include:

- internal controls and the independence of the entity's auditors
- oversight and management of risk
- review of the preparation of the entity's financial statements
- review of the compensation arrangements for the chief executive officer and other senior executives
- the resources made available to directors in carrying out their duties
- the way in which individuals are nominated for positions on the board
- dividend policy.

"Corporate Governance" despite some feeble attempts from various quarters has remained ambiguous and often misunderstood phrase. For Quite some time, it was confined to only corporate management. It is not so it is something much broader for it must include a fair, efficient and transparent administration to meet certain well defined objectives. Corporate governance also must go beyond law. The quantity, quality and frequency of financial and managerial disclosure, the degree and extent to which the Board of Director (BOD) exercise their trustee responsibilities and the commitment to run transparent organisation these should evolve due to interplay of many factors and the role played by more progressive dements within the corporate sector. In India, a strident demand for evolving a code of good practices by the corporate themselves is emerging.

MECHANISMS AND CONTROLS

Corporate governance mechanisms and controls are designed to reduce the inefficiencies that arise from moral hazard and adverse selection. For example, to monitor managers' behaviour, an independent third party (the auditor) attests the accuracy of information provided by management to investors. An ideal control system should regulate both motivation and ability.

Internal Corporate Governance Controls

Internal corporate governance controls monitor activities and then take corrective action to accomplish organisational goals. Examples include:

- Monitoring by the board of directors: The board of directors, with its legal authority to hire, fire and compensate top management, safeguards invested capital. Regular board meetings allow potential problems to be identified, discussed and avoided. Whilst non-executive directors are thought to he more independent, they may not always result in more effective corporate governance and may not increase performance. Different board structures are optimal for different firms. Moreover, the ability of the board to monitor the firm's executives is a function of its access lo information. Executive directors possess superior knowledge of the decision-making process and therefore evaluate top management on the basis of the quality of its decisions that lead to financial performance outcomes, *ex ante.* It could be argued, therefore, that executive directors look beyond the financial criteria.
- Remuneration: Performance-based remuneration is designed to relate some proportion of salary to individual performance. It may be in the form of cash or non-cash payments such as shares and share options, superannuation or other benefits. Such

incentive schemes, however, are reactive in the sense that they provide no mechanism for preventing mistakes or opportunistic behaviour, and can elicit myopic behaviour.

External Corporate Governance Controls

External corporate governance controls encompass the controls external stakeholders exercise over the organisation. Examples include:

- competition
- debt covenants
- demand for and assessment of performance information (especially financial statements)
- government regulations
- managerial labour market
- media pressure
- takeovers telephone lapping

SYSTEMIC PROBLEMS OF CORPORATE GOVERNANCE

- Demand for information: A barrier to shareholders using good information is the cost of processing it, especially to a small shareholder. The traditional answer to this problem is the efficient market hypothesis (in Finance, the efficient market hypothesis (EMH) asserts that financial markets are efficient), which suggests that the shareholder will free ride on the judgements of larger professional investors.
- Monitoring costs: In order to influence the directors, the shareholders must combine with others to form a significant voting group which can pose a real threat of carrying resolutions or appointing directors at a general meeting.

- Supply of accounting information: Financial accounts form a crucial link in enabling providers of finance 10 monitor directors. Imperfections in the financial reporting process will cause imperfection in the effectiveness of corporate governance. This should, ideally, be corrected by the working of the external auditing process.

ROLE OF THE ACCOUNTANT

Financial reporting is a crucial element necessary for the corporate governance system to function effectively. Accountants and auditors are the primary providers of information to capital market participants. The directors of the company should be entitled to expect that management prepare the financial information in compliance with statutory and ethical obligations, and rely on auditors' competence.

Current accounting practice allows a degree of choice of method in determining the method of measurement, criteria for recognition, and even the definition of the accounting entity. The exercise of this choice to improve apparent performance (popularly known as creative accounting) imposes extra information costs on users. In the extreme, it can involve non-disclosure of information.

One area of concern is whether the accounting firm acts as both the independent auditor and management consultant to the firm they are auditing. This may result in a conflict of interest which places the integrity of financial reports in doubt due to client pressure to appease management. The power of the corporate client to initiate and terminate management consulting services and, more fundamentally, to select and dismiss accounting firms contradicts the concept of an independent auditor. Changes enacted in the United States in the form of the Sarbanes-Oxley Act (in response to the Enron situation as noted below) prohibit accounting firms from providing both auditing and management consulting services. Similar provisions are in place under clause 49 of SEBI Act in India.

The Enron collapse is an example of misleading financial reporting. Enron concealed huge losses by dealing illusions that a third party was contractually obliged to pay the amount of any losses. However, the third party was an entity in which Enron had a substantial economic stake. In discussions of accounting practices with Arthur Andersen, the partner in charge of auditing, views inevitably led to the client prevailing

However. good 1'mancial reporting is not a sufficient condition for the effectiveness of corporate governance if users don't process it or if the informed user is unable to exercise a monitoring role due to high costs.

REGULATION

Rules versus Principles

Rules arc typically thought to be simpler to follow than principles, demarcating a clear line between acceptable and unacceptable behaviour. Rules also reduce discretion on the part of individual managers of auditors.

In practice rules can he more complex than principles. They may be ill-equipped to deal with new types of transactions not covered by the code. Moreover, even if clear rules are followed, one can still find a way to circumvent their underlying purpose—this is harder to achieve if one is bound by a broader principle.

Principles on the other hand is a form of self regulation. It allows the sector to determine what standards are acceptable or unacceptable. It also pre-empts over zealous legislations that might not lie practical.

Enforcement

Enforcement can affect the overall credibility of a regulatory system. They both deter bad actors and level the competitive playing Held. Nevertheless, greater enforcement is not always better for taken too far it can dampen valuable risk-taking. In practice however, this is largely a theoretical, as opposed to a real, risk

Action Beyond Obligation

Enlightened boards regard their mission as helping management lead the company. They are more likely to be supportive of the senior management team. Because enlightened directors strongly believe that it is their duty to involve themselves in an intellectual analysis of how the company should move forward into the future, most of the time the enlightened board is aligned on the critically important issues lacing the company.

Unlike traditional hoards, enlightened boards do not feel hampered by the rules and regulations of the Sarbanes-Oxley Act. Unlike standard boards that aim to comply with regulations, enlightened hoards regard compliance with regulations as merely a baseline for board performance. Enlightened directors go far beyond merely meeting the requirements on a checklist. They do not need Sarbanes-Oxley to mandate that they protect values and ethics or monitor CEO performance.

At the same time enlightened directors recognize that it is not their role to be involved in the day-to-day operations of the corporation. They lead by example. Overall, what most distinguishes enlightened directors from traditional and standard directors is the passionate obligation they feel to engage in the day-to-day challenges and strateging of the company. Enlightened boards can be found in very large, complex companies, as well as smaller companies.[8]

MODEL OF CORPORATE GOVERNANCE

Although the US model of corporate governance is the most notorious, there is a considerable variation in corporate governance models around the world. The intricated shareholding structures of keiretsus in Japan The heavy presence of banks in the equity of German firms, the chaebols in South Korea and many others arc examples of arrangements which try to respond to the same corporate governance challenges as in the US.

Anglo-American Model

There are many different models of corporate governance around the world. These differ according to the variety of capitalism in which they are embedded. The liberal model that is common in Anglo-American countries lends to give priority to the interests of shareholders. The coordinated model that one finds in Continental Europe and Japan also recognises the interests of workers, managers, suppliers, customers, and the community. Both models have distinct competitive advantages, but in different ways. The liberal model of corporate governance encourages radical innovation and cost competition, whereas the coordinated model of corporate governance facilitates incremental innovation and quality competition. However there are important differences between the U.S. recent approach to governance issues and what has happened in the U.K.

In the United States, a corporation is governed by a board of directors, which has the power to choose an executive officer, usually known as the chief executive officer. The CEO has broad power to manage the corporation on a daily basis, but needs to get board approval for certain major actions, such as hiring his/her immediate subordinates, raising money, acquiring another company, major capital expansions, or other expensive projects. Other duties of the board may include policy setting, decision making, monitoring management's performance, or corporate control.

The board of directors is nominally selected by and responsible to the shareholders, but the bylaws of many companies make it difficult for all but the largest shareholders to have any influence over the makeup of the board: normally, individual shareholders are not offered a choice of board choose, but are merely asked to rubberstamp the nominees of the sitting board. Perverse incentives have pervaded many corporate boards in the developed world, with board members beholden to the chief executive whose actions they are intended to oversee. Frequently, members of the boards of directors are CEOs of other corporations, which some[9] see as a conflict of interest.

The U.K. has pioneered a flexible model of regulation of corporate governance, known as the "comply or explain" code of governance. This is a principle based code that lists a dozen of recommended practices, such as-the separation of CEO and Chairman of the Board, the introduction of a time limit for CTOs' contracts. the introduction of a minimum number of non-executives Directors, of independent directors the designation of a senior non executive director, the formation and composition of remuneration, audit and nomination committees. Publicly listed companies in the U.K. have to either apply those principles of if they choose not to, to explain in a designated part of their annual reports why they not lo do so. The monitoring of those explanations is left to shareholders themselves. The tenet of the Code is that one size does not fit all in matters of corporate governance and that instead of a statuary regime like the Sarbanes-Oxley Act in the U.S., it is best to leave some flexibility to companies so that they can make choices most adapted to their circumstances. If they have good reasons lo deviate 1'roni the sound rule, they should be able to convincingly explain those to their shareholders.

The code his been in place since 1993 and has had drastic effects on the way firms are governed in the U.K. A study by Arcot, Bruno and Faure-Grimaud from the Financial Markets Group at the London School of Economics shows that shows that in 1993. about 10% of the UK companies member of the FTSE 350 were complaints on all dimensions while they were more than 60% in 2003. The same success was not achieved when looking it the explanation part for non compliant companies. Many deviations are simply not explained and a large majority of explanations fail to identify specific circumstances justifying those deviations. Still, the overall view is that the U.K.'s system works fairly well and in fact is often branded as a benchmark, followed by several countries.

Non Anglo-American Model

In East Asian countries, family-owned companies dominate. A study by Claessens, Djankov and Lang (2000) investigated the top 15 families in East Asian countries and found that they dominated listed corporate assets. In countries such as Pakistan, Indonesia and the Philippines, the top 15 families controlled over 50% of publicly owned corporations through a system of family cross-holdings, thus dominating the capital markets. Family-owned companies also dominate the Latin model of corporate governance, that is companies in Mexico, Italy, Spain, France (to a certain extent), Brazil, Argentina, and other countries in South America.

Europe and Asia exemplify the insider system: Shareholder and stakeholder

- a small number of listed companies,
- an illiquid capital market where ownership and control are not frequently traded
- high concentration of shareholding in the hands of corporations, institutions, families or government
- the insider model uses a system of interlocking networks and committees.

At the same lime that developing countries are undergoing a process of economic growth and transformation, they are also experiencing a revolution in the business and political relationships that characterize their private and public sectors. Establishing good corporate governance practices is essential to sustaining long-term development and growth as these countries move from closed, market-unfriendly, undemocratic systems towards open, market-friendly, democratic systems. Good corporate governance systems will allow organisations to realize their maximum productivity and efficiency, minimize corruption and abuse of power, and provide a system of managerial accountability.[10] These goals ire equally important for both private corporations and government bodies.

Because of the implicit relationship between private interests and the larger government, good corporate government, practices are essential to establishing good governance at the national level in developing countries.[11] A number of ties the keep the public and private sectors closely linked. On one hand, judiciary and regulatory bodies as well as legislatures play a role in corporate management and oversight. At the same time cartels arid large corporate interests use their size to exert not only economic, but also political power. These two sectors are so intertwined that a country cannot significantly change one without simultaneously instituting changes in the other.[12]

According to Nicolas Meisel, there are four priorities which developing countries should concentrate on while experimenting with new forms of corporate and public governance. The first is to focus on improving the quality of information and increasing the speed at which it is created and distributed to the public. Good communication is important to the functioning of any organisation. The second is to allow individual actors more autonomy while at the same time maintaining or increasing accountability. Thirdly, if a hierarchical organisation used to orient private activities toward the general interest, new countervailing powers should be encouraged to fill this role. Finally, the part the state plays and how government officials are selected must be considered if a developing economy is to achieve sustainable growth. This may involve making it easier for newcomers with new ideas incumbents who may hold to older, possibly outdated, models.

CODES AND GUIDELINES

Corporate governance principles and codes have been developed in different countries and issued from stock exchanges, corporations, institutional investors, or associations (institutes) of directors and managers will the support of governments and international organisations. As a rule, compliance with these governance recommendations is not mandated by law, although the codes linked to stock exchange listing requirements may have a coercive effect.

For example, companies quoted on the London and Toronto Stock Exchanges formally need not follow the recommendations of their respective national codes. However, they must disclose whether they follow the recommendations in those documents and, where not, they should provide explanations concerning divergent practices. Such disclosure requirements exert a significant pressure on listed companies for compliance.

In the United States, companies are primarily regulated by the state in which they incorporate though they are also regulated by the federal government and, if they are public, by their stock exchange. The highest number of companies are incorporated in Delaware, including more than half of the Fortune 500. Tills is due to Delaware's generally business-friendly corporate ,legal environment and the existence of a state court dedicated solely to business issues (Delaware Court of Chancery).

Most states' corporate law generally follow the American Bar Association's Model Business Corporation Act.

While Delaware does not follow the Act, it still considers its provisions and several prominent Delaware justices, including former Delaware Supreme Court Chief Justice E. Normay Veasey,

One issue that has been raised since the Disney decision in 2005 is the degree to which companies manage "heir governance responsibilities: in other words, do they merely try to supersede the legal threshold, or should they create governance guidelines that ascend to the level of best practice. For example, the guidelines issued by associations of directors, corporate managers and individual companies tend to be wholly voluntary. For example. The GM Board Guidelines reflect the company's effect to improve its own governance capacity. Such documents, however, may have a wider multiplying effect prompting other companies to adopt similar documents and standards of best practice.

One of the most influential guidelines has been the 1999 OECD Principles of Corporate Governance. This has revised in 2004. The OECD remains a proponent of corporate governance principles throughout the world.

Building on the work of the OECD, other international organisations, private sector associations and more than 20 national corporate governance codes, the United Nations Intergovernmental Working Group of Experts on International Standards of Accounting and Reporting (ISAR) has produced, voluntary Guidance on Good Practices in Corporate Governance Disclosure.

- Auditing
- Board and management structure and process
- Corporate responsibility and compliance
- Financial transparency and information disclosure
- Ownership structure and exercise of control rights

The World Business Council for Sustainable Development WBCSD has done work on corporate governance, particularly on accountability and reporting.

CORPORATE GOVERNANCE AND FIRM PERFORMANCE

In its 'Global Investor Opinion Survey' of over 200 institutional investors first undertaken in 2000 and updated in 2002. McKinsey found that 80% of the respondents would pay a premium for well-governed companies. They defined a well-governed company as one that had mostly out-side directors, who had no management ties, undertook formal evaluation of its directors, and was responsive to investors' requests for information on governance issues. The size of the premium varied by market, from 11% for Canadian companies to around 40% for companies where the regulatory backdrop was least certain (those in Moroeco. Egypt and Russia).

Other studies have linked broad perceptions of the quality of companies to superior share price performance. In a study of live year cumulative returns of Fortune Magazine's survey of most admired Firms'. Antunovich et al found that those "most admired" had an average return of 125%, while the 'least admired' Firms returned 80%. In a separate study Business Week enlisted institutional investors and 'experts' to assist in differentiating between boards with good and bad governance and found that companies with the highest rankings had the highest financial returns.

On the other hand, research into the relationship between specific corporate governance controls and firm performance has been mixed and often weak. The following examples are illustrative.

Board Composition

Some researchers have Found support for the relationship between frequency of meetings and profitability. Other have found a negative relationship between the proportion of external directors and firm performance, while others found no relationship between external board membership and performance. In a recent paper Bagahat and Black found that companies with more independent boards do mil perform better than other companies. It is unlikely that board composition has a direct impact on firm performance.

Remuneration/Compensation

The results of previous research on the relationship between firm performance and executive compensation have failed to find consistent and significant relationships between executives' remumeration and firm performance. Low average levels of pay-performance alignment do not necessarily imply that this form of governance control is inefficient. Not all firms experience the same levels of agency conflict, and external and internal monitoring devices may be more effective for some than for others.

Some researchers have Found that the largest CEO performance incentives came from ownership of the firm's shares. While other researchers found that the relationship between share ownership and firm performance was dependent on the level of ownership. The results suggest that increases in ownership above 20% cause management to become more entrenched, and less interested in the welfare of their sharcholders.

Some argue that firm performance is positively associated with share option plans and that these plans direct managers' energies and extend their decision horizons toward the long-term, rather than the short-term performance of the company. However, that point of view came under substantial criticism circa in the wake of various security scandals including mutual fund timing episodes and, in particular, the backdating of option grants as documented by University of Iowa academic Erik Lie and reported by lames Blander and Charles Forelle of the Wall Street Journal.

Even before the negative influence on public, opinion caused by the 2006 backdating scandal, use of options faced various criticisms. A particularly forceful and long running argument concerned the interaction of executive option with corporate stock repurchase programmes. Numerous authorities (including U.S. Federal Reserve Board economist Weisbenner) determined options may be employed in concert with stock buybacks in a manner contrary to shareholder interests. These authors argued that, in part corporate stock buybacks for U.S. Standard & Poors 500 companies surged to a $500 billion annual rate in late 2006 because of the impact of options. A compendium of academic works on the option/buyback issue is included in the study Scandal by author M. Gumport issued in 2006.

A combination of accounting changes and governance issues led options to become a less-popular means of remunertion as 2006 progressed, and various alternative implementations of buybacks surfaced to challenge the dominance of "open market" cash buybacks as the preferred means of implementing a share purchase plan.

REFERENCES

1. Dignam, A and Lowry, J (2006) *Company Law*, Oxford University Press.
2. *Corporate Governance International Journal*, "A Board Culture of Corporate Governance", Vol. 6 Issue 3 (2003)
3. Crawford, Curtis. J. (2007). The Reform of Corporate Governance: Major Trends in the U.S. Corporate Boardroom. 1977-1997. doctoral dissertation, Capella University. [1] (http://www.xceo.net/about_us/crawford_disertation.php)
4. SSRN Good Coporate Governance: An Instrument for Wealth Maximisation by Vrajlal Sapovadia
5. Bhagat & Black. "The Uncertain Relationship Between Board Com-position and Firm Performance", 54 Busines Lawyer).

6. National Association of Corporate Directors (NACD)-Directors Monthly. "Enlightened Baards: Action Beyond Obligation", Vol. 31 Number 12 (2007), Pg 13. [2]

7. Theyrule.net/admin/files/events/Crawford.Directors_Monthly. Dec07_final.pdf).

8. Business for Development: Fostering the Private Sector. OECD Development Centre, Paris: OECD Publication 2007 (149-152).

9. Nicolas is Meisel. Governance Culture and Development (Paris: OECD Publishing, 2004) Source OECD, 27 July 2007 http://masetto.sourceoeed.org/vl=215979/cl=14/nw=1/rpsv/cgi-bin/fulltextew.pl? prpsv=/ij/oecdthemes/99980010/v2004n9/s1/p11.idx(12).

10. Corporate Governnace in Development: The Experiences of Brazil, Chile, India, and South Africa, ed. Charles P. Oman, OECD Development Centre and CIPE, 2006.

11. Nicolas Meisel, Governance Culture and Development (Paris: OECD Publishing, 2004).

12. The Disney Decision of 2005 and the precedent it sets for corporate governance and fiduciary responsibiltiy, Kuckreja, Akin Gump, Aug. 2005.

Chapter 6

Corporate Social Responsibility: Challenges in the Era of Economic Liberalisation and Globalisation

Corporate Social Responsibility (CSR), also called corporate responsibility, corporate citizenship, responsible business and corporate social opportunity[1] is a concept, whereby organisations consider the interests of society by taking responsibility for the impact of their activities on customers, suppliers, employees, shareholders, communities and other stakeholders, as well as the environment. This obligation is seen to extend beyond the statutory obligation to comply with legislation and sees organisations voluntarily taking further steps to improve the quality of life for employees and their families as well as for the local community and society at large.

The practice of CSR is subject to much debate and criticism. Proponents argue that, there is a strong business case for CSR, in that corporations benefit in multiple ways by operating with a perspective broader and longer than their own immediate, short-term profits. Critics argue that CSR distracts from the fundamental economic role of businesses; others argue that it is nothing more than superficial window-dressing; still others argue that it is an attempt to preempt the role of governments as a watchdog over powerful multinational corporations.

EVOLUTION

Business ethics is a form of the art of applied ethics that examines ethical principles and moral or ethical problems that can arise in a business environment.

In the increasingly conscience-focused marketplaces of the 21st century, the demand for more ethical business processes and actions, known as ethicism, is increasing. Simultaneously, pressure is applied on' industry to improve business ethics through new public initiatives and laws (e.g. higher UK road tax for higher-emission vehicles).

Business ethics can be both a normative and a descriptive discipline. As a corporate practice and a career specialisation, the field is primarily normative. In academia, descriptive approaches are also taken. The range and quantity of business ethical issues reflects the degree to which business is perceived to be at odds with non-economic social values.

Historically, interest in business ethics accelerated dramatically during the 1980s and 1990s, both within major corporations and within academia. For example, today most major corporate websites lay emphasis on commitment to promoting non-economic social values under a variety of headings (e.g. ethics codes, social responsibility charters). In some cases, corporations have re-branded their core values in the light of business ethical considerations (e.g. BP's "beyond petroleum" environmental tilt).

The term CSR itself came into common use in the early 1970s, although it was seldom abbreviated. The term stakeholder, meaning those impacted by an organisation's activities, was used to describe corporate owners beyond shareholders from around 1989.

APPROACHES

Some commentators have identified a difference between the Continental European and the Anglo-Saxon approaches to CSR.[2] And even within Europe the discussion about CSR is very heterogenous.[3]

An approach for CSR that is becoming more widely accepted is community-based development projects, such as the Shell Foundation's involvement in the Flower Valley, South Africa. Here they have set up an Early Learning Centre to help educate the community's children, as well as develop new skills for the adults. Marks and Spencer is also active in this community through the building of a trade network with the community - guaranteeing regular fair trade purchases. Often alternative approaches to this is the establishment of education facilities for adults, as well as HIV/AIDS education programmes. The majority of these CSR projects are established in Africa. A more common approach of CSR is through the giving of aid to local organisations and impoverished communities in development countries. Some organisations do not like this approach as it does not help build on the skills of the people, whereas community-based development generally leads to more sustainable development.

SOCIAL ACCOUNTING, AUDITING AND REPORTING

Taking responsibility for its impact on society means in the first instance that a company accounts for its actions. Social accounting, a concept describing the communication of social and environmental effects of a company's economic actions to particular interest groups within society and to society at large, is thus an important element of CSR.[4]

A number of reporting guidelines or standards have been developed to serve as frameworks for social accounting auditing and reporting:

- Account Ability's AA1000 standard, based on John Elkington's triple bottom line (3BL) reporting
- Global Reporting Initiative's Sustainability Reporting Guidelines

- Verite's Monitoring Guidelines
- Social Accountability International's SA8000 standard
- Green Globe Certification / Standard
- The ISO 14000 environmental management standard
- The United Nations Global Compact promotes companies reporting in the format of a Communication on Progress (COP). A COP report describes the company's implementation of the Compact's ten universal principles.
- The United Nations Intergovernmental Working Group of Experts on International Standards of Accounting and Reporting (ISAR) provides voluntary technical guidance on eco-efficiency indicators, corporate responsibility reporting and corporate governance disclosure.

In some nations legal requirements for social accounting, auditing and reporting exist (e.g. in the French bilan social), though agreement on meaningful measurements of social and environmental performance is difficult. Many companies now produce externally audited annual reports that cover Sustainable Development and CSR issues ("Triple Bottom Line Reports"), but the reports vary widely in format, style, and evaluation methodology (even within the same industry). Critics dismiss these reports as lip service, citing examples such as Enron's yearly "Corporate Responsibility Annual Report" and tobacco corporations' social reports.

POTENTIAL BUSINESS BENEFITS

The scale and nature of the benefits of CSR for an organisation can vary depending on the nature of the enterprise, and are difficult to quantify, though there is a large body of literature exhorting business to adopt measures beyond financial ones (e.g., Deming's Fourteen

Points, balanced scorecards). Orlizty, Schmidt and Rynes[5] found a correlation between social/environmental performance and financial performance. However, businesses may not be looking at short-run financial returns when developing their CSR strategy.

The definition of CSR used within an organisation can vary from the strict "stakeholder impacts" definition used by many CSR advocates and will often include charitable efforts and volunteering. CSR may be based within the human resources, business development or public relations departments of an organisation[6] or may be given a separate unit reporting to the CEO or in some cases directly to the board. Some companies may implement CSR-type values without a clearly defined team or programme. The business case for CSR within a company will likely rest on one or more of these arguments:

Human Resources

A CSR programme can be seen as an aid to recruitment and retention,[7] particularly within the competitive graduate student market. Potential recruits often ask about a firm's CSR policy during an interview, and having a comprehensive policy can give an advantage. CSR can also help to improve the perception of a company among its staff, particularly when staff can become involved through payroll giving, fundraising activities or community volunteering.

Risk Management

Managing risk is a central part of many corporate strategies. Reputations that take decades to build up can be ruined in hours through incidents such as corruption scandals or environmental accidents. These events can also draw unwanted attention from regulators, courts, governments and media. Building a genuine culture of doing the right thing' within a corporation can offset these risks.[8]

Brand Differentiation

In crowded marketplaces, companies strive for a unique selling proposition which can separate them from the competition in the minds of consumers. CSR can play a role in building customer loyalty based on distinctive ethical values.[9] Several major brands, such as The Co-operative Group and The Body Shop are built on ethical values. Business service organisations can benefit too from building a reputation for integrity and best practice.

License to Operate

Corporations are keen to avoid interference in their business through taxation or regulations. By taking substantive voluntary steps, they can persuade governments and the wider public that they are taking issues such as health and safety, diversity or the environment seriously, and so avoid intervention. This also applies to firms seeking to justify eye-catching profits and high levels of boardroom pay. Those operating away from their home country can make sure they stay welcome by being good corporate citizens with respect to labour standards and impacts on the environment.

CRITICISMS AND CONCERNS

Critics of CSR as well as proponents debate a number of concerns related to it. These include CSR's relationship to the fundamental purpose and nature of business and questionable motives for engaging in CSR. including concerns about insincerity and hypocrisy.

CSR and the Nature of Business

Corporations exist to provide products and/or services that produce profits for their shareholders.[10] Milton Friedman and others take this a step further, arguing that a corporation's purpose is to maximize returns to its shareholders, and that since (in their view), only people can have social responsibilities, corporations are only responsible to their shareholders and not to society as a whole. Although they accept that corporations should obey the laws of the countries within which they work, they assert that corporations have no other obligation to society. Some people perceive CSR as incongruent with the very nature and purpose of business, and, indeed, a hindrance to free trade. Those who assert that CSR is incongruent with capitalism and are in favor of neoliberalism argue that improvements in health, longevity and/or infant mortality have been created by economic growth attributed to free enterprise.[11]

Critics of this argument perceive neoliberalism as opposed to the well-being of society and a hindrance to human freedom. They claim that the type of capitalism practiced in many developing countries is a form of economic and cultural imperialism, noting that these countries usually have fewer labor protections, and thus their citizens are at a higher risk of exploitation by multinational corporations.[12]

A wide variety of individuals and organisations operate in between these poles. For example, the RHAL eadership Alliance asserts that the business of leadership (be it corporate or otherwise) is to change the world for the better.[13] Many religious and cultural traditions hold that the economy exists to serve human beings, so all economic entities have an obligation to society (e.g., Economic Justice for All). Moreover, as discussed above, many CSR proponents point out that CSR can significantly improve long-term corporate profitability because it reduces risks and inefficiencies while offering a host of potential benefits such as enhanced brand reputation and employee engagement.

CSR and Questionable Motives

Some critics believe that CSR programmes are undertaken by companies such as British American Tobacco (BAT).[14] the petroleum giant BP (well-known for its high-profile advertising campaigns on environmental aspects of its operations), and McDonald's to distract the public from ethical questions posed by their core operations. They argue that some corporations start CSR programmes for the commercial benefit they enjoy through raising their reputation with the public or with government. They suggest that corporations which exist solely to maximize profits are unable to advance the interests of society as a whole.[15]

Another concern is when companies claim to promote CSR and be committed to sustainable development whilst simultaneously engaging in harmful business practices. For example, since the 1970s. the McDonald's Corporation's association with Ronald McDonald House has been viewed as CSR and relationship marketing. More recently, as CSR has become mainstream, the company has beefed up its CSR programmes related to its labor, environmental and other practices[16] All the same, in McDonald's Restaurants v Morris & Steel, Lord Justices Pill, May and Keane ruled that it was fair comment to say that McDonald's employees worldwide 'do badly in terms of pay and conditions'[17] and true that 'if one eats enough McDonald's food, one's diet may well become high in fat etc., with the very real risk of heart disease.'[18]

Similarly, Shell has a much-publicised CSR policy and was a pioneer in triple bottom line reporting, however, this did not prevent the 2004 scandal concerning its misreporting of oil reserves—an act which seriously damaged its reputation and led to charges of hypocrisy. Since then, the Shell Foundation has become involved in many projects across the world, including a partnership with Marks and Spencer (UK) in three flower and fruit growing communities across Africa.

Critics concerned with corporate hypocrisy and insincerity generally suggest that better governmental and international regulation and enforcement, rather than voluntary measures, are necessary to ensure that companies behave in a socially responsible manner.

MOTIVATIONS FOR CSR

Corporations may be influenced to adopt CSR practices by several motivating fines[19].

Ethical Consumerism

The rise in popularity of ethical consumerism over the last two decades can be linked to the rise of CSR. As global population increases, so does the pressure on limited natural resources required to meet rising consumer demand (Grace and Cohen 2005). Industrialisation in many developing countries is booming as a result of technology and globalisation. Consumers are becoming more aware of the environmental and social implications of their day-to-day consumer decisions and are beginning to make purchasing decisions related to their environmental and ethical concerns. However, this practice is far from consistent or universal.

Globalisation and Market Forces

As corporations pursue growth through globalisation, they have encountered new challenges that impose limits to their growth and potential profits. Government regulations, tariffs, environmental restrictions and varying standards of what constitutes labour exploitation are problems that can cost organisations millions of dollars. Some view ethical issues as simply a costly hindrance. Some companies use CSR methodologies as a strategic tactic to gain public support for their presence in global markets, helping them sustain a competitive advantage by using their social contributions to provide a subconscious level of advertising.(Fry, Keim, Mieners 1986) Global competition places particular pressure on multinational corporations to examine not only their own labour practices, but those of their entire supply chain, from a CSR perspective.

Social Awareness and Education

The role among corporate stakeholders to work collectively to pressure corporations is changing. Shareholders and investors themselves, through socially responsible investing are exerting pressure on corporations to behave responsibly. Non-governmental organisations are also taking an increasing role, leveraging the power of the media and the Internet to increase their scrutiny and collective activism around corporate behaviour. Through education and dialogue, the development of community in holding businesses responsible for their actions is growing (Roux 2007).

Ethics Training

The rise of ethics training inside corporations, some of it required by government regulation, is another driver credited with changing the behaviour and culture of corporations. The aim of such training is to help employees make ethical decisions when the answers are unclear. Tullberg believes that humans are built with the capacity to cheat and manipulate, a view taken from (Trivers 1971, 1985), hence the need for learning normative values and rules in human behaviour (Tullberg 1996). The most direct benefit is reducinfljthe likelihood of "dirty hands" (Grace and Cohen 2005), fines and damaged reputations for hreaehlug laws or moral norms. Organisations also see secondary benefit in increasing employe loyalty and pride in the organisation. Caterpillar and Best Buy are examples of organisations that have taken ' such steps (Thilmany 2007).

Laws and Regulation

Another driver of CSR is the role of independent mediators, particularly the government, in ensuring that corporations are prevented from harming the broader social good, including people and the environment. CSR critics such as Robert Reich argue that governments should set the agenda for social responsibility by the way of laws and regulation that will allow a business to conduct themselves responsibly.

The issues surrounding government regulation pose several problems. Regulation in itself is unable to cover every aspect in detail of a corporation's operations. This leads to burdensome legal processes bogged down in interpretations of the law and debatable grey areas (Sacconi 2004). General Electric is an example of a corporation that has failed to clean up the Hudson River after contaminating it with organic pollutants. The company continues to argue via the legal process on assignment of liability, while the cleanup remains stagnant. (Sullivan & Schiafo 2005). The second issue is the financial burden that regulation can place on a nation's economy. This view shared by Bulkeley, who cites as an the Australian federal government's actions to avoid compliance with the Kyoto Protocol in 1997, on the concerns of economic loss and national interest. The Australian government took the position that signing the Kyoto Pact would have caused more significant economic losses for Australia than for any other OECD nation (Bulkeley 2001, pg 436). Critics of CSR also point out that organisations pay taxes to government to ensure that society and the environment are not adversely affected by business activities.

Crises and their Consequences

Often it takes a crisis to precipitate attention to CSR. One of the most active stands against environmental management is the CERES Principles that resulted after the Exxon Valdez incident in Alaska in 1989 (Grace and Cohen 2006). Other examples include the lead poisoning paint used by toy giant Mattel, which required a recall of millions of toys globally and caused the company to initiate new risk management and quality control processes. In another example, Magellan Metals in the West Australian town of Esperance was responsible for lead contamination killing thousands of birds in the area. The company had to cease business immediately and work with independent regulatory bodies to execute a cleanup.

LATIN AMERICA AND THE CARIBBEAN (LAC)

The move towards CSR is relatively new in Latin America and the Caribbean and is gaining ground as companies are pressed to adapt to the demands of the global economy. For small and medium enterprises (SMEs) in this region, adopting CSR practices can open doors to new market opportunities and bring a number of other benefits including reduced costs, improved bottom lines and public image, and greater opportunities to do business with other SMEs or larger firms.

The levels of corporate citizenship are corporate governance law, corporate philanthropy and corporate social responsibility. Corporate citizenship means adhering to laws, and complying with some standards. Corporate philanthropy means helping communities via social investments. Corporate social responsibility requires performance of one's obligations to stakeholders

In addition to these benefits, adopting responsible management practices can also help smaller businesses access the capital, they need to grow.[20]

To further promote the expansion of CSR among small and medium enterprises in the region, there are a number of obstacles to overcome: the lack of understanding among SMEs about CSR; the scarcity of trained experts in the region to build business capacity in this area; and insufficient shareholder or government pressure on companies to make their management records public. The Multilateral Investment Fund (MIF) is working to address these challenges through projects aiming to raise awareness among SMEs in Latin America and the Caribbean about the benefits of CSR and to support smaller companies in their efforts to implement CSR measures. MIF also partners with large companies foundations and universities interested in building awareness and spreading CSR knowledge to businesses throughout the region.[21]

REFERENCES

1. Grayson, D. and Hodges, A., (2004). *Corporate Social Opportunity! Seven Steps to Make Corporate Social Responsibility Work for your Business.*
2. Williams, Cynthia A.; Ruth V. Aguilera (2008). "Corporate Social Responsibility in a Comparative Perspective (http://vww.business,uinc.edu/aguilera in Crane. A., et.al.: *The Oxford Handbook of Corporate Social Responsibility.* Oxford University Press.
3. Habisch, Andre; Jan Jonker, Martha Wegner, R. Schmidpeter (eds.) (2005), *Corporate Social Responsibility across Europe.* Heidelberg: Springer.
4. R.H. Gray, D.L. Owen & K.T. Maunders, *Corporate Social Reporting: Accounting and accountability* (Hemel Hempstead: Prentice Hall, 1987).
5. Orlitzky, Marc: Frank L. Schmidt. Sara L. Rynes (2003). "Corporate Social and Financial Performance: A 24 (3): 403-41. London: SAGE Publications.
6. "Corporate Social Responsibility and Ethical Careers (http://www.careers.ed.ac.uk/. Careers Service).
7. Bhattacharya, C.B., Sankar Sen and Daniel Korschun (2008), "Using Corporate Social Responsibility to Win the War for Talent," MIT Sloan Management Review, 49 (2), 37-44; "The Good Company (http://wwvv.econoinist.com/surveys/display Story. cfm?Story_id=3555212)", *The Economist* (2005-01-20).
8. Kytle, Beth: John Gerard Ruggie (2005). "Corporate Social Responsibility as Risk Management: A Model for Multinationals (http://www.ksg.harvard.edu/m-rebg/CSRI/publications/workingpaper_" (PDF). *Social Responsibility*

Initiative Working Paper No. 10., John F. Kennedy School of Government, Harvard University.

9. Paluszek, John (April 6-7, 2005). "Ethics and Brand Value: Strategic Differentiation (http://www.scu.edu/ethics/practicing/focusareas/business/ethics-and-brand-value.ppt)" *Business and Organisational Ethics Partnership Meeting.* Markkula Center for Applied Ethics, Santa Clara University.

10. Malloy, D.C. (2003). "Understanding the Nature of Ethics, and Purposes of Business Health Care and Law (http://www.cces.ca/pdfs/CCES-PAPER-Malloy-E.)", *The Sport We Want* (PDF), Canadian Centre for Ethics in Sport (http://www.cces.ca/).

11. Friedman, Milton (1970-09-13). "The Social Responsibility of Business is to Increase its Profits (http://www.colorado.edu/studentgroups/libertarians/issues/friedman-soc-resp-business.html)", *The New York Times Magazine.*

12. Aquino, M.P., Nuestro Clamor por la Vida. Teologia Latinoamericana desde la Perspectiva de la Mujer (San José, Costa Rica: Departamento Ecuménico de Investigaciones, 1992), et al.

13. Real Leadership Alliance (http://www.realeadership.com/)

14. Friends of the Earth (2005-04-28). "British American Tobacco Report Shows Truth Behind Greenwash (http://www.foe.co.uk/resource/press_release/british_american_ tobacco_r)

15. McKibben, Bill (November/December 2006). "Hope vs. Hype (http://www.motherjones.com/news/teature/2006/11/hype_vs_hope.html)", *Mother Jones.*

16. McDonald's Corporation CSR information (http://www.medonalds.com/corp/values.)

17. Appeal Judgment, p. 247.

18. Judgment, p. 264.

19. Corporate Social Responsibility: It's No Longer an Option (http://www.towersperrin.com/tp/showdctmdoc.jsp?country=global&url=Master_Brand_2/USA/News/Spotlights/2008/2008_07_30_Spotlight_Corporate_Social.

20. Cici, Carlos; Federica Ranghieri (2008) *"Recommended Actions to Foster the Adoption of CSR Practices in SMEs" (http://idbdocs.iadh.org/wsdocs/getdocument.),* Inter-American Development Bank Report.

21. "Multilateral Investment Fund: Corporate Social Responsibility (http://www.iadb.org/mif/subtopic.cfm? language= English & SUBTOPIC = CSOR & TOPIC = SME)".

Chapter 7

Good Governance and Sustainable Human Development: Challenges and Prospects

Sustainable development is a buzzword found in much environmental and some economics literature these days. Certainly, the idea of sustainable development has become increasingly popular in the contemporary world. New literature on sustainable development have been appearing with increasing rapidity since the United Nations Conference on Environment and Development (UNCED) also known as the Earth Summit, held in Rio de Janeiro. Brazil in June 1992, and the number of research papers appearing in professional journals has been expanding at what seems to be an exponential rate.

The questions are what is all the fuss about? What is sustainable development anyway? And more importantly, why does sustainable development matter?

The word sustainable conies to us from the foresters of the 18th and 19th century in Europe. At that time, much of Europe was being deforested, and the foresters became increasingly concerned since wood was one of the driving forces in the European economy. Wood heated homes, built homes and factories, became furniture and other articles of manufacture, and the forests that provided the wood were central to romanitic literature and ideas.

Forests were best harvested from an economic standpoint using clear-cutting techniques. This meant that the loggers moved into a tract of forest and removed all of the trees in the tract. But the forests that grew back after clear-cutting did not always provide the wood fiber needed for the European economy. The foresters, and especially the German foresters, in response to this crisis developed scientific, or sustainable, forestry. The idea at the time was simple. If enough trees were planted to replace the wood provided by the trees that were harvested every year and the growth rate of the entire forest was grow in ensure this happened, then the forest would be sustainable. It would always grow enough wood fiber to replace the wood fiber lost to harvesting.

Thus, in this original idea sustainable means that as a resource is used it is replaced by growing additional amounts of the resource. In the modern context of the word sustainable, this is a difficult context because there are many resources, such as oil or iron ore, that cannot be grown. Still, these resources, like the trees in Europe's forests, are finite. If all the oil is extracted, there will not be any more oil. Still, if humanity is to survive with a civilisation for another 1,000 years, we are still going to need to heal our homes and fulfill many of the same purposes that oil now fulfills.

The word development, at least, as it is used in the phrase sustainable development, has a different history. During the cold war the United States needed to respond to the Communist challenge in the Third World that said that communism would briny with it a new standard of living. Walt Rostow, a prominent U.S. government official and economist, developed a competing ideology that he called economic development. Under the Communist model, societies that staged a revolution the proletariat and threw off the shackles of capitalism would begin a transformation that would lead to economic equality between all people.

All of the wealth of a nation could then be used to raise the standard of living and well-being of all the people within that society. The attractiveness of this model to the poor people of the First World is obvious. It promised masses people a significantly better way of life.

Rostow's answer to this challenge was that it was the civilised world's task to economically develop the Third World Rostow, and then the U.S. government and the governments of the Western Europe and Japan believed that all the civilised world had to do was to prime the economic pump of capitalism in the Third World, and just like a real pump when enough dollars were inserted into an economy, the Third world economy would lake off. This would eventually result in a better standard of living, a developed rather than a developing society, and a world safe for democracy and capitalism. Thus, according to this model, the poor would be much better off in the long run by embracing democracy and capitalism. If the Third World country would remain anti-communist, they would receive foreign aid, at some point in the future, take off and become equal to the economies of Western Europe, the U.S. and Japan.

Thus. development, in the context of sustainable development, means that the Third World's economies will become equal to the developed world's economies. This, in turn, will alleviate poverty and suffering in poor countries and make the World more equitable for all human beings.

Evolution of Sustainable Development as a Policy Concept

There are a number of important antecedents to Our Common Future, the report by the United Nation's Brundtland Commission (1987) that marks the beginning of the sustainable development concept that has generated all the literature and recent commentary. Divergent economic theorists like E.F. Sehumaker of Britain, environmentalists like Barry Commoner and Lester R. Brown, population analysts like Paul Ehrlich, politicians like Willy Brandt of what was then West Germany and Jimmy Carter of the United States, discussions within the United Nations and United Nations agencies, and a number of environmental organisations spread throughout the world all played roles in formulating ideas dial became part of the Brundtland Commission's message. But, even though many of the concepts of sustainable development existed before Our Common Future was published, the Commission's report, appearing in 1987, started the process of making sustainable development an important issue on the world stage.

The Commission identified a number of "common challenges" facing the earth: Population and human resources, food security, species and ecosystems, energy, industrial development, and urbanisation. In the context of these challenges they discussed international environmental problems, what successes had been registered in trying to address those problems, the scope and nature of the environmental problems still ,facing the world community, and the role of the world's economic systems in developing solutions to these problems and providing long-term relief for what they perceived to be the related problems of poverty and under development.

In the process of describing these challenges and proposing potential policy directions the world community could take to address the problem they had identified, the Commission presented and defined the phrase, sustainable development (World Commission on Environment and Development). "Sustainable development requires meeting the major needs of all and extending to all the opportunely to satisfy their aspirations for a better life." However, "living standards that go the basic' minimum are sustainable only if consumption standards everywhere have regard for long-term sustainability" (World Commission on Environment and Development).

Thus, sustainable development, as a concept, has two primary pillars: Economic development and the consumptive use of the world's natural resources in ways that are sustainable. We have to consume, in oilier words, with the realisation that resources are finite, and part of our job as human beings is to preserve the human future on this planet into a limitless future. In this concept of the limitless future, the Commission also called for what it termed "equity and the common interest." The Commission declared that "ecological interactions do not respect the boundaries Of individual ownership and political jurisdiction." Nor has the local nature of human interaction with the environment been confined, as the result of the creation of ever more sophisticated technologies, to local environmental effects. "Rapid growth in production has extended it [production] to the international plane, with both political and economic manifestations. To the Commission "the enforcement of common interest often suffers because areas of political jurisdiction and areas of impact do not coincide" (World Commission on Environment and Development).

In addition, the Commission continues, there is currently an inequitable distribution in resource consumption:

> The search for common interest would be less difficult if all development and environment problems had solutions that would leave everyone better off. This is seldom the case, and there are usually winners and losers... 'Losers' in the environmental/development conflicts include those who suffer more than their fair share of the health, property, and ecosystem damage costs of pollution (The World Commission on Environment and Development).

This inequitable distribution is of increasing concern because, "as a system approaches ecological limits, inequalities sharpen," and "hence, our inability to promote the common interest in sustainable development is often a product of the relative neglect of economic and social justice within and amongst nations" (The World Commission on Environment and Development). In other words the winners in the battle to consume from the earth's many commons create a dilemma for those who recognize the need for sustainable use since efforts to preserve the commons' various assets, as the system approaches ecological limits, increases both economic and social injustice "within and amongst nations."

The Commission then outlined a series of "strategic imperatives," or "critical objectives," inherent in their concept of sustainable development. These included:

- reviving growth;
- changing the quality of growth;
- ensuring essential needs for jobs, food, energy, water, and sanitation;
- ensuring a sustainable level of population;
- conserving and enhancing the resource base;
- reorienting technology and managing risk; and
- merging environment and economics in decision making (World Commission on Environment and Development).

The Responses to Our Common Future

Generally, as Michael Carley and Ian Christie have pointed out, there have been two primary responses to the Commission's sustainable development initiative, along with many variants on common themes. One approach calls for continued economic growth with the growth made more environmentally sensitive "in order to raise living standard globally and break the link between poverty and environmental degradation," and the other calls for radical changes in the world's economic order (Carley and Christie).

A good example of the reactions of those calling for economic growth with environmental responsibility is the report, "Choosing a Sustainable Future," released by the National Commission on the Environment. The report begins with a warning that "if America continues down its current path, primarily reading to environmental injuries and trying the repair them, the quality of our environment will continue to deteriorate, and eventually our economy will decline as well." Then the report's message is presented.

> If, however, our country pioneers new technologies, shifts its policies, makes bold economic changes, and embraces a new ethic of environmentally responsible behaviour, it is far more likely that the coming years will bring a higher quality of life, a healthier environment, and a more vibrant economy for all Americans (National Commission on the Environment, 1993).

In other words, if we keep our heads, recognize the seriousness of the environmental crisis, and then act boldly to meet the various challenges of that crisis, we can not only turn around the quality of the environment but we can keep a vibrant economy as well. We do not have to choose between an environmentally healthy and economically robust nation. We can have it all. We are smart enough, have the ability to develop enough new technologies, and can change our behaviours enough to confront all the problems lacing us and create the optimal solutions.

A more radical approach to sustainable development was published by tester W. Milbrath in a book entitled Envisioning a Sustainable Society, released only two years after publication of Our Common Future. Calling for: an end to the idea of a growth economy, an end to the culture that always accepts scientific advancement as a positive good, and the beginning of a society that learns its way to an in infrastructure designed for sustainability, among other proposals. Professor Milbrath begins his last chapter by saying that:

> Anyone who calls for a massive transformation of society is bound to be an impractical dreamer. This calls for people to

transform the most basic of all relationships, their relationship to nature. The changes 1 have proposed will surely be difficult to adopt. Yet, modern society's only choice is to change (Milhrath, 1989).

Both Milhrath's dreams and the work of the National Commission on the Environment are idealistic and formed from an intellectual, rather than an observation, base. Much of the sustainable development literature has similar Haws. Milbrath's thesis that "modern society's only choice is to change" is repeated over and over again in a multitude of ways in the literature. The authors catalog the planet's or nation's or region's environmental ills in substantial detail, then they culminate the case they have built, using statistics, charts, graphs, scientific research, and sometimes social science or anthropological research, by concluding that the environment's deterioration is guaranteed to continue and that this fact makes change, whether it is within a more conservative, mainstream approach such as that presented by the National Commission on the Environment, or a more radical structure such as presented by Milbrath, inevitable. We are in trouble, and something positive must be done.

The Earth Summit

Alter, and in the midst of the literary ferment arising from the Brundtland Commission report, including some powerful, deep ecology work by poets and essayists like Wendell Berry and Gary Snyder and novelists and essayists like Edward Abbey, the Earth Summit was proposed and planned by the United Nations. Called the United Nations Conference on Environment and Development (UNCED), it was held from June 3rd through June 14th in 1992 in Rio de Janeiro, Brazil. One hundred and fifty nations sent representatives. 1,400 non-governmental organisations were in attendance, 8,000 journalists covered the event and thousands of Brazilians attended one or more sessions. At the same time a major gathering of non-governmental organisations conducted what was billed as "The Global

Forum" only 40 kilometers from where the Earth Summit was meeting.

The major accomplishments of UNCED centered around the creation of United Nation's organisations formed either at the Summit or as the result of the process of preparing for the conference. The most important of these bodies is the Sustainable Development Commission that was given the task of furthering the work of creating sustainable development policies and procedures throughout the world. Other bodies were created out of "conventions" passed at the Summit on climate change and biodiversity. These particular organisations are to be dedicated to developing scientific and technical advice related to the development and implementation of international treaties. The basic ideas are that treaties entered into by the world's nations should, in the future, make sure that treaty provisions do not contribute to climate changes that have the potential to harm life on the planet earth and should help protect the planet's biodiversity. The Planet Earth Council and the Business Council for Sustainable Development were also created as the result of the Summit.

In addition to the UN organisations created, the Summit also considered and adopted treaties on climate change and biodiversity and a non-binding statement of forest principles. The treaty on climate change was signed at the Conference. but the treaty on biodiversity was resisted by the United States government until Bill Clinton became President, after which the biodiversity treaty was completed, although it has still not been ratified by the U.S. Senate. The non-binding statement on forest principles was signed at the conference (Haas. Levy. and Parson. 1992).

The Summit also adopted the Rio Declaration that includes 27 principles. These principles, though very general, are especially significant since they represent a series of difficult to reach compromises between industrialised and developing countries. Much of the developing world feels that the industrialised countries have used up the world's environmental resources in their pursuit of development and now wish to protect what environmental resources are remaining at the expense of the possibility of economically improving the lot of poor nations. These principles, then, provide a framework the world's diplomats in their efforts to improve both environmental and economic conditions around the world. The Rio principles included:

> a state's sovereign right to exploit its own resources in accordance with its own policies, without harming the environment elsewhere (principle 2); the right to development (principle 3); environmental protection as an integral part of development (principle 4); sustainable development that requires reducing 'unsustainable patterns of production and consumption' and that promotes 'appropriate demographic policies' (principle 8): access to information and citizen participation (principle 10)... and the polluter pays principles, including the internalisation of costs and the use of economic instruments (principle 16) (Parson, Haas, and Levy, 1992).

The major question that has to be asked about the Rio principles is whether they are substantive enough to lead to any significant changes in the world's approach to either environmental or economic conditions. In the end the world's governments are still centered on the concept of national sovereignty. Thus, inevitably each nation-state will interpret the Rio principles in light of their national interest rather than in the earth's interest. The principles are general in nature because that was the only way the diplomats could convince a large enough set of signatories to affix their signatures to the final document. Therefore, even though the principles are significant, their long-term success at improving conditions on the ground, in the air. and in water is yet to be determined.

Alter the Earth Summit the literature and discussions about sustainable development exploded. Newspapers, business magazines, science journals and magazines, popular magazines, television, radio, and a host of other forums and conferences centered on a discussion of sustainable development. In some parts of the world, such as in New Zealand, sustainable resource management concepts designed to improve the environment while, at the same time, helping New Zealand meet economic goals, were adopted into new legislation (Roberlson, 1993). The first stirrings of a national sustainable development policy in the United Suites were also felt when President-elect Bill Clinton declared in December of 1992 that "our future depends on maintaining a sustainable environment, and in so doing we can create economic opportunity" (Appenzeller, 1993).

The Critiques

There are those, of course. who question the whole sustainable development concept. Stephen R. Dovers and John W. Handmer. writing in Environmental Conservation, discovered what they described as eight "obvious" contradiction in the new movement. "The apparent ease with which these [eight contradictions] run be classified should not be allowed to hide the fact that, within each there exist many levels and tensions" (Dovers and Handmer, 1993). At the heart of the Dovers and Handmer criticism is a sense that the sustainable development discussion to date has been more rhetoric than an honest attempt to deal with facts and numbers. They admit that humans can live with logical inconsistencies and still work toward solutions, but overall they are pessimistic in that"... our numbers, per *caput* consumption, and total load on The Biosphere, continue to increase." They are afraid that the contradictions they see in the sustainable development movement "are perhaps insurmountable in any morally-defensible way." and that "the magnitude of the problems of environment and development can he overwhelming enough, let alone when matched with the magnitude of the cultural and political obstacles to change" inherent in the concept of sustainable development. In other words, they are afraid the contradictions within the various ideas that make up sustainable development as a concept are both too profound and insurmountable to overcome (Dovers and Handmer, 1993).

Professor Stanley Temple of the University of Wisconsin-Madison questions the very use of the phrase, sustainable development, pointing out that the word sustainable has been used in too many situations today, and ecological sustainability is one of those terms that confuse a lot of people. You hear about sustainable development, sustainable growth, sustainable economies sustainable societies, sustainable agriculture. Everything is sustainable (Temple, 1992).

The result of the overuse of the word, sustainable, in Temple's view, is that it has come to mean too much and nothing at the same time. Therefore sustainable development as a concept is too largely drawn to have any particular usefulness.

This discussion does not any more completely describe the criticisms of sustainable development than the description of the work of the World Commission on the Environment and Development, Lester W. Milbrath and the Earth Summit provides a complete picture of the sustainable development movement. It only provides some of the flavor of the total discussion.

The major point to be derived from reading the literature critical of the idea of sustainable development is that this is a movement that is more ethereal than concrete. There are a lot of discussions about the pending doom of biosphere if the environment is not protected more vigorously and efficiently than in the past in the pro-sustainable development literature. There is a call for economic and resource equity between the peoples currently living on the earth and between living generations and unborn generations. But, as the critics are pointing out, there is a lot of fuzziness that does not make the concept of sustainable development concrete. The word sustainable, as Temple points out, has become a buzz word dial is used lo the point of distraction. What does it really mean? Does it mean that resources must he protected at all cost. Should they be protected to the seventh generation, as would be the position of many Native Americans in the United States? Or, as the Menominee Indian Tribe of Wisconsin contends should resources be protected forever? And which resources should be protected? Are we really going to try to live without oil or a whole host of useful mineral resources? What, exactly, does sustainable mean in the context of sustainable development?

Equally difficult questions can be raised about the word, development, in the sustainable development context. The Brundtland Commission appears in "Our Common Future" to want to primarily improve the economies of the Third World so that the living standards of those living in countries mired in poverty can be raised to a more acceptable level. Development in Europe, Japan, the United States, and in places like Korea. Taiwan, Thailand. and other rising economies, has a much different meaning. Neo-classical economists like, Milton Friedman believe passionately that the free market demands that all people in all places at all limes have the right to improve their economic well being. In his book. Free To Choose, written with his wile Rose Friedman is the declaration that

> The two ideas of human Freedom and economic freedom working together came to their greatest fruition in 'lie United States. Those ideas are still very much with us. We are all of us imbued with them. They are in the United States the very fabric of our being. But we have been straying from them. We have been forgetting the basic truth that the greatest threat to human freedom is the concentration of power, whether in the hands of government or anyone else. We have persuaded ourselves that is safe to grant power, provided it is for good purposes.

Fortunately, we are waking up. We are again recognising the dangers of an overgoverned society, coming to understand that good objectives can be perverted by bad means, that reliance on the freedom of people to control their own lives in accordance with their own values is the surest way to achieve the full potential of a great society (Friedman and Friedman).

Are the great societies, as the Friedmans describe them, ready to limit their consumption, their pursuit of economic and human freedom, in order to guarantee equity between either current populations or future generations if that is a necessary pre-requisite of achieving the ideal of sustainable development? Can the idea of economic freedom be maintained in a sustainably developed society? A society that can sustain its use of natural resources and the environment forever? Or is the whole idea of sustainable development a buzz-word pipe dream conjured up by idealists who fail to realize that the world and humankind are realities'?

The work of the idealists like Milbrath is both entertaining and a dead end road. The entertainment value derives from the power of speculations about the future. But, in the end fiction, although it may give insights into realities, cannot resolve the conflicts and contradictions that are part of both the human and the earth's condition. No blueprint of Shang-gri-la will bring Shang-gri-la into existence. No road map to Shang-gri-la will lead to the creation of paradise. The task of those who believe that the idea of sustainable development is more than a pleasant fiction is to construct a model of sustainable development based upon the characteristics of an observable model, even if the model is incomplete in that it is not as fully sustainable or as fully developed as the proponents of the sustainable development concept would desire. The value of such a model is that it can be used to eliminate some of the fuzziness surrounding the idea of sustainable development and can also be used to encourage policies and practices that can really, lead to a more sustainable developed world.

This is only the lightest of introductions to the idea of sustainable development and the controversies surrounding the idea. Sustainable development has a legion of practical problems that stand between the world today and its eventual realisation. To those that believe the free market is the answer to all of the world's problems, sustainable development is a dangerous notion that can bring the prosperity of the U.S.. Western Europe, and Japan crashing into a prolonged economic dark age. To environmentalists who are worried about concepts like the carrying capacity of the earth and the long-term needs of human survival. sustainable development is a shining promise that must be reached if the world is saved. For those in poor countries who are desperate for a more equitable distribution of wealth, it is an idea with enormous appeal.

One important note to make is that not even all of those who are quoted as critics of one aspect or another of the sustainable development concept are opposed to the concept. In some cases their comments are designed to move the discussion forward by applying critical thinking to the problems inherent in the idea of sustainable development. In other cases, such as that of the Friedmans, it is safe to assume that they find the whole idea of sustainable development dangerous and in need of serious revision.

The work of the Menominee Sustainable Development Institute is to look at sustainable development through the prism provided by Menominee efforts to sustain their Forest and society for the last century or so in the face of steadily increasing assimilation pressures by both the U.S. economy and U.S. society. This prism provides clues about the kind of values, economic system, and social order might be necessary it a sustainable world is to be created. It also provides clues about what kind of path might be taken by me modern world toward sustainable development. This home page is dedicated to examining all of the issues raised by Menominee's efforts to create a society based on sustainable development. Comments to the home page are always welcome.

UNIVERSALISATION OF HUMAN DEVELOPMENT

"It is justice, not charity, that is wanting in the world", wrote Mary Wollstonecraft, the pioneering feminist, in A Vindication of the Rights of Woman, published in 1792, the same year in which her friend Thomas Paine published the second part of the Rights of Man. Both were concerned with giving everyone-women and men-power over their own lives and opportunities to live the way they had reasons to value. One particular feature of their common approach is particularly worth emphasising in the context of policy discussions today, viz. universalism. It is of specific interest in interpreting the task of "human development" in a world that is characterised, on the one hand, by enormous inequities in contemporary living conditions, and on the other, by real threats to the prospects of human life in the figure.

The rights that Wollstonecraft and Paine spoke about applied to all—irrespective of class, gender, race, community, or generation. These divisions often bias the analysis of claims of different groups, and partisanship is a recurrent threat to the equality of concern and respect that can be the only sustainable basis of a just social order. Appeals to rights and entitlements that have moved the world forcefully have often tended to ignore the freedoms of particular groups. For example, while ancient Greek philosophers presented some of the most far-reaching analyses of individual independence and autonomy, they typically did not hesitate to leave out the slaves—and often women too—from the discourse. The language and the rhetoric as well as the reality of rights in the contemporary world are often characterised by the neglect of particular sections of the population—less privileged ethnic groups, exploited classes, sequestered women.

The basic idea of "human development" involves the assertion of the unacceptability of such biases and discrimination. The contemporary debates on public policy require that this feature of universalism be kept firmly in view. The growing concern with "sustainable development reflects a basic belief that the interests of future generations should receive the same kind of attention that those in the present generation get. We cannot abuse and plunder our common stock of natural assets and resources leaving the future generations unable to enjoy the opportunities we take for granted today. We cannot use up, or contaminate, our environment as we wish, violating the rights and the interests of the future generations. The demand of sustainability" is, in fact, a particular reflection of universality of claims-applied to the future generations vis-a-vis us.

But, that universalism also requires that in our anxiety to protect the future generations, we must not overlook the pressing claims of the less privileged today. A universality approach cannot ignore the deprived people today in trying to prevent deprivation in the future. The recognition of this need for integration is much in the spirit of the "human development approach" to economic and social progress. The focus of this approach is on the kind of life that all the people—irrespective of nationality, class, race, gender, of community—can lead, and this non-sectarianism clearly must apply to generational divisions as well. The prospects of future people command respect in the same way that the opportunities of the present generation do. Universalism in acknowledging the life claims of everyone is the common thread that binds the demands of human development today with the exigencies of environmental preservation for the future.

Perhaps, the strongest argument in favor of giving priority to the protection of the environment, is the ethical need for guaranteeing that future generations would continue to enjoy similar opportunities of leading worthwhile lives that are enjoyed by generations that precede them. This, is the central idea underlying the demand for "sustainable development", and it has many important implications. But this goal of sustainability— increasingly recognised to be legitimate- would make little sense if the present life opportunities that are to be "sustained" in the future were miserable and indigent. Sustaining deprivation cannot be our goal, nor should we deny the less privileged today the attention that we bestow on generations in the future.

The living standard of a substantial part of humanity has radically moved forward in a way that would have been hard to anticipate in Paine's or Wollstonecraft's time. While it would have been, then, difficult to dispute that human life everywhere was "nasty, brutish and short" (as Thomas Hobbes had put it in Leviathan), people today in many countries in Europe, North America and elsewhere have lives that are much longer, less miserable, and far less battered by forces beyond the person's control. And yet a great many people in the world still continue to suffer from the absence of fundamental opportunities to lead decent and satisfying lives. The continued high incidence of premature mortality, ill health, undernourishment, illiteracy, poverty, insecurity, and other forms of deprivation indicate the failure of the modem world to bring even the most basic capabilities within the reach of all. A new born child may be doomed to a life of extreme brevity or intense misery if that child happens to be born in a "wrong class", in a "wrong country", or to be of the "wrong sex".

Universalism is basically an elementary demand for impartiality—applied within generations and between them. It is the recognition of a shared claim to the basic capability to lead worthwhile lives. Not working towards guaranteeing the basic capabilities to the future generations would be scandalous, but in the same way, not working towards bringing those elementary capabilities within the reach of the deprived in the present generation would also be outrageous. Given the implicit biases in many policy debates, there is a real need for jealously guarding that universalist perspective. The Human Development Reports have been systematically concerned with uncovering the nature and extent of these deprivations and with identifying the challenges involved in reducing such deficiencies and in advancing human development across the globe. The fifth Report, for which this essay is being written, provides an opportunity to examine critically how the analysis of the problem is standing up to the growing understanding of the nature of these deprivations and their manifold implications.

The promotion of human development in the contemporary world has 'to be integrated with the Safeguarding of their, fruits for the future. As the full significance of the issues forcefully discussed in the environmental conference in Rio in 1992 begins to be more fully understood, the integration of human progress and environmental conservation has emerged as one of the central challenges faced by the modern world (Pronk and Haq 1992, Speth 1992). The moral value of sustaining what we now have depends on the quality of what we have, and the entire approach of sustainable development directs us as much towards the present as towards the future. There is, in fact, no basic difficulty in broadening the concept of human development, as outlined in the previous Human Development Reports, to accommodate the claims of the future generations and the urgency of environmental protection.

The perspective of human development translates readily into a critical—and in many ways overdue-recognition of the need for active international efforts to preserve the quality of the environment in which we live. We have to see how the human developments we have achieved in the past, and what we are trying to achieve right now, can be sustained in the future—and further extended—rather than being threatened by cumulative pollution, exhaustion of natural resources, and other deteriorations of global and local environments. But, this safeguarding of the future prospects has to be done without giving up the efforts towards rapid human development and the speedy elimination of widespread deprivation of basic human capabilities which characterize the unequal and unjust world in which we live. This is partly n matter of cooperation across the frontiers, but the basis of that collaboration must-take full note of the inequalities that exist now and the urgency of rapid human development in the more deprived parts of the world. The basic underlying principle is universalism, and here again, the key concept, as Mary Wollstonecraft had noted, is justice, not charity.

DEVELOPMENT APPROACHES: CONTRASTS AND CONVERGENCE

Human Development, Aggregate Wealth and Universalism

The foundational task of scrutinising the demands of sustainable huma development also provides an appropriate occasion to see how the "human development" approach relates to the more conventional analyses to be found in the standard economic literature—from Adam Smith onwards. Interest in human development is not new in economics. Indeed, as was argued in the first Human Development Report (UNDP 1990), this motivating concern is explicitly present in the writings of the early founders of quantitative economics (such as William Petty, Gregory King, Franois Quesnay, Antoine Lavoisier, and Joseph Lagrange) as well as the pioneers of political economy (such as Adam Smith, David Ricardo, Robert Maltha, Karl Marx, and John Stuart

Mill). There is, in this sense, no foundational departure in making economic analysis and policy take extensive note of the demands of human development. The approach reclaims an old and established heritage, rather than importing or implanting a new diversion.

But, economics has never been a subject of one tradition only. The interest in human development has had to compete with other priorities and pursuits within the same body of mainstream economics. The preoccupation with commodity production, opulence and financial success can also be traced in professional economics through several centuries-involving many leading economists as well as businessmen and bureaucrats, who have preferred to concentrate more on the characteristics of overall maternal success than on the deprivation and development of human lives. Indeed, the dominant contemporary tradition of focusing on such variables as per-capita gross national product or national Wealth is a continuation—perhaps even an intensification—of the old opulence-oriented approach.

The focus on wealth maximisation can be taken at different levels, and at the common aggregative level, the spotlight is put entirely on making the community as a whole as opulent as possible, irrespective of distribution and of what that wealth does to human lives. It is, of course, true that being rich, wealthy and affluent can be among the most important contributory factors in generating well-being, and the opulence-oriented approach to economic progress certainly cannot be criticised for being irrelevant to the success of human living. On the other hand, insofar as it neglects other crucial factors, such as public care and social organisation, which also contribute to the well-being and freedom of individuals, the approach is deeply limited and defective. And insofar as the concern is with overall wealth maximisation-irrespective of distribution—there is a serious disregard of individual predicaments in favor of some conglomerative achievement, which can be blind to the most extreme deprivations suffered by many, while others make use—possibly excellent use—of the accomplishment of wealth and opulence.

Thus, the fundamental difficulty with the approach of wealth maximisation and with the tradition of judging success by overall opulence of a society is a deep-seated failure to come to terms with the universalist unbiasedness needed for an adequate understanding of social justice and human development. in this sense, the wealth-based approach is not, by any means, inconsequential, but it certainly is significantly partisan. The most basic problem with the opulence view is its comprehensive failure to take note of the need for impartial concern in providing entitlements to the ingredients of human living, and thus with the universalism of human development.

Conflicts and Misapplications

The long history of economic analysis provides plentiful examples of both types of approaches, concentrating respectively on (1) opulence and overall wealth, and (2) the quality of human lives. While the latter is the tradition on which the contemporary literature on human development draws, the importance of the former tradition—despite its limitations—must not be overlooked in trying to integrate economic analysis with the demands of human development. The tension between the two approaches has often been, powerful and explosive, particularly when the conflicts between the two outlooks have involved practical policy issues of major dimension. However, it is necessary to different both these approaches (with distinguished traditions of their own) from simple policy mistakes based m appeals to allegedly appropriate prerequisites of either economic opulence, or of human development. Many of those policies have, in fact, ended up serving neither the quality of human life, nor the actual promotion of economic opulence.

The Irish famines of the 1840s might have left a train of tremendous bitterness and anger with which the British Isles have to wrestle even today, but the non-interventionist leaders in London at that time were not only rather callous, they were also, in many ways, deeply mistaken in seeing no conflict between their particular view of "economic propriety" and the real ingredients of economic prosperity, not to mention the security of life and liberty of millions of vulnerable people. Similarly, those who carried out the disastrous economic policies that intensified the Great Depression of the 1980s may not have been any less humane than their opponents, but they certainly took quite a flawed view of the effects of so-called "sound finance"—even on production and wealth, and a fortiori on jobs and the lives of human beings.

Policy mistakes of similar kinds—allegedly in pursuit of "economic soundness" and even of "human well-being"—have occurred fairly plentifully in the contemporary world as well. There are extensive literatures that throw light on the failures of national governmental policies and of bureaucracies of powerful international institutions. It is, obviously, important to avoid such mistakes, which sometimes do not even promote the objectives they are chosen to promote. But, nevertheless, in assessing the alternative intellectual approaches, it would be unfair to judge them in terms of mistakes that have been committed in their respective names. Instead, both the approaches have to be scrutinised in their own terms-rather than concentrating primarily on misapplication and wrong use—even though the propensity to generate erroneous applications can be itself a limitation of an approach and, in that form, must be taken into account.

Objectives and Instruments

How cogent and illuminating are the two traditions of focusing respectively on (1) human development, and (2) overall wealth and opulence? These traditions can be seen as differing, directly or indirectly, in two distinct respects. The first concerns divergences in the ultimate objectives, and the second relates to differences in the effectiveness of distinct instruments.

While the human development approach has conformed broadly to the line of reasoning enunciated by Aristotle more than two millennia ago ("wealth is evidently not the good we are seeking, for it is merely useful and for the sake of something else"), there have been many professional experts, who have seen their task as being confined to the maximisation of opulence (an old illustration is the seventeenth century monograph by the pioneering mercantilist author, Thomas Mun, England's Treasure by Foreign Trade, or the balance of Our Foreign Trade is the Rule of Our Treasure). That division about our basic objectives still surfaces in the debates on current policies in different parts of the world, and also in discussions about what importance to attach to various indicators and criteria of progress (such as GNP per capita).

At the level of objectives, the case for following Aristotle rather than Mun is not hard to appreciate. How can we possibly give priority to the means of living, which is what treasures and wealths are, over the ends of good and free human lives? While much of economic and financial writing proceeds as if there is nothing beyond opulence with which we need be concerned, it is fair to see that as a problem of presentation, rather than a reflection of some deep-seated eccentricity about ends and means. The really interesting debates must relate to instrumental effectiveness of overall wealth and opulence in promoting those things for which wealth and opulence are sought.

There is, in fact, much more substance in the opulence-centered approach than the implausible view that is an end in itself. This takes us to the second difference, which relates to the cause-effect relationships in the pursuit of the deeper objectives. Some have taken the view that while opulence is not at all valued at all for its own sake, it still is the most important instrument in promoting the more basic objectives—even the Aristotelian one of rich and fulfilling lives.

For example, W. Arthur Lewis, one of the leading modern development economists, did not entertain much doubt that the appropriate objective to pursue is increasing "the range of human choice." He did also acknowledge the causal role of many factors in advancing the freedom to choose. But, nevertheless he decided to concentrate specifically on "the growth of output per head", because it "givens man greater control over his environment, and thereby increases his freedom" (Lewis 1955). Indeed the focus of his classic book was sufficiently precise to permit him to assert: "Our subject is growth, and not distribution."

Lewis's faith in the instrumental efficacy of total growth has proved to be quite disputable in terms of the experiences observed in the actual world. Many countries have grown fast without a commensurate impact on living conditions, and more importantly, some countries have achieved high quality of life respite relatively moderate growth of GNP or GDP per head. It has also been observed that even when there is a generally positive and statistically significant relationship between GNP per head and indicators of quality of life in the gross inter country data, much of that relationship turns on the use of extra income in the specific fields of public education and health, and in reducing absolute poverty.

It is certainly true that the higher the average income of a country, the more likely it is—given other things-that it will tend to have a higher average life expectancy, lower infant and child mortality rates, higher literacy, and in fact, a higher value of the "Human Development Index" (HDI). A number of recent studies have confirmed this general pattern. However, the associations are far from perfect. For example, in intercountry comparisons, income variations tend to explain not much more than half the differences in life expectancy, or in infant or child mortality, and it explains a smaller proportion of differences in adult literacy rates. Many countries, such as Sri Lanka, China, Jamaica, Costa Rica, and the state of Kerala in India, have achieved levels of human development that are enormously higher than what would be expected on the basis of their GNP or real income per head. What is also of importance—perhaps even more so-is the route through which growth of GNP most effectively influences human development. Economic growth not only involves increase in private incomes, it can also significantly contribute to generating resources that can be marchalled to improve social services (such as public health care, epidemiological protection, basic education, safe drinking water, etc.). In some cases such marshalling is effectively done, while in other cases, the fruits of growth are put to little use of this kind. This can make a big difference to the outcome in terms of the expansion of basic human capabilities.

Similarly, while the expansion of private income certainly is of instrumental importance in enhancing basic capabilities, the effectiveness of that impact depends much on the distribution of the newly generated incomes. In particular, the biggest impact may be expected to occur if the rise in average GNP per head goes with a sharp reduction in the poverty of the worst off people, rather going in oilier directions. To what extent this will happen depends on a variety of economic and social circumstances related to the labor-intensive nature of techniques of production, the sharing of education and skills across the population, the success of land reforms and the sharing of rural resources, and so on. Here again the experiences of different countries and of different policy regimes have been quite divergent.

There is considerable evidence that the statistical correlation between GNP per head and human development tends to work through the impact of GNP expansion on higher public expenditure and lower poverty. For example, it is found in Anand and Ravallion (1993) that when life expectancy variations are linked with public health spending per person and an index of poverty, the addition of GNP per person as a further explanatory variable yields a coefficient that is not significantly different from zero. This and related results that focus on other characteristics of quality of life—must not, of course, be interpreted to imply that economic growth does not matter in expanding the quality of life. Rather, what they indicate is that the connections are seriously contingent, and much depends on how the fruits of economic growth are shared (in particular what the poor get) and how far the additional resources are used to support public services (for example, public health services, which are particularly crucial in influencing life expectancy).

Thus, the opulence-oriented view of progress, which has little intrinsic merit (as was discussed earlier), has a conditionally important instrumental role-and that conditionality»relates specifically to features on which the human development approach has tended to focus, to wit, public action and poverty reduction. There is no basic conflict between (1) regarding economic growth to be very important, and (2) taking it to be in itself an insufficient basis of human development. Insofar as growth of GNP or GDP promotes enhancement of living conditions, its biggest impact comes through the expanded ability to undertake public action to promote human development, and the share of the additional income that is enjoyed by the poor. In recognising the importance of economic growth as a means for human development, we must also take lull note the contingent nature of its effectiveness as means (depending on the use of the means for promoting human development), and (2) its non-uniqueness as means (there are other means as well, including social organisation).

Again the central issue turns out to be the need for universalist attention in valuing the enhancement of human capabilities, as opposed to partisan interest in promoting aggregate growth—while overlooking how the fruits are distributed and what is done to make those fruits serve the interests of the least privileged. The discipline of universalism directs the focus of our attention on those whose needs are greatest and whose deprivations are most acute, and that attention can be extremely effective when it is translated into practical policy.

Capability and Reproduction

The human development approach concentrates on the capability to lead worthwhile lives as the object of importance. It applies the universalist perspective to the freedom to lead lives that people today and in the future would value. This focus on freedom includes a concern with reproductive freedom as well. Since the population problem has tended to attract a good deal of attention lately, it is worth discussing whether the support for reproductive freedom might not be self-defeating—leading to such an increase in population that the well-being and freedom of all would be threatened.

Alarmist views have been expressed in this field quite plentifully in recent years. To some extent, this is a positive development since the subject of population is indeed an important one. On the other hand, to argue for violation of reproductive freedom in the cause of population control (for example, through libligatory limits on the size of families) may not be the right way to think about this complex question. Nor is a sense of alarm and panic the most favorable circumstance for reflecting rationally on matters of there is, in a wealth of evidence to indicate that given the real opportunity to choose smaller without adverse economic and social consequences, smaller families are indeed chosen.

In the experience of the industrialised West, fertility rates have come down sharply with economic and social development, reduction of mortality rates, and expansion of basic education. Similar processes can now DC observed in many parts of the so-called Third World (Easterlin 1980, Summers 1992, Barro and Lee 1993, and the references cited there). In particular, female education seems to play a critical part in reducing the birth rate, along with the availability of medical care and reduction of mortality rates.

It appears, therefore, that human development contributes to solving—rather than intensifying the population problem. This is not surprising, since people—women in particular—have good reasons not to choose a life of continuous child-bearing and child-rearing. A family's effective freedom in having a mailer number of children is favorably influenced by the availability of medical facilities (including the opportunity of birth control), the reduction of death rates (making it unnecessary to give birth to many children to make sure that some do survive), and the expansion of basic education (especially female education, giving women the opportunity to understand better the options that exist and the social values associated with a smaller family size in a modern community). These factors have been very important even in China's remarkably rapid decline in the birth-rate, even though the advocates of coercion in birth control tend to cite mainly the use of some compulsion in family planning in China. As a matter of fact, the state of Kerala in India, which has similar mortality rates, health facilities and basic education levels as China (somewhat higher female education levels), but no compulsion whatever, has a similar birth rate as (in lad, a little lower than) China's. In intercountry comparisons, human development-related to longevity, health, education and security-seems to be significantly influential in reducing the birth rate.

If reproductive freedom is seen as a part of human freedom in general, we achieve a better perspective of challenges and demands of the population problem. The personal and social problems that are generated by over-rapid population increase are seized by educated, secure and unharassed parents when the opportunity for sensible reflection exists. The promotion of human development not only reflects itself in expanded longevity, enhanced education levels, more secure and less harassed lives, it also makes it possible for people to opt for smaller families. The solution of the population problem can be sought through expanding the options that people have, rather than through reducing options (Sen, 1994). Human beings have to be seen as persons who are capable of sensible reflection and responsible decision, rather than being treated as a stock of breeding animals who are to be led against their will into some bureaucratically ordained path.

ENVIRONMENT AND SUSTAINABLE DEVELOPMENT

Environmental Challenge

The idea of sustainable development arose essentially from concerns relating to the overexploitation of natural and environmental resources. Early discussions stressed the limits to economic activity imposed by the physical environment, and concluded that species and ecosystems should be utilised in ways that allow them to go on renewing themselves indefinitely (IUCN 1980). The anxieties expressed by environmental scientists and ecologists were recognised by policymakers and economists, who attempted to formulate concepts of sustainable development". An early formulation by Robert Repetto (1985) was as follows:

> "At the core of the idea of sustainability, then, is the concept that current decisions should not damage the prospects for maintaining or improving living standards in the future...This implies that our economic systems should be managed so

> that we live off the dividend of our resources, maintaining and improving the asset base so that the generations that follow will be able to live equally well or better. This principle also has much in common with the ideal concept of income that accountants seek to determine: the greatest amount that can be consumed in the current period without reducing prospects for consumption in the future."

As we snail presently argue, this connection between the ideal of sustainable development and the economic accountant's concept of maintaining the income level (discussed, in particular, by Hicks 1946) is an important one to explore.

A more recent characterisation has been suggested by Robert Solow (1992): "The duty imposed by sustainability to bequeath to posterity not any particular thing—with rare exceptions such as Yosemite, for example, but rather to endow them with whatever it takes to achieve a standard of living least as good as our own and 10 look after their next generation similarly. We are not to consume humanity's capital, in the broadest sense."

The term "sustainable development", in fact, owes its widespread usage to the Brundtland Commission Report (1987), Our Common Future, which defined it as "development that meets the needs of the present without compromising the ability of future generations to meet their own needs. It contains within it two key concepts:

- the concept of 'needs', in particular the essential needs of the world's poor, to which overriding priority should be given; and
- the idea of limitations imposed by the state of technology and social organisation on the environment's ability to meet present and future needs" (WCED 1987).

The Brundtland Commission definition is often cited and has become very influential. As ageneral statement, it reminds us that sustainability is about an obligation to future generations (towards meeting their "needs"), and thus it is necessarily about intergenerational allocation. Unlike some earlier statements, n also helpfully shifts attention away from conserving specific resources and "leaving the world as we found it" in every particular. The latter would appear to be neither feasible nor necessarily sensible: resources are basically fungible and can be substituted for one another. The Brundtland Commission's notion of sustainable development is indeed broader and invites examination even independently of environmental concerns.

Moreover, the obligation of sustainability cannot be left entirely to the market. The future is not adequately represented in the market—at least not the distant future—and there is no reason that ordinary market behaviour with take care of whatever obligation we have to the future. Universalism demands that the state should serve as a trustee for the movement of future generations. Government policies such as taxes, subsidies, and regulation can adapt the incentive structure in ways that protect the global environment and resource base for people yet to be born. As A.C. Pigou (1932) had noted, "there is wide agreement that the State should protect the interests of the future in some degree against the effects of our rational discounting and of our preference for ourselves over our descendants. The whole movement for 'conservation' in the United States is based on this conviction. It is the clear duty of Government, which is the trustee for unborn generations as well as for its present citizens, to watch over, and, if need be, by legislative enactment, to defend, the exhaustible natural resources of the country from rash and reckless spoliation."

Intergenerational Equity and Sustainable Development

What are our obligations to future generations? Joseph Addison, writing in The Spectator of 1714 was dismissive any duty to posterity: "Most people are of the humour of an old fellow of a college, who, when he Was pressed by the Society to come into something that might redound to the good of their successors, grew very peevish; 'We are always doing,' says he, 'something for posterity, but I would fain see posterity do something for us." Yet, of course, there is something posterity can do for us: it can inherit less physical and natural capital, and thus allow us to achieve—though not out of its choice-a higher standard of living al its expense.

How much capital should the future inherit from us? This has been the subject matter of optimal growth theory since the pioneering article of Frank P. Ramsey (1928). The theory has formed the basis of development policy and social cost-benefit analysis in the less developed countries. In the Appendix we present a simply two-period model which captures the central features of intergenerational allocation as seen in this approach.

This framework is founded on the essentially utilitarian criterion of maximising the sum total of welfare of different generations. It allows the welfare of one generation to be traded off one-for-one against that of another generation. If the benefit to us from economic activities which continue to emit greenhouse gases it the present rates outweighs the harm done to future generations from global warming, then the criterion would recommend no change in our activities. Other ethical notions of the total "good" may allow for different tradeoffs—for example, those that take account of welfare inequality between generations. Yet, others may allow no tradeoff in certain ranges —for example, those based on the "rights" of future generations to the same quality of environment and levels of clean air as the present generation has. This latter view of justice would give priority to specific rights that generations have over decisions based on a calculation of aggregate welfare (Rawls 1971, Dworkin 1978, Sen 1982a, b).

Within the broadly welfarist framework of optimal growth theory-by far the main economic approach used to analyze questions of intergenerational justice—it is relevant to enquire whether sustainable development is necessarily a consequence of growth being optimal. If it were, then a (derived) justification for sustainability could be found in maximising the total good. Let us take sustainable development to mean non-declining welfare over time—although other definitions are formulated in terms of non-declining income, consumption, or capital stock.

Even though Ramsey (1928) had argued for treating the welfare of different generations impartially, much of the subsequent literature assumes a positive rate of pure time preference according to which well-being at a later lime counts for less than well-being at an earlier time. Now if the social rate of return to investing in environmental capital (protection) is not large, and in particular it is smaller than the rate of pure time discount, it is not worthwhile for the present generation to reduce its consumption and increase investment: the gain in well-being to the future generation will not compensate for the sacrifice in well-being of the present generation. This can lead to a decline in well-being over time. Moreover, a similar result obtains with a positive rate of pure time preference even in an economy with exhaustible resources (Solow 1974b, Dasgupta and Heal 1979). On the other hand, universalism in the space of generational welfares—in the special form of no pure time discount—will typically lead to rising welfare over time in such models.

Yet, there is no general presumption that sustainability will be implied by optimality in models of intertemporal allocation. It becomes an even less likely consequence once we incorporate environmental productivity and quality into production and welfare, respectively (Pezzey 1992). Hence, a justification for sustainability will have to be sought outside the framework of maximising aggregate intergenerational well-being.

For Robert Solow (1974b, 1991), sustainability is simply a matter of distributional equity, about sharing the capacity for well-being between present people and future people: "[It is] an obligation to conduct ourselves so that we leave or the future the option or the capacity to be as well off as we are. It is not clear [to me] that one can be more precise than that. Sustainability is an injunction not to satisfy ourselves by impoverishing our successors" (Solow 1991: 3).

The notion appears to be founded on a forward-looking application of Rawls's Difference Principle, even though Solow (1974b) recognises the difficulties of applying this principle to the problem of saving. Still, his concern for intergenerational equity leads him to the view that we have done rather well at the hands of our ancestors, who were much poorer than we are and hence might properly have saved less and consumed more. According to Solow (1991: 7): "You could make a good case that out ancestors, who were considerably poorer than we are, whose standard of living was considerably less than our own, were probably excessively generous in providing for us. They cut down a lot of trees, but they saved a lot and they built a lot of railroad rights-of-way. Both privately and publicly they probably did better by us than a sort of fair minded judge in thinking about the equity (whether they got their share and we got our share or whether we profited at their expense) would have required. It would have been day for them to save a little less, to enjoy a little more and give us a little less of a start than our generation has had." For Solow, then, sustainability would appear to be an obligation to preserve the present-day economic opportunities (such as productive capacity) for the future, not necessarily to increase them. This can be seen as an interpretation of the demands of universalism" applied to intergenerational equity, and as such has much intuitive appeal.

The principle of preserving productive capacity, or society's broad "stock of capital", can also be defended in deontological terms without a direct appeal to distributional equity. The relevant notion here is that of usufruct rights. We may enjoy the fruits of the accumulated capital and environmental resources that we inherit (in the form of the income and amenities to which they give rise), but we may not deplete the total stock. This principle requires us to pass on to future generations what we have inherited from past generation—since we did not accumulate or produce it ourselves. It is not based on a claim of equal well-being for die next generation.

Preserving productive capacity intact is not, however, an obligation to leave the world as we found it in every detail. What needs to be conserved are the opportunities of future generations to lead worthwhile haves. The fact of substitutability (in both production and consumption) implies that what we are obligated to leave behind is a generalised capacity to create well-being, not any particular thing or any particular resource. Since we do not know what the tastes and preferences of future generations will be, and what they will do, we can talk of sustainability only in terms of conserving a capacity to produce well-being. As Solow again emphasises: "Sustainability as a moral obligation is a general obligation not a specific one. It is not an obligation to preserve this or preserve that. It is an obligation, if want to make sense out of it to preserve the capacity to be well off, to be as well off as we. That does not preclude preserving specific resources, if they have an independent value and no good substitutes. But, we shouldn't kill ourselves, that is part of the value of specific resources. It is not a consequence of any interest in sustainability".

The idea that "income" is what can be spent while leaving the asset base intact is precisely the concept of sustainable income established by John Hicks (1946: 172) almost fifty years ago: "The purpose of income calculations in practical affairs is to give people an indication of the amount which they can consume without impoverishing themselves. Following out this idea, it would seem that we ought to define a man's income as the maximum value which he can consume during a week, and still expect to be as well off at the end of the week as he was at the beginning.

Thus, when a person saves, he plans to be better off in the future. When he lives beyond his income, he plans to be worse off. Remembering that the practical purpose of income is to serve as a guide for prudent conduct, I think it is fairly clear that this is what the central meaning must be." It is easily seen why Repetto (1985) saw an analogy between the idea of sustainable development and the economic accountant's notion of what spendable income is.

Preservation of the resource base does not imply that all exhaustible (e.g. mineral and fossil fuel) resources must be conserved, that is likely to be unfeasible. But if society's broad stock of capital is to be maintained, we have to replace the non-renewable resources that are used up with something else. That has to be reproducible capital, whether physical or human. The idea that the proceeds from a "wasting asset" should be set aside and reinvested so that the yield from these investments compensates for the dwindling resource is also traceable to Hicks (1946: 187). He argued that: "If a person's receipts are derived from the exploitation of a wasting asset, liable to give out at some future date, we should say that IJS receipts are in excess of his income, the difference between them being reckoned as an allowance for depreciation. In this case, if he is to consume no more than his income, he must re-lend some part of his receipts; and the lower the rate of interest is, the greater the sum he will have to re-lend in order for the interest on it to make up for the expected failure of receipts from his wasting asset in the future".

It is essentially this Hicksian logic which lies behind Hartwick's (1977) Rule of rule that has become, justly, which used in the recent environmental literature. He showed exactly how much from the use of a depletable resource should be set aside and invested in reproducible capital so that the total return (i.e. income) could be sustained over time. Hartwick's Rule says that if the entire competitive rents from an economy's use of a wasting resource are invested in reproducible capital, then it will be able perpetually to maintain a constant level of consumption. The competitive rents, or pure return to the non-renewable resource, are given by Hotelling's (1931) classic result that the shadow value of the resource rises at a rate equal to the current marginal product of reproducible capital. The accumulation of reproducible capital through investment of the Hotelling rents exactly offsets the (efficient) depletion of the exhaustible resource.

Although Hartwiek's original rule applied to rather simple economies (with constant returns to scale, a given stock of exhaustible resources, no technical progress, and no population growth), there have been significant generalisations and elaborations of it, including the incorporation of resource amenities (Dixit *et al.* 1980). Solow (1986) suggests that Hartwick's Rule can be given the interpretation that an appropriately defined stock of capital is being maintained intact, and that income is the interest on that patrimony. The broad notion of the stock of capital allows for exhaustible and renewable resources, for oilman capital, for freedom from pollution, and for other suitable forms of "environmental capital". Moreover, the rule has considerable intuitive appeal within the general framework of universalist ethics. It seems appropriate enough to meet our obligation to the future by channelling the rents on our use of non-renewable resources into capital formation, any kind of capital formation-physical or human. The policy allows future generations to sustain indefinitely the income, or capacity to consume, of the present generation.

Intergenerational Justice and Human Development

We have emphasised that sustainability is a matter of distributional equity in a very broad sense, that is, of sharing the capacity for well-being between present people and future people in an acceptable way-that is in a way which neither the present generation nor the future generations can readily reject. This is a criterion of justice that has been forcefully used-though not in the context of intergenerational equity-by Thomas Scanlon (1982) and, more recently, by John Rawls (1993).

There would, how ever, be something distinctly odd if we were deeply concerned for the well-being of the future— and as yet unborn-generations while ignoring the plight of the poor today. The moral obligation underlying sustainability is an injunction to preserve the capacity for future people to be as well off as we are. This has a terribly hollow ring if it is not accompanied by a moral obligation to protect and enhance the well-being of people who are poor and deprived. If one thinks that people will be deprived in the future unless different policies are followed, then one is morally obliged to ask whether people are deprived right now. It would be a gross violation of the universalist principle, if we were to be obsessed about intergenerational equity without at the same seizing the problem of intragenerational equity: the ethic of universalism certainly demands such impartiality.

A concern for equity right now, and not merely for equity between periods of time, requires redistribution to the deprived contemporaries. But, redistribution to poor people today might be felt to be disadvantageous from the standpoint of sustainability. It might be interpreted as leading to an increase in current consumption, not lo an increase in investment. However, much depends on what form that redistribution takes.

This is precisely where the significance of human development as a means comes in. Redistribution to the poor in the form of improving their health, education and nutrition is not only intrinsically important in enhancing their capabilities to lead more fulfilling lives-but it is also instrumentally important in increasing their "human capital" with lasting influence in the future. A general increase in educational levels, for example, will raise productivity and the ability to generate higher incomes, now and in the future. The importance of maternal education in raising the quality of life and agency of later generations has also been well established (Summers 1992). Thus human development should be seen as a major contribution to the achievement of sustainability.

This argument should be contrasted with other arguments that have been proposed in the context of sustainable development. For example, poverty alleviation has been suggested as an instrument to protect the environment from degradation (World Bank 1992). There it is argued that alleviating poverty is a prerequisite for environmental conservation:

> "The poor arc both victims and agents of environmental damage. About half of the world's poor live in rural areas»that are environmentally fragile, and they rely on natural resources ever over which they have little legal control. Land-hungry farmers resort to cultivating unsuitable areas—steeply sloped, erosion-prone hillsides; semiarid land where soil degradation is rapid; and tropical forests where crop yields on cleared fields frequently drop sharply after just a few years. Poor families often lack the resources to avoid degrading their environment. The very poor, struggling at the edge of subsistence, are preoccupied with day-to-day survival. It is not that the poor have inherently short horizons; poor communities often have a strong ethic of stewardship in managing their traditional lands. But, their fragile and limited resources, their often poorly defined property rights, and their limited access to credit and insurance markets prevent them from investing as much as they should in environmental protection" (World Bank 1992).

This argument provides an instrumental justification for poverty alleviation, as a means of protecting the environment. There is much substance in this. But, the human development argument goes beyond that. Human development is defended as a goal in itself; it directly enhances the capability of people to lead worthwhile lives, so there are immediate gains in what is ultimately important, while safeguarding similar opportunities in the inline. There is hardly any example in the world of the expansion of education and health being anything other than monotone; good education and good health seem to generate powerful demand for these opportunities and more for our children. This is a relationship that goes well beyond the redistribution of income to the poor at a given point of time—important though that is. It should also be noted that any instrumental justification for human development is not gripped by some impersonal objective such as conserving the environment, but relates concretely to people's ability to generate for themselves more income and other means of good living.

Chapter 8

Exploring Strategy for Promoting Sustainable Human Development

In in industrialised countries, the consumption patterns of cities are severely stressing the global ecosystem, while settlements in the developing world need more raw material, energy, and economic development simply to overcome basic economic and social problems. Human settlement conditions in many parts of the world, particularly the developing countries, are deteriorating mainly as a result of the low levels of investment in the sector attributable to the overall resource constraints in these countries.

In the low-income countries, for which recent data are available, an average of only 5.6 per cent of central government expenditure went to housing, amenities, social security and welfare. Expenditure by international support and finance organisations is equally low. For example, only 1 per cent of the United Nations system's total grant-financed expenditures in 1988 went to human settlements, while in 1991, loans from the World Bank and the International Development Association (IDA) for urban development and water supply and sewerage amounted to 5,5 and 5.4 per cent, respectively, of their total lending.

On the other hand, available information indicates that technical cooperation activities in the human settlement sector investment. For public and private sector investment.

For example, every dollar of UNDP technical cooperation expenditure on human settlements in 1988 generated a follow-up investment of $122, the highest of all UNDP sectors of assistance.

This is the foundation of the "enabling approach" advocated for the human settlement sector External assistance will help to generate the internal resources needed to improve the living and working environments of all people by the year 2000 and beyond, including the growing number of unemployed - the no-income group. At the same time, the environmental implications of urban development should be recognised and addressed in an integrated fashion by all countries, with high priority being given to the needs of the urban and rural poor, the unemployed and the growing number of people without any source of income.

Human Settlement Objective

The overall human settlement objective is to improve the social, economic and environmental quality of human settlements and the living and working environments of all people, in particular the urban and rural poor. Such improvement should be based on technical cooperation activities, partnerships among the public, private and community sectors and Participation in the decision-making process by community groups and special interest groups 'such as women, indigenous people, the elderly and the disabled. These approaches should form the core principles of national settlement strategies.

In formulating these strategies, countries with need to set priorities among the eight programme areas in this chapter in accordance with their national plans and objectives, taking fully into account their social and cultural capabilities. Furthermore, countries should make appropriate provision to monitor the impact of their strategies on marginalised and disenfranchised groups, with particular reference to the needs of women.

The programme areas included in this study are:

(a) Providing adequate shelter for all;

(b) Improving human settlement management;

(c) Promoting sustainable land-use planning and management;

(d) Promoting the integrated provision of environmental infrastructure: water, sanitation, drainage and solid-waste management;

(e) Promoting sustainable energy and transport systems in human settlements;

(i) Promoting human settlement planning and management in disaster-prone areas;

(g) Promoting sustainable construction industry activities;

(h) Promoting human resource development and capacity-building for human settlement development.

PROGRAMME AREAS

A. Providing Adequate Shelter for All

Basis for Action

Access to safe and healthy shelter is essential to a person's physical, psychological, social and economic well-being and should be a fundamental part of national and international action. The right adequate housing as a basic human right is enshrined in the Universal Declaration of Human Rights (UDHR) and the International Covenant on Economic, Social and Cultural Rights (ICESCR). Despite this it is estimated that at the present time, at least 1 billion people do not have access to safe and healthy shelter and that if appropriate action is not taken, this number will increase dramatically by the end of the century and beyond.

A major global programme to address this problem is the Global Strategy for Shelter to the Year 2000, adopted by the General Assembly in December 1988 (resolution 43/181, annex). Despite its widespread endorsement, the Strategy needs a much greater level of political and financial support to enable it to reach its goal of facilitating adequate shelter for all by the end of the century and beyond.

Objective

The objective is to achieve adequate shelter for rapidly growing populations and for the currently deprived urban and rural poor through an enabling approach to shelter development and improvement that is environmentally sound.

Activities

The following activities should be undertaken:

(a) As a first step towards the goal of providing adequate shelter for all, all countries should take immediate measures to provide shelter to their homeless poor, while the international community and financial institutions should undertake actions to support the efforts of the developing countries to provide shelter to the poor;

(b) All countries should adopt and/or strengthen national shelter strategies, with targets based, as appropriate, on the principles and recommendations contained in the Global Strategy for Shelter to the Year 2000. People should be protected by law against unfair eviction from their homes or land;

(c) All countries should, as appropriate, support the shelter efforts of the urban and rural poor, the unemployed and the no-income group by adopting and/or adapting existing codes and regulations, to facilitate their access to land, finance and low-cost building materials and by actively promoting the regularisation and upgrading of informal settlements and urban slums as an expedient measure and pragmatic solution to the urban shelter deficit;

(d) All countries should, as appropriate, facilitate access of urban and rural poor to shelter by adopting and utilising housing and finance schemes and new innovative mechanisms adapted to their circumstances;

(e) All countries should support and develop environmentally compatible shelter strategies at national, state/provincial and municipal levels through partnerships among the private, public and community sectors and with the support of community-based organisations;

(f) All countries, especially developing ones, should, as appropriate, formulate and implement programmes to reduce the impact of the phenomenon of rural to urban drift by improving rural living conditions;

(g) All countries, where appropriate, should develop and implement resettlement programmes that address the specific problems of displaced populations in their respective countries;

(h) All countries should, as appropriate, document and monitor the implementation of their national shelter strategies by using, inter alia, the monitoring guidelines adopted by the Commission on Human Settlements and the shelter performance indicators being produced jointly by the United Nations Centre for Human Settlements (Habitat) and the World Bank;

(i) Bilateral and multilateral cooperation should be strengthened in order to support the implementation of the national shelter strategies of developing countries;

(j) Global progress reports covering national action and the support activities of international organisations and bilateral donors should be produced and disseminated on a biennial basis, as requested in the Global Strategy for Shelter to the Year 2000.

Means of Implementation

(A) Financing and cost evaluation

The Conference secretariat has estimated the average total annual cost (1993-2000) of implementing the activities of this programme to be about $75 billion, including about $10 billion from the international community on grant or concessional terms. These are indicative and order-of-magnitude estimates only and have not been reviewed by Governments. Actual costs and financial terms, including any that are non-concessional, will depend upon, inter alia, the specific strategies and programmes Governments decide upon for implementation.

(B) Scientific and technological means

The requirements under this heading are addressed in each of the other programme areas included in the present chapter.

(C) Human resource development and capacity-building

Developed countries and funding agencies should provide specific assistance to developing countries in adopting an enabling approach to the provision of shelter for all, including the no-income group, and covering research institutions and training activities for government officials, professionals, communities and non-governmental organisations and by strengthening local capacity for the development of appropriate technologies.

B. Improving Human Settlement Management

Basis for Action

By the turn of the century, the majority of the world's population will be living in cities. While urban settlements, particularly in the developing countries, are showing many of the symptoms of the global environment and development crisis, they nevertheless generate 60 per cent of gross national product and, if properly managed, can develop the capacity to sustain their productivity, improve the living conditions of their residents and manage natural resources in a sustainable way

Some metropolitan areas extend over the boundaries of several political and administrative entities (counties and municipalities) even though they conform to a continuous urban system In many cases this political heterogeneity hinders the implementation of comprehensive environmental management programmes.

Objective

The objective is to ensure sustainable management of all urban settlements, particularly in developing countries, in order to enhance their ability to improve the living conditions of residents, especially the marginalised and disenfranchised, thereby contributing to the achievement of national economic development goals.

Activities

(A) Improving urban management

One existing framework for strengthening management is in the United Nations Development Programme/World Bank/United Nations Centre for Human Settlements (Habitat) Urban Management Programme (UMP), a concerted global effort to assist developing countries in addressing urban management issues. Its coverage should be extended to all interested countries during the period

1993-2000. All countries should, as appropriate and in accordance with national plans, objectives and priorities and with the assistance of non-governmental organisations and representatives of local authorities, undertake the following activities at the national, state/provincial and local levels, with the assistance of relevant programmes and support agencies:

(a) Adopting and applying urban management guidelines in the areas of land management, urban environmental management, infrastructure management and municipal finance and administration;

(b) Accelerating efforts to reduce urban poverty through a number of actions, including:

(i) Generating employment for the urban poor, particularly women, through the provision, improvement and maintenance of urban infrastructure and services and the support of economic activities in the informal sector, such as repairs, recycling, services and small commerce;

ii Providing specific assistance to the poorest of the urban poor through, inter alia, the creation of social infrastructure in order to reduce hunger and homelessness, and the provision of adequate community services;

iii Encouraging the establishment of indigenous community-based organisations, private voluntary organisations and other forms of non-governmental entities that can contribute to the efforts to reduce poverty and improve the quality of life for low-income families;

(c) Adopting innovative city planning strategies to address environmental and social issues by:

(i) Reducing subsidies on, and recovering the full costs of, environmental and other services of high standard (e.g. water supply, sanitation, waste collection, roads, telecommunications) provided to higher income neighbourhoods;

(ii) improving the level of infrastructure and service provision in poorer urban areas;

(d) Developing local strategies for improving the quality of life and the environment, integrating decisions on land use and land management, investing in the public and private sectors and mobilising human and material resources, thereby promoting employment generation that is environmentally sound and protective of human health.

(B) Strengthening urban data systems

During the period 1993-2000 all countries should undertake, with the active participation of the business sector as appropriate, pilot projects in selected cities for the collection, analysis and subsequent dissemination of urban data, including environmental impact analysis, at the local statc/provincial, national and international levels and the establishment of city data management capabilities. United Nations organisations, such as Habitat, UNEP and UNDP, could provide technical advice and model data management systems.

C) Encouraging intermediate city development

In order to relieve pressure on large urban agglomerations of developing countries, policies and strategies should be implemented towards the development of intermediate cities that create employment opportunities for unemployed labour in the rural areas and support rural-based economic activities, although sound urban management is essential to ensure that urban sprawl does not expand resource degradation over an ever wider land area and increase pressures to convert open space and agri-cultural/buffer lands for development.

Therefore, all countries should, as appropriate, conduct reviews of urbanisation processes and policies in order to assess the environmental impacts of growth and apply urban planning and management approaches specifically suited to the needs, resource capabilities and characteristics of their growing intermediate-sized cities. As appropriate, they should also concentrate on activities aimed at facilitating the transition from rural to urban lifestyles and settlement patterns and at promoting the development of small-scale economic activities, particularly the production of food, to support local income generation and the production of intermediate goods and services for rural hinterlands.

All cities, particularly those characterised by severe sustainable development problems, should, in accordance with national laws, rules and regulations, develop and strengthen programmes aimed at addressing such problems and guiding their development along a sustainable path. Some international initiatives in support of such efforts, as in the Sustainable Cities Programme of Habitat and the Healthy Cities Programme of WHO, should be intensified. Additional initiatives involving the World Bank, the regional development banks and bilateral agencies, as well as other interested stakeholders, particularly international and national representatives of local authorities, should be strengthened and coordinated. Individual cities should' as appropriate:

(a) Institutionalise a participatory approach to sustainable urban development, based on a continuous dialogue between the actors involved in urban development (the public sector, private sector and communities), especially women and indigenous people;

(b) Improve the urban environment by promoting social organisation and environmental awareness through the participation of local communities in the identification of public services needs, the provision of urban infrastructure, the enhancement of public amenities and the protection and/or rehabilitation of older buildings, historic precincts and other cultural artifacts. In addition, "green works" programmes should be activated to create self-sustaining human development activities and both formal and informal employment opportunities for low-income urban residents;

(c) Strengthen the capacities of their local governing bodies to deal more effectively with the broad range of developmental and environmental challenges associated with rapid and sound urban growth through comprehensive approaches to planning that recognize the individual needs of cities and are based on ecologically sound urban design practices;

(d) Participate in international "sustainable city networks" to exchange experiences and mobilise national and international technical and financial support;

(e) Promote the formulation of environmentally sound and culturally sensitive tourism programmes as a strategy for sustainable development of urban and rural settlements and as a way of decentralising urban development and reducing discrepancies among regions;

(f) Establish mechanisms, with the assistance of relevant international agencies, to mobilise resources for local initiatives to improve environmental quality;

(g) Empower community groups, non-governmental organisations and individuals to assume the authority and responsibility for managing and enhancing their immediate environment through participatory tools, techniques and approaches embodied in the concept of environmental care.

Cities of all countries should reinforce cooperation among themselves and cities of the developed countries, under the aegis of non-governmental organisations active in this field, such as the International Union of Local Authorities (IULA), the International Council for Local Environmental Initiatives (ICLEI) and the World Federation of Twin Cities.

Means of Implementation

(A) Financing and cost evaluation

The Conference secretariat has estimated the average total annual cost (1993-2000) of implementing the activities of this programme to be about $100 billion, including about $15 billion from the international community on grant or confessional terms. These are indicative and order-of-magnitude estimates only and have not been reviewed by Governments. Actual costs and financial terms, including any that are non-concessional, will depend upon, inter alia, the specific strategies and programmes Governments decide upon for implementation.

(B) Human resource development and capacity-building

Developing countries should, with appropriate international assistance, consider focusing on training and developing a cadre of urban managers, technicians, administrators and other relevant stakeholders who can successfully manage environmentally sound urban development and growth and are equipped with the skills necessary to analyse and adapt the innovative experiences of other cities. For this purpose, the full range of training methods from formal education to the use of the mass media —should be utilised, as well as the "learning by doing" option.

Developing countries should also encourage technological training and research through joint efforts by donors, non-governmental organisations and private business in such areas as the reduction of waste, water quality, saving of energy, safe production of chemicals and less polluting transportation.

Capacity-building activities carried out by all countries, assisted as suggested above, should go beyond the training of individuals and functional groups to include institutional arrangements, administrative routines, inter-agency linkages, information flows and consultative processes.

In addition, international efforts, such as the Urban Management Programme, in cooperation with multilateral and bilateral agencies, should continue to assist the developing countries in their efforts to develop a participatory structure by mobilising the human resources of the private sector, non-governmental organisations and the poor, particularly women and the disadvantaged.

C. Promoting Sustainable Land-use Planning and Management

Basis for Action

Access to land resources is an essential component of sustainable low-impact lifestyles. Land resources are the basis for (human) living systems and provide soil, energy, water and the opportunity for all human activity. In rapidly growing urban areas, access to land is rendered increasingly difficult by the conflicting demands of industry, housing, commerce, agriculture, land tenure structures and the need for open spaces. Furthermore, the rising costs of urban land prevent the poor from gaining access to suitable land. In rural areas, unsustainable practices, such as the exploitation of marginal lands and the encroachment on forests is and ecologically fragile areas by commercial interests and landless rural populations, result in environmental degradation, as well as in diminishing returns for impoverished rural.

Objective

The objective is to provide for the land requirements of human settlement development through, environmentally sound physical planning and land use so as to ensure access to land to all households and, where appropriate, the encouragement of communally and collectively owned and managed land. Particular attention should be paid to the needs of women and indigenous people for economic and cultural reasons.

Activities

All countries should consider, as appropriate, undertaking a comprehensive national inventory of their land resources in order to establish a land information system in which land resources will be classified according to their most appropriate uses and environmentally fragile or disaster-prone areas will be identified for special protection measures.

Subsequently, all countries should consider developing national land-resource management plans to guide land-resource development and utilisation and, to that end, should:

(a) Establish, as appropriate, national legislation to guide the implementation of public policies for environmentally sound urban development, land utilisation, housing and for the improved management of urban expansion;

(b) Create, where appropriate, efficient and accessible land markets that meet community development needs by, inter alia, improving land registry systems and streamlining procedures in land transactions;

(c) Develop fiscal incentives and land-use control measures, including land-use planning solutions for a more rational and environmentally sound use of limited land resources:

(b) Encourage partnerships among the public, private and community sectors in managing land resources for human settlements development;

(e) Strengthen community-based land-resource protection practices in existing urban and rural settlements;

(f) Establish appropriate forms of land tenure that provide security of tenure for all land-users, especially indigenous people, women, local communities, the low-income urban dwellers and the rural poor;

(g) Accelerate efforts to promote access to land by the urban and rural poor, including credit schemes for the purchase of land and for building/acquiring or improving safe and healthy shelter and infrastructure services;

(h) Develop and support the implementation of improved land-management practices that deal comprehensively with potentially competing land requirements for agriculture, industry, transport, urban development, green spaces, preserves and other vital needs;

(i) Promote understanding among policy makers of the adverse consequences of unplanned settlements in environmentally vulnerable areas and of the appropriate national and local land-use and settlements policies required for this purpose.

At the international level, global coordination of land-resource management activities should be strengthened by the various bilateral and multilateral agencies and programmes, such as UNDP, FAO, the World Bank, the regional development banks, other interested organisations and the UNDP/World Bank/Habitat Urban Management Programme, and action should be taken to promote the transfer of applicable experience on sustainable land-management practices to and among developing countries.

Means of Implementation

(A) Financing and cost evaluation

The Conference secretariat has estimated the average total annual cost (1993-2000) of implementing the activities of this programme to be about $3 billion, including about $300 million from the international community on grant or concessional terms. These are indicative and order-of-magnitude estimates only and have not been reviewed by Governments. Actual costs and financial terms, including any that are non-concessional, will depend upon, inter alia, the specific strategies and programmes Governments decide upon for implementation.

(B) Scientific and technological means

All countries, particularly developing countries, alone or in regional or subregional groupings, should be given access to modern techniques of land-resource management, such as geographical information systems, satellite photography/imagery and other remote-sensing

(C) Human resource development and capacity-building

Environmentally focused training activities in sustainable land-resources planning and management should be undertaken in all countries, with developing countries being given assistance through international support and funding agencies in order to:

(a) Strengthen the capacity of national, state/provincial and local educational research and training institutions to provide formal training of land-management technicians and professionals;

(b) Facilitate the organisational review of government ministries and agencies responsible for land questions, in order to devise more efficient mechanisms of land-resource management, and carry out periodic in-service refresher courses for the managers and staff of such ministries and agencies in order to familiarize them with up-to-date land-resource-management technologies;

(c) Where appropriate, provide such agencies with modern equipment, such as computer hardware and software and survey equipment;

(d) Strengthen existing programmes and promote an international and interregional exchange of information and experience in land management through the establishment of professional associations in land-management sciences and related activities, such as workshops and seminars.

D. Promoting the Integrated Provision of Environmental Infrastructure: Water, Sanitation, Drainage and Solid-waste Management

Basic for Action

The sustainability of urban development is defined by many parameters relating to the availability of water supplies, air quality and the provision of environmental infrastructure for sanitation and waste management. As a result of the density of users, urbanisation, if properly managed, offers unique opportunities for the supply of sustainable environmental infrastructure through adequate pricing policies, educational programmes and equitable access mechanisms that are economically and environmentally sound. In most developing countries, however, the inadequacy and lack of environmental infrastructure is responsible for widespread ill-health and a large number of preventable deaths each year. In those countries conditions are set to worsen due to growing needs that exceed the capacity of Governments to respond adequately.

An integrated approach to the provision of environmentally sound infrastructure in human settlements, in particular for the urban and rural poor, is an investment in sustainable development that can improve the quality of life, increase productivity, improve health and reduce the burden of investments in curative medicine and poverty alleviation.

Most of the activities whose management would be improved by an integrated approach, are covered in Agenda 21 as follows: chapter 6 (Protecting and promoting human health conditions), chapters 9 (Protecting the atmosphere), 18 (Protecting the quality and supply of freshwater resources) and 21 (Environmentally sound management of solid wastes and sewage-related issues).

Objective

The objective is to ensure the provision of adequate environmental infrastructure facilities in all settlements by the year 2025. The achievement of this objective would require that all developing countries incorporate in their national strategies programmes to build the necessary technical, financial and human resource capacity aimed at ensuring better integration of infrastructure and environmental planning by the year 2000.

Activities

All countries should assess the environmental suitability of infrastructure in human settlements, develop national goals for sustainable management of waste, and implement environmentally sound technology to ensure that the environment, human health and quality of life are protected. Settlement infrastructure and environmental programmes designed to promote an integrated human settlements approach to the planning, development, maintenance and management of environmental infrastructure (water supply, sanitation, drainage, solid-waste management) should be strengthened with the assistance of bilateral and multilateral agencies.

Coordination among these agencies and with collaboration from international and national representatives of local authorities, the private sector and community groups should also be strengthened. The activities of all agencies engaged in providing environmental infrastructure should, where possible, reflect an ecosystem or metropolitan area approach to settlements and should include monitoring, applied research, capacity-building, transfer of appropriate technology and technical cooperation among the range of programme activities.

Developing countries should be assisted at the national and local levels in adopting an integrated approach to the provision of water supply, energy, sanitation, drainage and solid-waste management, and external funding agencies should ensure that this approach is applied in particular to environmental infrastructure improvement in informal settlements based on regulations and standards that take into account the living conditions and resources of the communities to be served.

All countries should, as appropriate, adopt the following principles for the provision of environmental infrastructure:

(a) Adopt policies that minimise if not altogether avoid environmental damage, whenever possible;

(b) Ensure that relevant decisions are preceded by environmental impact assessments and also take into account the costs of any ecological consequences;

(c) Promote development in accordance with indigenous practices and adopt technologies appropriate to local conditions;

(d) Promote policies aimed at recovering the actual cost of infrastructure services, while at the same time, recognising the need to find suitable approaches (including subsidies) to extend basic services to all households:

(e) Seek joint solutions to environmental problems that affect several localities.

The dissemination of information from the existing programmes should be facilitated and encouraged among interested countries and local institutions.

Means of implementation

(A) Financing and cost evaluation

The Conference secretariat has estimated most of the costs of implementing the activities this programme in other chapters. The secretariat estimates the average total annual cost (1993-200) of technical assistance from the international community grant or concessional terms to be about $50 million. These are indicative and order of magnitude estimates only and have not been reviewed by Governments. Actual costs and financial terms, including any that are non-concessional, will depend upon, inter alia, the specific strategies and programmes Governments decide upon for implementation.

(B) Scientific and technological means

Scientific and technological means within the existing programmes should be coordinated wherever possible and should:

(a) Accelerate research in the area of integrated policies of environmental infrastructure programmes and projects based on cost/benefit analysis and overall environmental impact;

(b) Promote methods of assessing "effective demand", utilising environment and development data as criteria for selecting technology.

(C) Human resource development and capacity-building

With the assistance and support of funding agencies, all countries should, as appropriate, undertake training and popular participation programmes aimed at:

(a) Raising awareness of the means, approaches and benefits of the provision of environmental infrastructure facilities, especially among indigenous people, women, low-income groups and the poor;

(b) Developing a cadre of professionals with adequate skills in integrated infrastructure service planning and maintenance of resource-efficient, environmentally sound and socially acceptable systems;

(c) Strengthening the institutional capacity of local authorities and administrators in the integrated provision of adequate infrastructure services in partnership with local communities and the private sector;

(d) Adopting appropriate legal and regulatory instruments, including cross-subsidy arrange-ments, to extend the benefits of adequate and affordable environmental infrastructure to unserved population groups, especially the poor.

E. Promoting Sustainable Energy and Transport Systems in Human Settlements

Basis for action

Most of the commercial and non-commercial energy produced, today, is used in and for human settlements, and a substantial percentage of it is used by the household sector. Developing countries are at present faced with the need to increase their energy production to accelerate development and raise the living standards of their populations, while at the same tune reducing energy production costs and energy-related pollution. Increasing the efficiency of energy use to reduce its polluting effects and to promote the use of renewable energies must be a priority in any action taken to protect the urban environment.

Developed countries, as the largest consumers of energy, are faced with the need for energy planning and management, promoting renewable and alternate sources of energy, and evaluating the life-cycle-costs of current systems and practices as a result of which many metropolitan areas are suffering from pervasive air quality problems related to ozone, particulate matters and carbon monoxide. The causes have much to do with technological inadequacies and with an increasing fuel consumption generated by inefficiencies, high demographic and industrial concentrations and a rapid expansion in the number of motor vehicles.

Transport accounts for about 30 per cent of commercial energy consumption and for about 60 per cent of total global consumption of liquid petroleum. In developing countries, rapid motorisation and insufficient investments in urban-transport planning, traffic management and infrastructure, are creating increasing problems in terms of accidents and injury, health, noise, congestion and loss of productivity similar to those occurring in many developed countries A; of these problems have a severe impact on urban populations, particularly the.... low-income and no-income groups

Objectives

The objectives are to extend the provision of more energy-efficient technology and alternative/renewable energy for human settlements and to reduce negative impacts of energy production and use on human health and on the environment.

Activities

The principal activities relevant to this programme area are included in chapter 9 (Protection of the atmosphere), programme area B, subprogramme 1 (Energy development, efficiency and consumption) and subprogramme 2 (Transportation).

A comprehensive approach to human settlements development should include the promotion of sustainable energy development in all countries, as follows:

(a) Developing countries, in particular, should:

i. Formulate national action programmes to promote and support reafforestation and national forest regeneration with a view to achieving sustained provision of the biomass energy needs of the low-income groups in urban areas and the rural poor, in particular women and children;

ii. Formulate national action programmes to promote integrated development of energy-saving and renewable energy technologies, particularly for the use of solar, hydro, wind and biomass sources;

iii. Promote wide dissemination and commercialisation of renewable energy technologies through suitable measures, inter alia, fiscal and technology transfer mechanisms;

iv. Carry out information and training programmes directed at manufacturers and users in order to promote energy-saving techniques and energy-efficient appliances;

(b) International organisations and bilateral donors should:

(i) Support developing countries in implementing national energy programmes in order to achieve widespread use of energy-saving and renewable energy technologies, particularly the use of solar, wind, biomass and hydro sources;

ii. Provide access to research and development results to increase energy-use efficiency levels in human settlements.

Promoting efficient and environmentally sound urban transport systems in all countries should be a comprehensive approach to urban-transport planning and management. To this end, all countries should:

(a) Integrate land-use and transportation planning to encourage development patterns reduce transport demand;

(b) Adopt urban-transport programmes favouring high-occupancy public transport in countries, as appropriate;

(c) Encourage non-motorised modes of transport by providing safe cycleways and footways in urban and suburban centres in countries, as appropriate;

(d) Devote particular attention to effective traffic management, efficient operation of public transport and maintenance of transport infrastructure;

(e) Promote the exchange of information among countries and representatives of local and metropolitan areas;

(f) Re-evaluate the present consumption and production patterns in order to reduce the use of energy and national resources.

Means of Implementation

(A) Financing and cost evaluation

The Conference secretariat has estimated the costs of implementing the activities of this programme in chapter 9 (Protection of the atmosphere).

(B) Human resource development and capacity-building

In order to enhance the skills of energy service and transport professionals and institutions, all countries should, as appropriate:

(a) Provide on-the-job and other training of government officials, planners, traffic engineers and managers involved in the energy-service and transport section;

(b) Raise public awareness of the environmental impacts of transport and travel behaviour through mass media campaigns and support for non-governmental and immunity initiatives promoting the use of non-motorised transport, shared driving and improved traffic safety measures;

(c) Strengthen regional, national, state/provincial, and private sector institutions that provide education and training on energy service and urban transport planning and management.

F. Promoting Human Settlement Planning and Management in Disaster-prone Areas

Basis for action

Natural disasters cause loss of life, disruption of economic activities and urban productivity particularly for highly susceptible low-income groups, and environmental damage, such as loss of fertile agricultural land and contamination of water resources, and can lead to major resettlement of populations. Over the past two decades, they are estimated to have caused some 3 million deaths and affected 800 million people. Global economic losses have been estimated by the Office of the United Nations Disaster Relief Coordinator to be in the range of $30-50 billion per year.

The General Assembly, in resolution 44/236, proclaimed the 1990s as the International Decade for Natural Disaster Reduction. The goals of the Decade bear relevance to the objectives of the present programme area.

In addition, there is an urgent need to address the prevention and reduction of man-made dusters and/or disasters caused by, inter alia, industries, unsafe nuclear power generation and toxic wastes.

Objective

The enable all countries, in particular those that are disaster-prone, to mitigate the of natural and man-made disasters on human settlements, national economies and the environment.

Activities

Three distinct areas of activity are foreseen under this programme area, namely, the development of a "culture of safety", pre-disaster planning and post-disaster reconstruction.

(A) Developing a culture of safety

To promote a "culture of safety" in all countries, especially those that are disaster-prone, the following activities should be carried out:

(a) Completing national and local studies on the nature and occurrence of natural disasters, their impact on people and economic activities;

(b) Implementing nationwide and local awareness campaigns through all available media, translating the above knowledge into information easily comprehensible to the general public and to the populations directly exposed to hazards;

(c) Strengthening, and/or developing global, regional, national and local early warning systems to alert populations to impending disasters;

(d) Identifying industrially based environmental disaster areas at the national and international levels and implementing strategies aimed at rehabilitation of these areas through, inter alia:

i) Restructuring of the economic activities and promoting new job opportunities in environmentally sound sectors;

ii) Promoting close collaboration between governmental and local authorities, local communities and non-governmental organisations and private business;

iii) Developing and enforcing strict environmental control standards.

(B) Developing pre-disaster planning

Pie-disaster planning should form an integral part of human settlement planning in all countries. The following should be included:

(a) Undertaking complete multi-hazard research into risk and vulnerability of human settlements and settlement infrastructure, including water and sewerage, communication and transportation networks, as one type of risk reduction may increase vulnerability to another (e.g., an earthquake-resistant house made of human ill be more vulnerable to wind storms);

(b) Developing methodologies for determining risk and vulnerability within specific human settlements and incorporating risk and vulnerability reduction into the human settlement planning and management process;

(c) Redirecting inappropriate new development and human settlements to areas not prone to hazards;

(d) Preparing guidelines on location, design and operation of potentially hazardous industries and activities;

(e) Developing tools (legal, economic etc.) to encourage disaster sensitive development, including means of ensuring that limitations on development options are not punitive to owners, or incorporate alternative means of compensation;

(f) Further developing and disseminating information on disaster resistant building materials and construction technologies for buildings and public works in general;

(g) Developing training programmes for contractors and builders on disaster-resistant construction methods. Some programmes should be directed particularly to small enterprises, which build the great majority of housing and other small buildings in the developing countries, as well as to the rural populations, which build their own houses;

(h) Developing training programmes for emergency site managers, nongovernmental organisations and community groups which cover all aspects of disaster mitigation, including urban search and rescue, emergency communications, early warning techniques, and pre-disaster planning:

(i) Developing procedures and practices to enable local communities to receive information about hazardous installations or situations in these areas, and facilitate their participation in early warning and disaster abatement and response procedures and plans;

(j) Preparing action plans for the reconstruction of settlements, especially the reconstruction of community lifelines.

(C) Initiating post-disaster reconstruction and rehabilitation planning

The international community, as a major partner in post-reconstruction and rehabilitation, should ensure that the countries involved derive the greatest benefits from the funds allocated by undertaking the following activities:

(a) Carrying out research on past experiences on the social and economic aspects of post-disaster reconstruction and adopting effective strategies and guidelines for post-disaster reconstruction, with particular focus on development-focused strategies in the allocation of scarce reconstruction resources, and on the opportunities that post-disaster reconstruction provides to introduce sustainable settlement patterns;

(b) Preparing and disseminating international guidelines for adaptation to national and local needs:

(c) Supporting efforts of national Governments to initiate contingency planning, with participation of affected communities, for post-disaster reconstruction and rehabilitation

Means of implementation

(A) Financing and cost evaluation

The Conference secretariat has estimated the average total annual cost (1993-2000) of implementing the activities of this programme to be about $50 million from the international community on grant or concessional terms. These are indicative and order of magnitude estimates only and have not been reviewed by Governments. Actual costs and financial terms, including any that are non-concessional, will depend upon, inter alia, the specific strategies and programmes Governments decide upon for implementation.

(B) Scientific and technological means

Scientists and engineers specialising in this field in both developing and developed countries should collaborate with urban and regional planners in order to provide the basic knowledge and means to mitigate losses owing to disasters as well as environmentally inappropriate development.

(C) Human resource development and capacity-building

Developing countries should conduct training programmes on disaster-resistant construction methods for contractors and builders, who build the majority of housing in the developing countries. This should focus on the small business enterprises, which build the majority of housing in the developing countries.

Training programmes should be extended to government officials and planners and community and non-governmental organisations to cover all aspects of disaster mitigation, such as early warning techniques, pre-disaster planning and construction, post-disaster construction and rehabilitation.

G. Promoting Sustainable Construction Industry Activities

Basis for Action

The activities of the construction sector are vital to the achievement of the national socio-economic development goals of providing shelter, infrastructure and employment. However, they can be a major source of environmental damage through depletion of the natural resource base, degradation of fragile eco-zones, chemical pollution and the use of building materials harmful to human health.

Objectives

The objectives are, first, to adopt policies and technologies and to exchange information on them in order to enable the construction sector to meet human settlement development goals, while avoiding harmful side-effects on human health and on the biosphere, and, second, to enhance the employment-generation capacity of the construction sector. Governments should work in close collaboration with the private sector in achieving these objectives.

Activities

All countries should, as appropriate and in accordance with national plans, objectives and priorities:

(a) Establish and strengthen indigenous building materials industry, based, as much as possible, on inputs of locally available natural resources;

(b) Formulate programmes to enhance the utilisation of local materials by the construction sector by expanding technical support and incentive schemes for increasing the capabilities and economic viability of small-scale and informal operatives which make use of these materials and traditional construction techniques:

(c) Adopt standards and other regulatory measures which promote the increased use of energy-efficient designs and technologies and sustainable utilisation of natural resources in an economically and environmentally appropriate way;

(d) Formulate appropriate land-use policies and introduce planning regulations specially aimed at the protection of eco-sensitive zones against physical disruption be construction and construction-related activities;

(e) Promote the use of labour-intensive construction and maintenance technologies which generate employment in the construction sector for the underemployed labour force found in most large cities, while at the same time, promoting the development of skills in the construction sector;

(f) Develop policies and practices to reach the informal sector and self-help housing builders by adopting measures to increase the affordability of building materials on the part of the urban and rural poor, through, inter alia, credit schemes and bulk procurement of building materials for sale to small-scale builders.

All countries should:

(a) Promote the free exchange of information on the entire range of environmental and health aspects of construction, including the development and dissemination of databases on the adverse environmental effects of building materials through the collaborative efforts of the private and public sectors;

(b) Promote the development and dissemination of databases on the adverse environmental and health effects of building materials and introduce legislation and financial incentives to promote recycling of energy-intensive materials in the construction industry and conservation of waste energy in building-materials production methods:

(c) Promote the use of economic instruments, such as product charges, to discourage the us of construction materials and products that create pollution during their life cycle;

(d) Promote information exchange and appropriate technology transfer among all countries; with particular attention to developing countries, for resource management in construction, particularly for non-renewable resources;

(e) Promote research in construction industries and related activities, and establish and strengthen institutions in this sector.

Means of Implementation

(A) Financing and cost evaluation

The Conference secretariat has estimated the average total annual cost (1993-2000) of implementing the activities of this programme to be about $40 billion, including about $4 billion from the international community on grant or concessional terms. These are indicative and order of magnitude estimates only and have not been reviewed by Governments. Actual costs and financial terms, including any that are non-concessional, will depend upon, inter alia, the specific strategies and programmes Governments decide upon for implementation.

(B) Human resource development and capacity-building

Developing countries should be assisted by international support and funding agencies in upgrading the technical and managerial capacities of the small entrepreneur and the vocational skills of operatives and supervisors in the building materials industry, using a variety of training methods. These countries should also be assisted in developing programmes to the use of non-waste and clean technologies through appropriate transfer of technology.

General education programmes should be developed in all countries, as appropriate, to increase builder awareness of available sustainable technologies.

Local authorities are called upon to play a pioneering role in promoting the increased use of environmentally sound building materials and construction technologies, e.g., by pursuing an innovative procurement policy.

H. Promoting Human Resource Development and Capacity-building for Human Settlements development

Basis for Action

Most countries, in addition to shortcomings in the availability of specialised expertise in the areas of housing, settlement management, land management, infrastructure, construction, energy transport, pre-disaster planning and reconstruction, face three cross-sectoral human resource development and capacity-building shortfalls. First is the absence of an enabiling policy environment capable of integrating the resources and activities of the public sector, the private sector and the community, or social sector; second is the weakness of specialised training and research institutions; and third is the insufficient capacity for technical training and assistance for low-income communities, both urban and rural.

Objective

The objective is to improve human resource development and capacity-building in all countries by enhancing the personal and institutional capacity of all actors, particularly indigenous people and women, involved in human settlement development. In this regard, proper consideration should be taken of traditional cultural practices of indigenous people and their relationship to the environment.

Activities

Specific human resource development and capacity-building activities have been built into each of the programme areas of this chapter. More importantly, however, additional steps should be taken to reinforce those activities. In order to do so, all countries, as appropriate, should take the following action:

(a) Strengthening the development of human resources and of capacities of public sector institutions through technical assistance and international cooperation so as to achieve by the year 2000 substantial improvement in the efficiency of governmental activities;

(b) Creating an enabling policy environment supportive of the partnership between the public, private and community sectors;

(c) Providing enhanced training and technical assistance to institutions providing training for technicians, professionals and administrators, and appointed, elected and professional members of local governments and strengthening their capacity to address priority training needs, particularly in regard to social, economic and environmental aspects of human settlements development;

(d) Providing direct assistance for human settlement development at the community level, inter alia, by:

i) Strengthening and promoting programmes for social mobilisation and raising awareness of the potential of women and youth in human settlements activities;

ii) Facilitating coordination of the activities of women, youth, community groups and non-governmental organisations in human settlements development;

iii) Promoting research on women's programmes and other groups, and evaluating progress made with a view to identifying bottlenecks and needed assistance;

(e) Promoting the inclusion of integrated environmental management into general local government activities.

Both international organisations and non-governmental organisations should support the above activities by, inter alia, strengthening subregional training institutions, providing updated training materials and disseminating the results of successful human resource and capacity-building activities, programmes and projects.

Means of implementation

(A) Financing and cost evaluation

The Conference secretariat has estimated the average total annual cost (1993-2000) of implementing the activities of this programme to be about $65 million from the international community on grant or concessional terms. These are indicative and order of magnitude estimates only and have not been reviewed by Governments. Actual costs and financial terms, including any that are non-concessional, will depend upon, inter alia, the specific strategies and programmes Governments decide upon for implementation.

(B) Scientific and technological means

Both formal training and non-formal types of human resource development and capacity-building programmes should be combined, and use should be made of user-oriented training methods, up-to-date training materials and modern audio-visual communication systems.

REFERENCES

1. No aggregate figures are available on internal expenditure or official development assistance on human settlements. However, data available in the World Development Report, 1991, for 16 low-income developing countries show that the percentage of central government expenditure on housing, amenities and social security and welfare for 1989 averaged 5.6 per cent, with a high of 15.1 per cent in the case of Sri Lanka, which has embarked on a vigorous housing programme. In OECD industrialised countries, during the same year, the percentage of central government expenditure on housing, amenities and social security and welfare ranged from a minimum of 29.3 per cent to a maximum of 49.4 per cent, with an average of 39 pre cent World Bank. World Development Report, 1991, World Development Indicators (Washington, D.C., 1991)).
2. The report of the Director-General for Development and International Economic Cooperation containing preliminary statistical data on operational activities of the United Nations system for 1988 (A/44/324-E/1989/106/Add.4, annex).
3. World Bank, Annual Report, 1991 (Washington, D.C., 1991).
4. UNDP "Reported investment commitments related to UNDP-assisted projects, 1988", table 1, 'Sectoral distribution of investment commitment in 1988-1989".
5. A pilot programme of this type, the City Data Programme (CDP), is already in operation in the United Nations Centre on Human Settlements (Habitat) aimed at the production and dissemination to participating cities of microcomputer application software designed to store, process and retrieve city data for local, national and international exchange and dissemination.
6. This calls for integrated land-resource management policies, which are also addressed in chapter 10 of Agenda 21 (Integrated approach to planning and management of land resources).

7. The goals of the International Decade for Natural Disaster Reduction, set out in the annex to General Assembly resolution 44/236, are as follows:
   (a) To improve the capacity of each country to mitigate the effects of natural disasters expeditiously and effectively, paying special attention to assisting developing countries in the assessment of disaster damage potential and in the establishment of early warning systems and disaster-resistant structures when and where needed;
   (b) To devise appropriate guidelines and strategies for applying existing scientific technical knowledge, taking into account the cultural and economic diversity among nations:
   (c) To foster scientific and engineering endeavours aimed at closing critical gaps in knowledge in order to reduce loss of life and property;
   (d) To disseminate existing and new technical information related to measures for the assessment, prediction and mitigation of natural disasters;
   (e) To develop measures for the assessment, prediction, prevention and mitigation of natural disasters through programmes of technical assistance and technology transfer, demonstration projects, and education and training, tailored to specific disasters and locutions and to evaluate the effectiveness of those programmes.

APPENDICES

APPENDIX - I

Administrative Reforms Commission's (ARC) Approach to Improve Governance in India

In the words of Kofi Annan: "Good governance is perhaps the single most important factor in eradicating poverty and promoting development".

Governance is the exercise of economic, political and administrative authority to manage a country's affairs at all levels. It consists of the mechanisms, processes and institutions through which citizens and groups articulate their interests, exercise their legal rights, meet their obligations and resolve their differences. Without good governance, no amount of developmental schemes can bring in improvements in the quality of life of the citizens. On the contrary, if the power of the state is abused, or exercised in weak or improper ways, those with the least power in the society – the poor- are most likely to suffer. In that sense, poor governance generates and reinforces poverty and subverts efforts to reduce it. Strengthening governance is an essential precondition to improving the lives of the poor.

The Tenth Plan document identified good governance as the single most important factor in ensuring that the Plan objectives are achieved. Among other things, decentralisation of power and citizens' empowerment, effective people's participation through state and non-state mechanisms, greater synergy and consolidation among various agencies and programmes of government, civil service reforms, transparency, rationalisation of government schemes and mode of financial assistance to states, improved access to formal justice system to enforce rights, reforms and strengthening of land administration and harnessing the power of technology for governance have been identified as the key priorities.

Over the past three years, several significant initiatives have been launched to improve the quality of governance. A series of political reforms have been enacted by Parliament by unanimous consent. These include the electoral funding reforms promoting transparency and fairness and creating tax incentives to donors, disclosure of antecedents of candidates contesting for public office, and the 97th Constitutional Amendment limiting the size of the Council of Ministers to 15 per cent of the strength of the Lower House and considerably strengthening anti-defection provisions.

A new value added tax (VAT) regime has been introduced recently, which is seen as the most ambitious tax reform after Independence. The path-breaking Right to Information Act has come into effect recently. This new law applies to union and state agencies, local governments and even societies and trusts which receive public funds. This far-reaching law also provides for independent information commissioners, proactive disclosures and reporting mechanisms and has the potential to impact our governance process in a profound and positive way by empowering citizens.

These welcome initiatives indicate that our political system is willing to respond to the growing challenges of governance. The reasonably swift and efficient response of our administration to a series of major natural calamities –

the Tsunami of December 2004, the Mumbai floods of July, 2005, and the recent earthquake in Jammu & Kashmir - demonstrates that in times of crisis we are able to marshal our resources effectively. All these and competent election management show that we have an impressive administrative infrastructure and it responds well when objectives are clearly defined, resources are made available and accountability is surely enforced.

However, a lot more remains to be done. There is increasing lawlessness in several pockets of the country, and armed groups are resorting to violence with impunity for sectarian or ideological reasons. The state apparatus is generally perceived to be largely inefficient, with most functionaries serving no useful purpose. The bureaucracy is generally seen to be tardy, inefficient, and unresponsive. Corruption is all pervasive, eating into the vitals of our system, undermining economic growth, distorting competition, and disproportionately hurting the poor and marginalised citizens. Criminalisation of politics continues unchecked, with money and muscle power playing a large role in elections. In general, there is high degree of volatility in society on account of unfulfilled expectations and poor delivery.

Abuse of authority at all levels in all organs of state has become the bane of our democracy. The perception that every political party and politician is corrupt needs to be seriously addressed, and restructuring the systems in all sectors–political, bureaucratic and judicial–is of paramount importance. There is a need to restructure our political and governance institutions and rejuvenate our Republic. Otherwise, the growing cynicism and despair among large sections may shatter public confidence in democratic institutions.

Globalisation in an interconnected world is inevitable, but it should not be at the cost of the people. The institutions of state–legislative, executive, and judicial–will have to be strengthened to meet the challenges of globalisation. The aspirations of the younger generations, uninhibited by past baggage, and emerging from institutions of higher learning and frontier technologies, will have to be fulfilled as they become the torchbearers of the new century.

In general, the positive power to promote public good seems to be severely restricted, making it difficult for even the most conscientious and competent functionaries to deliver optimal results. The systemic rigidities, needless complexity and over centralisation have made most elected politicians and appointed public servants ineffective and helpless. But, the negative power of abuse of authority in pursuit of pelf, privilege and patronage, or harassment of public through flagrant violation of law, petty tyranny and nuisance value is virtually unchecked.

This imbalance in the exercise of power is at the heart of the crisis of governance. As a result, most agencies of government are functioning sub-optimally, and government programmes have not yielded the desired results. At most levels authority is divorced from accountability, leading to a system of realistic and plausible alibis for non-performance. Most functionaries are, thus, caught in a vicious cycle.

This situation is further aggravated by the phenomenal asymmetry of power in our society. Only about 8 per cent of our work force is employed in the organised sector with a secure monthly wage and attendant privileges, and over 70 per cent of these workers are employed in government at various levels and public sector undertakings. Such a privileged position gives even the lowliest of public servants enormous power over most of the citizens, given the abject poverty, illiteracy, excessive centralisation of power, a culture of exaggerated deference to authority, hierarchical tradition in society, and the legacy of colonial traditions and practices. Any serious effort to make our governance apparatus an instrument of service to the people and a powerful tool to achieve national objectives needs to take into account these two cardinal factors plaguing our polity – the imbalance in the exercise of power, and asymmetry in the wielding of power.

There are two fundamental, interrelated objectives, which need to be achieved in the coming decades. The first is the fulfillment of human potential, prevention of avoidable suffering and ensuring human dignity, access to justice and opportunity to all Indians so that every citizen is a fulfilled and productive human being. The second is the rapid economic growth realizing the nation's potential and allowing India to play her rightful role in the global arena in order to protect the vital interests of present and future generations, and become an important actor in promoting global peace, stability and prosperity. We need to sharply focus the state's role and fashion instruments of governance as effective tools in our quest for these national goals.

The economic reform process initiated in 1991 has posed fresh challenges of governance. In the light of the changing domestic and global situation, the role of the Indian state in the coming decade has to be clearly defined. The assumption that market is the answer to all our challenges is a dangerous and irrational one. The state needs to focus on the irreducible role of government that is required to fulfill human potential and promote rapid economic growth. Abdication of the state or its inefficiency in these critical sectors will spell disaster to our future.

The non-negotiable role of the state in four broad areas needs to be clearly recognized and reemphasized. The first is in the area of public order, justice and rule of law. Deficiencies on this front have led to decline in trust in the state's capacity to protect life and liberty and enforce rights.

This in turn has aggravated the tendency to resort to violence and crime to obtain rough and ready justice, promote sectarian interests, or achieve ideological goals. Ensuring access to speedy and efficient justice, protecting rights of citizens, enforcing rule of law, and maintaining public order are all inseparable and they form the bedrock of a civilized society and sound liberal democracy. The deficiencies in this vital area need to be plugged through judicial and police reforms, better citizen participation in governance, transparency and more effective and integrated approach to public order maintenance.

The alacrity with which we constitute various committees and commissions of enquiry is matched only by the inaction on the voluminous reports laboriously produced. Public trust and confidence is shaken by such ritualism and tokenism. We need to institutionalize mechanisms for independent enquiry and mandatory implementation so that public confidence and social cohesion are strengthened. Governance at all levels must ensure orderly justice and peaceful resolution of conflicts in a complex and dynamic society.

The second area is human development through access to good quality education and healthcare to make every citizen productive and fulfilled. Despite our long-standing commitment to these goals, the results are uneven and far from satisfactory. Allocation of resources is undoubtedly inadequate leading to huge unmet demand. Even what is spent not very productive in outcomes. Yet, even private sector is not delivering effectively because of systemic inadequacies. We need to reorient public finances in order to direct resources to human development. But, even more vitally, we need to redesign our delivery mechanisms in an innovative manner based on past experience and best practices and deploy the nation's finest talent in these sectors. Most of the nation's gene pool is wasted because of inadequate and poor quality of school education.

Higher education too is not very successful in promoting excellence of producing service providers, leaders, managers and wealth creators, for the future. There are other clear danger signals, which need to be acknowledged and addressed immediately. For instance as public health system has been unsatisfactory and inadequate, private health expenditure, which already accounts for about 80% of total expenditure, is growing (14% per annum) much faster than GDP. The resultant high cost and poor access would seriously undermine our human development and perpetuate misery and poverty. The governance system should be geared to address these fundamental challenges through sensible and innovative policy, effective and competent delivery, and meaningful incentives and accountability mechanisms.

The third broad area is infrastructure and sustainable natural resource development. While the economic aspects of these are well-recognised, the governance challenges are not adequately addressed. For instance, effective land administration is crucial to capital formation in agriculture and soil conservation. Energy plantation and biofuel production would require great administrative innovation and grassroots coordination. Urban management involves much more than resource allocation for infrastructure and poses formidable challenges of governance. Power distribution management through local people's involvement and ownership in a consumer-friendly way is more a governance issue than an economic or tariff problem. We need to create innovative modes of governance in dealing with many such growing challenges.

Social security is a relatively new and growing area of state activity to which the administrative system must respond with alacrity, sensitivity and efficacy. The recent enactment of the employment guarantee law, the efforts in the pipeline to provide a measure of social security to the unorganized sector workers, and many healthcare risk-pooling mechanisms contemplated require effective delivery system, which can address the special challenges posed in this emerging sector of state activity.

All these and other governance and administrative challenges have to be addressed in the context of serious resource constraints. The Fiscal Responsibility and Budget Maintenance Act (FRBMA) enacted in 2001 is a useful measure, but has obviously not fulfilled the expectations. Laws alone cannot address fundamental fiscal problems. We need to raise resources, reduce unproductive subsidies, and get better outcomes for every rupee utilised. Past experience shows that revenue cannot be increased by enhancing tax rates in a centralized administration.

There has to be an increasingly transparent link between taxes and services rendered, and better tax administration to ensure greater compliance. Subsidy reduction is politically painful, and the people have to see an alternative and better application of the resources saved in order to accept de-subsidisation. And the administration must become far more accountable and effective in delivering results with the same expenditure. In order to accomplish these goals, there should be conscious efforts to establish the links between the citizen's vote and public good, and taxes and services, and fuse authority with accountability at every level. Therefore, effective empowerment of local governments and stakeholders, and reform to ensure effective and sufficient delegation with accountability at every level to deliver should be the cornerstone of governance reform.

One emerging area which needs special attention is the changing nature of federalism. The last decade has witnessed significant maturing of our federalism. The states are increasingly empowered to determine their own policies and programmes, and the union is evermore sensitive to local needs. However, the role of the Union is expanding in a substantial measure in recent years in new ways. Education, healthcare, rural and urban development and social security are either state subjects, or largely under state jurisdiction. And yet, the services are increasingly driven by union policies and funds. Paucity of resources at state level, need for standardisation of services, compulsions of reducing regional disparities, and the imperatives of meeting the challenges of a growing economy in the modern world have necessarily enlarged the Union's role in these sectors.

Such a shift in the Union's role in a federal democracy is quite in keeping with the evolution of other large federal states like the US. But, large Union funding with state control could easily erode accountability. We need to carefully design mechanisms to monitor these programmes and enforce accountability, even as the desired outcomes are achieved, and the constitutional scheme of division of powers is fully respected. Poor implementation will only lead to waste, corruption, lack of accountability, and growing regional disparities. At the same time, if non-performing states are punished by withdrawal of the programmes, the poor and disadvantaged, who need preferential support, suffer even more, and regional inequalities are further accentuated. Therefore, innovative, viable and effective mechanisms need to be put in place to protect public money, guarantee intended outcomes, and enforce accountability.

In any system, the quality of public servants is critical in determining outcomes. We have well-established procedures for initial recruitment of civil servants in India. However, there is growing concern that our civil services and administration in general have become wooden, inflexible, self-perpetuating, and inward-looking. While the bureaucracy responds to crisis situations with efficacy, colossal tardiness and failure to deal with 'normal' situations is evident in most cases. Effective horizontal delegation and a clear system of accountability at every level should be at the heart of our administrative reform. At the same time, we also need to recognize the complex challenges of modern administration in critical sectors like policing, justice delivery, education, healthcare, transportation, land management, infrastructure, skill promotion, employment generation, and urban management. All these are intricate issues, which need domain expertise, long experience in the sector, and deep insights.

Processes of civil service recruitment, periodic training, promotion and posting strategies and career management have to be reformed urgently. We need to foster excellence in the public system, and attract continuously the best talent and expertise. The barrier between government and the rest of the economy and society must be lowered, allowing free movement based on competence and leadership qualities.

Propensity to centralise has been the dominant feature of our administration. We need to truly redesign government on the basis of the principle of subsidiary. A task which can be performed by a small unit should never be entrusted to a large unit. Only when economies of scale and technical complexity demand entrustment to the larger tier should it be done so. All the financial devolution and personnel transfer should match functional domain determined on this basis. Only then will the citizen see the link between his vote and public good, and monies can be traced to services delivered.

The structure of local governments envisaged in the 73rd and 74th Constitutional amendments is now in place, but the soul of self-governance and empowerment is largely missing. As a result of the economic reform process, the states have come into their own, and yet the Union has in recent years discovered a more meaningful and strategic role for itself. Similarly, local government empowerment need not mean weakening of states. States must be enabled to discover their vital role in providing strategic inputs and leadership even as local governments deliver most of the basic services. Wherever a community of stakeholders can be clearly identified, responsibility for services must be transferred to them, so that the stakeholders wield authority and are directly in control of their lives.

The Tenth Plan document emphasised the role of civil society in improving delivery. Conscious efforts have since been made to make citizens partners in policy-making and implementation of various programmes. However, despite long debate, two serious lacunae remain. First, cooperatives, which are citizens' enterprises for collective benefit, are still largely state-controlled, despite the constitutional freedoms guaranteed in Article 19. A clear and unambiguous inclusion of the right to form and run cooperatives in the Fundamental Rights chapter of our Constitution would liberate them from state fetters, and release the energies and enterprise of millions of ordinary citizens. Societies are largely free, thanks to the protection afforded under Article 19 (1) (c).

But, most voluntary organisations are excessively dependant on state funding or foreign donor organisations. A culture of self-reliance needs to be fostered among the vibrant civil society and community-based organisations. For this, private, indigenous charities need to be encouraged and incentivised. The current law allows tax exemption to a tune of 50% to most contributions to charitable activities. A full tax exemption on such contributions will promote self-help and reduce over dependence on state or foreign donors.

Pervasive corruption is the most disturbing element of our governance. Happily, recent years witnessed encouraging trends in certain sectors. Wherever competition, choice, transparency and technology have been introduced, corruption has dramatically declined. However, in other core sectors where the state's role is critical, corruption continues unchecked. There are signs of growing corruption in some of these state-controlled sectors, indicating a shift from the traditional forms of corruption. Police, criminal justice system, healthcare delivery, public procurement and contracting, transfers and postings of officials, tax collection and land administration are areas, which are by nature fully or substantially state-controlled. Corruption is either continuing or growing in these sectors, as the inexhaustible demand for illegitimate funds in our governance system continues unabated. Clearly far-reaching political and electoral reforms to transform our political culture and alter the nature of incentives in public life are the need of the hour.

In addition, real decentralisation of power with effective institutional checks will give citizens greater control and curb the rapacity of state functionaries. Judicial and police reforms ensuring speedy, efficient and accessible justice and swift, sure and severe punishment for abuse of office will increase risks of unacceptable behaviour. Self-regulatory mechanisms to uphold standards in professional groups are another area that requires urgent attention in the changing context. Finally, measures of accountability including the recently enacted Right to Information, well-designed citizen's charters with penalties for non-performance, independent, empowered and effective anti corruption agencies, innovative tools to involve citizens in the fight against graft and leakages will surely expose corruption much more easily, minimize wrong incentives, and enforce compliance with acceptable norms of public conduct.

A comprehensive approach involving political, electoral, judicial, and police reforms coupled with decentralisation and accountability must be the essence of an all out assault on corruption. *In the wake of economic liberalisation, changing forms of corruption, and technological sophistication in economic offences, there is a need for pan-Indian institutional framework for effective enforcement of criminal justice with focus on speed and dexterity.*

One weakness in our governance is the incapacity to institutionalise the best practices from our own country and elsewhere. A conscious effort not only to identify and document best practices but also build policy and create new structures and institutions to allow mass replication needs to be made. The communications revolution sweeping across India offers us a great opportunity to innovate and replicate. Many models of improved use of technology for better governance are now available to us. But again convergence of many services at the citizen's doorstep, with greater citizen power and local control are critical for the future. The impressive postal network with its high efficiency and citizen-friendly approach, and the railways with their vast reach and proven track record offer us great opportunities for convergence of a variety of services in the next decade. Our scientists and technologists have the proven ability to meet the challenges of a modern economy. We need to harness their skills to make real improvements in governance possible in real time.

Governance is admittedly a weak link in our quest for prosperity and equity. We have an impressive governance infrastructure and significant successes to our credit. But, we need to refashion the instruments to suit the emerging challenges. *Unemployment and discrimination are two malignant factors afflicting our society, and militating against the principles of equality of opportunity enshrined in our Constitution. Our governance process must be redesigned to combat these two scourges, so that the productive potential of our people is liberated.* The political system has the resilience and capacity to mobilize public opinion and transform our governance. What we need is the will and painstaking effort and energy to innovate, design and reform.

APPENDIX - II

United Nations Economic Commission for Africa's (UNECA) Strategy for Promoting Good Governance

During the past two decades, governance has become a key concept in the international development debate and policy discourse. In Africa, where there has been a historical record of bad governance, improving the governance environment has been given a central place in the New Partnership for Africa's Development (NEPAD), an initiative that represents the latest attempt by African leaders to place the African continent on a path of sustainable development encompassing good governance and prosperity with a consolidation of peace, security, and stability. The NEPAD lists a number of prerequisites for African countries to move forward in their quest for sustainable development. Key among these is the proper adherence to good political, economic, and corporate governance.

Governance and Development in Africa

Governance has to do with the manner in which responsibility is discharged. Such a responsibility may by acquired through election; appointment or delegation in the public domain or in the area of commerce—corporate governance. Therefore, good governance is taken here to mean a condition whereby such responsibility is discharged in an effective, transparent, and accountable manner while bad governance is associated with maladministration in the discharge of responsibility.

Good governance entails the existence of efficient and accountable institutions-political, judicial, administrative, economic, corporate and entrenched rules that promote development, protects human rights, respects the rule of law, and ensures that people are free to participate in, and be heard on, decisions that affect their lives.

It can be noted that good governance, in all its facets, has been demonstrated to be positively correlated with the achievement of better growth rates, and particularly through the building of institutions in support of markets. Recent empirical analysis suggests a positive correlation between democratic governance and the levels of income, investment, human capital, economic liberalisation, and distributive income growth in society. Indeed, some analysts, have successfully argued that good governance, and particularly its aspects of democratic consolidation, is a *sine qua non* for development. Consequently, the new maxim for Africa in the twenty-first century should be "no democracy, no development".

Similarly, former UN Secretary-General Kofi Anan has said that "good governance is perhaps the single most important factor in eradicating poverty and promoting development". And a former Kenyan Vice-President has also noted that "good political and economic governance underpins sustainable development".

Through the NEPAD framework document, African leaders have recognized the salient importance of good governance for achieving sustainable development in Africa and they have set out principles pertaining to the strengthening of democracy and political governance as well as economic and corporate governance. On democracy and political governance, the NEPAD states that development is impossible in the absence of democracy, respect for human rights, peace, and good governance. The purpose of the principles here is to contribute to the strengthening of the political and administrative framework of African countries, in line with the principles of democracy, transparency, accountability, integrity, respect for human rights, and promotion of the rule of law.

The necessity for institutional reform has been recognised to drive the process forward, given the capacity limitations across African countries. As identified in the NEPAD framework document, the institutional reforms to strengthen political governance in Africa will need to focus on:

(1) the administrative and civil services;

(2) the strengthening of parliamentary oversight;

(3) the promotion of participatory decision-making;

(4) the adoption of effective measures to combat corruption and embezzlement; and

(5) the undertaking judicial reforms.

These five areas of focus have been exhaustively discussed elsewhere. Suffice to say here that for the first time in post-independence Africa, African leaders themselves are pointing to the shortcomings of the institutional structure over which they preside directly and/or have much say.

Institutions, and public institutions in particular, have been a failure in Africa. Many of these institutions have been captured by the elite to serve narrow personal interests. The resultant effect has been the lack of the ability of the state to provide the requisite institutional framework to support good governance. In too many African countries, both the public and private sectors do not operate according to widely accepted rules that are transparent and enforced by accountable institutions. Consequently, the challenge for African policy-makers, under the NEPAD, is to shape policies and institutional development in ways that enhance good governance and sustainable development.

With respect to economic and corporate governance, the NEPAD framework document states that the objective here is to promote a set of concrete and time-bound programmes aimed at enhancing the quality of economic and public financial management, as well as good corporate governance. Good economic and corporate governance is urgently needed for Africa. Countries attract more investment and achieve higher rates of per capita growth, where the state improves certain basic aspects of its performance. A state that applies rules and policies predictably and fairly, ensures order and the rule of law, and protects property rights will generate confidence and attract more domestic and foreign investment. That, in turn, generates trade and faster economic growth as well as provides the where withal for sustainable development.

Here again, the role of institutions looms large. The existence of weak institutions of economic and corporate governance, as a constraint on sustainable development in Africa, is clear and convincing. This has, accordingly, limited the public sector in the fulfillment of its economic functions. Those economic functions can be broadly classified into three distinct categories:

(1) Making and implementing economic policy
(2) Delivering services; and
(3) Ensuring accountability for the use of public resources and public regulatory power.

Institutions are needed to maintain fiscal and monetary discipline, mobilise resources; and set priorities among the competing demands for those resources as integral aspects of the making and implementation of good economic policy. Similarly, institutional arrangements are required for the efficient delivery of public services that are also pro-poor. In addition, there must be institutional mechanisms that ensure accountability through the capacity to monitor and enforce rules and to regulate economic activities in the public interest. However, regulatory frameworks should be minimal, simple and easy to implement.

Good governance is worth pursuing in its own right in Africa. Much has been observed and volumes have been written about the deleterious effects of bad governance in Africa. Through the NEPAD, a new generation of enlightened leaders is aiming to reverse that trend. Respect for human rights and democratic principles, honest and good quality administration, and protecting the rights and freedoms under the rule of law are concerned with values that apply equally to every state and citizen. Democracy, for example, is a universally recognised ideal, based on values common to people everywhere regardless of cultural, social, or economic differences. These transcend the functional importance of aspects of good governance, such as for sustainable development.

President Mbeki of South Africa has argued quite convincingly, for example, that Africa wishes to realise the goal of good governance, in all its elements, "not because we seek to improve our relations with the rest of the world as a first objective, critically important as this is, but to end political and economic mismanagement on our continent, and the consequential violent conflicts, instability, denial of democracy and human rights, deepening poverty and global marginalisation". Nonetheless, as noted above, the various components of good governance are also necessary and functional for sustainable development processes.

Quite clearly, growth and development cannot be achieved in the absence of good governance. Among other things, good governance ensures the most efficient utilisation of already scarce resources in the promotion of development; enhances participation, responsibility, and accountability; and has the potential to emancipate people from poverty as state legitimacy is recognised and entrenched. As a matter of fact, any effort to reduce poverty and sustain development must start with and build upon good governance. Good governance can, therefore, be also regarded as governance on behalf of development-oriented policy.

According to the 2002 Human Development Report of UNDP, good governance advances sustainable development for three reasons. First, enjoying political freedom and participating in the decisions that shape one's life are fundamental human rights. In those African countries, where leaders are not elected or selected by election (Libya, for example), or where elections are flawed (Zimbabwe, for example), choices are severely restricted. The denial of these rights is a denial of human development. Second, good governance helps to protect people from economic and political catastrophes such as famines and other crises. There is a direct correlation between bad governance and famines, for example, in Africa. In other words, those countries frequently suffering from famines in Africa tend not to have good governance. Third, good governance can promote sustainable development by empowering citizens to influence policies that promote growth and prosperity and which reflect their priorities.

Monitoring and Measuring Progress Towards Good Governance in Africa: The UNECA Project

From the forgoing, it should be quite clear that achieving good governance is one of Africa's greatest challenges. In recent years, good governance has gained much currency in Africa and the need for democratic consolidation is now well understood by the majority of the continent's leaders. This has taken imperative expression in the NEPAD. However, there exists a gap between the desire to improve governance and the capacity to measure and monitor progress towards that improvement. The UNECA project makes a contribution in the latter direction.

Project Objective

The overall objective of the project is to monitor the progress of African states towards good governance. To accomplish that, we first defined good governance in a comprehensive manner, so as to include both state and non-state actors within the political and economic spaces; we conceptualised indicators to measure good governance; and we devised a research methodology and instruments to provide us with the data for the various indicators that will serve as the mechanism for the analysis on what, if any, progress is being achieved over time with respect to good governance. The results from the project will also be used as inputs into a number of other governance-related outcomes as discussed later in the paper.

Essential Components of Good Governance: Underlying Assumptions

The project posits that achieving good governance encompasses a range of actions aimed at creating more open, participatory societies, and promoting greater accountability and transparency in public affairs. Among the primary factors that, are taken to improve governance are:

- A political system which provides opportunities for all its citizens, including the poor and disadvantaged by creating the conditions that encourage broad input in governance and development decision-making from all elements of civil society.
- A political system that provides for effective transfer of power and periodic renewal of the leadership through representative and competitive multi-party and multi-candidate elections; impartial and credible electoral administration; effective oversight of the electoral process; and an informed and active citizenry.
- Strengthened public sector legislative and administrative institutions, including efficient parliamentary oversight, judicial independence, and adequacy of the audit machinery-providing and verifying that government decisions are in line with its legal commitments.

- Greater transparency, predictability, and accountability in political, oversight, and regulatory decisions by government and public bodies. Reliable, relevant, and timely information about the activities of government being available to the public. And, systems being in place that are facilitated by public institutions to hold public officials to account for their behaviour, actions, and decisions.
- Effective public sector management with stable macroeconomic policy, effective resource mobilisation and efficient use of public resources; increased government responsiveness to citizens at the local level including a pro-poor orientation as well as create conditions for economic prosperity.
- Adherence to the rule of law in a manner that protects personal and civil liberties and gender equity and ensures public safety and security with equal access to justice for all; and provides effective and fair institutions in the legal arena.

Methodology

Three survey instruments were designed to obtain data and pertinent information with respect to governance in a sample of approximately 28 countries covering the five sub-regions of Africa-North, South, East, West, and Central (see Annex I).

The first instrument, seeks the opinion from an expert panel. It is opinion-based and is used to collect responses from an appropriately represented segment of experts on issues pertaining to governance in their country. The expert panel is comprised of at least 100 people. They include academics; researchers, in constitutional, social, or economic areas; lawyers; professionals working with independent civil society organisations; educated and experienced business leaders; retired professionals; and religious leaders active in community affairs.

The second instrument seeks the perception of the general adult population. In all cases, the ultimate sampling unit is the household-the respondent being the head of the household or the next senior member. The sample population was suitably stratified using administrative regions and levels of urbanisation, in most cases.

The final instrument seeks factual information and hard data through investigations or desk research on the prevailing political, social, and economic life of the country. It is used to reinforce the perceptions delivered in the other two instruments. The outcomes of this instrument tend to parallel those obtained in the expert panel survey.

The contents of the three instruments provide us with 83 indicators covering three categories:

(1) Political Representation—includes the political system and distribution of power, the electoral process, and the competitive environment for political parties;

(2) Institutional Effectiveness and Accountability—includes the independence and effectiveness of the legislative, executive, and judicial branches of government, as well as civil society organisations; and

(3) Economic Management and Corporate Governance—includes public financial management and accountability, the integrity of the monetary and financial systems, the efficiency of the tax system and domestic resource mobilisation, budget transparency, central bank independence, accounting and auditing standards, private sector development, and corporate governance issues such as shareholders' rights and board oversight.

(4) The 83 indicators have been further disaggregated and grouped into five clusters as follows:

- Political Representation 15
- Institutional Checks and Balances 16
- Effectiveness and Accountability of the Executive 18
- Human Rights, Law Enforcement and Rule of Law 19
- Economic Management and Corporate Governance 15

To assist in the undertaking of the project, we have engaged a number of local institutions with the requisite capacity and track record of research and consultancy engagements. For each country, a local institution conducts the work required for the three instruments and prepares a country report.

Project Outputs

The outputs from the project will be the following:

- Country Reports
- Sub-Regional Reports
- Africa Governance Report
- Research Papers

The country reports will be prepared by the local institutions tasked to do so based on the three instruments we have provided them as previously discussed. The country reports will then feed into the preparation of sub-regional reports. Both the country reports and sub-regional reports will be used to inform the preparation of the Africa Governance Report. A number of research papers are also expected to be produced based on the data collected.

The Africa Governance Report (AGR) will be produced annually covering specific themes. This year's report—which will be the first—will be all encompassing taking a much more macro approach and based on all of the indicators we would have compiled within the three categories and five clusters. The focus of the report will be on "Measuring and Monitoring Progress Towards Good Governance in Africa".

This year's AGR will also be the primary input to the Fourth African Development Forum (ADF IV) to be held at our conference Center in Addis Ababa in December of this year. The theme of ADF IV is "Towards Good Governance in Africa".

In addition, the various country reports and the AGR will be used as critical inputs to the African Peer Review Mechanism (APRM). The APRM was originally developed by the UNECA in response to a request by the Heads of State and Government Implementation Committee of the New Partnership for Africa's Development (NEPAD). The mandate of the APRM is to ensure that the policies and practices of participating states conform to the political, economic, and corporate governance codes and standards that they have agreed to.

The primary purpose of the APRM is to assess and monitor the progress of African countries in meeting the goals of achieving good governance and sustainable development based on a number of relevant indicators pertaining to political governance, economic governance and management, corporate governance, and socio-development as contained in that ARM.

Conclusion

The UNECA governance project, through the data collected via the three instruments I described, will provide a sound basis for monitoring progress in governance by providing information on the quality of governance in various countries as perceived by expert panels and scientifically selected representative samples of entire population. These hard, primary and current data are reinforced by factual information provided in the desk research segment. All three instruments, together, will provide a balanced and complete picture of the state of governance at the country, sub-regional and continental levels.

The specific outcomes from the outputs from the project are intended to include:

(1) monitoring progress in achieving good governance;
(2) identifying gap between policy, constitutional and other legal provisions and actual practice;
(3) identifying areas of governance regarded as particularly poor or lacking;
(4) identifying capacity needs;
(5) sharing country experience and best practices; and
(6) contributing to the realisation of the objects of the NEPAD with respect to consolidating good political, economic and corporate governance on the African continent.

ANNEX 1

Countries in the UNECA Governance Survey

Phase I		*Phase II*		*Phase III*	
No.	*Country*	*No.*	*Country*	*No.*	*Country*
1.	Benin	1	Burkina Faso	1	Cameroon
2	Botswana	2	Cote d'Ivoire[1]	2	Chad
3	Ghana	3	Gabon	3	Morocco
4	Kenya	4	The Gambia	4	Mozambique
5	Malawi	5	Egypt	5	Niger
6	Mali	6	Ethiopia	6	Rwanda
7	Nambia	7	Lesotho		
8	Nigeria	8	Mauritius		
9	Senegal	9	Swaziland		
10	South Africa	10	Zambia		
11	Tanzania				
12	Uganda				

1. The appointed institution in Cote d'Ivoire has advised that it may not be able to implement the project in that country because of the state of unrest there.

APPENDIX - III

Millennium Development Goals

Millennium Development Goals (MDGs): Goals and Targets Adopted by the United Nations, 2001

Goal 1: Eradicate extreme poverty and hunger

- Halve, between 1990 and 2015, the proportion of people whose income is less than $ 1 a day
- Halve, between 1990 and 2015, the proportion of people who suffer from hunger.

Goal 2: Achieve universal primary education

- Ensure that, by 2015, children everywhere, boys and girls alike, will be able to complete a full course of primary schooling.

Goal 3: Promote gender equality and empower women

- Eliminate gender disparity in primary and secondary education preferably by 2005 and in all levels of education no later than 2015.

Goal 4: Reduce child mortality

- Reduce by two-thirds, between 1990 and 2015, the under-five mortality rate.

Goal 5: Improve maternal health

- Reduce by three-quarters, between 1990 and 2015, the maternal mortality ratio.

Goal 6: Combat HIV/AIDS, malaria, and other diseases.

- Have halted by 2015 and begun to reverse the spread of HIV/AIDS
- Have halted by 2015 and begun to reverse the incidence of malaria and other major diseases.

Goal 7: Ensure environmental sustainability

- Integrate the principles of sustainable development into country policies and programmes and reverse the loss of environmental resources
- Halve by 2015, the proportion of people without sustainable access to safe drinking water
- Have achieved by 2020, a significant improvement in the lives of at least 100 million slum dwellers.

Goal 8: Develop a global partnership for develop-ment

- Develop further an open rule-based, predictable, nondiscriminatory trading and financial system (includes a commitment to good governance, development, and internationally)
- Address the special needs of the least developed countries (includes tariff- and quota-free access for exports, enhanced programme of debt relief for and cancellation of official bilateral debt, and more generous ODA for countries committed to poverty reduction)
- Address the special needs of landlocked countries and small island developing states (through the Programme of Action for the Sustainable Development of Small island Developing States and 22nd General Assembly provisions)
- Deal comprehensively with the debt problems of developing countries through national and international measures in order to make debt sustainable in the long term
- In cooperation with developing countries, develop and implement strategies for decent and productive work for youth

- In cooperation with pharmaceutical companies, provide access to affordable essential drugs in developing countries
- In cooperation with the private sector, make available the benefits of new technologies, especially information and communications technologies.

Source: Mini Atlas of Global Development, the World Bank, Washington, D.C. 2004.

Bibliography

Angang Hu, Public Exposure of Economic Losses Resulting from Corruption, 4, *China and World Economy*, 44, 44 (2002).

Bardhan, Pranab, Corruption and Development: A Review of Issues, 35, *J. Econ. Literature,* 1320, 1322 (1997).

Bhattacharya, C.B., Sankar Sen and Daniel Korschun (2008), "Using Corporate Social Responsibility to Win the War for Talent," *MIT Sloan Management Review,* 49 (2), 37-44.

Cynthia A., Ruth V. Aguilera (2008). "Corporate Social Responsibility in a Comparative Perspective (http://vww.business, uinc.edu/aguilera in Crane. A., et.al.: *The Oxford Handbook of Corporate Social Responsibility.* Oxford University Press.

Dick, Howard, *Corruption and Good Governance: The New Frontier of Social Engineering, in* Corruption in Asia: Rethinking the Governance Paradigm 71, 72 (Tim Lindsey & Howard Dick, eds., 2002).

Dignam, A. and Lowry, J. (2006) *Company Law*, Oxford University Press.

Ehrlich, Isaac & Francis T. Lui, Bureaucratic Corruption and Endogenous Economic Growth, 107(S6), *Journal of Political Economy*, 270, S271 (Dec. 1999).

Fan, C. Simon & Herschel I. Grossman, *Incentives and Corruption in Chinese Economic Reform* 3, March 2000.

Fan, Chengze Simon & Herschel I. Grossman, Entrepreneurial Graft in China, *Providence J.*, May 3, 2001.

Gillespie, Kate & Gwenn Okruhlik, The Political Dimensions of Corruption Cleanups: A Framework for Analysis, V. 24 No. 1, *Comparative Politics,* 77, 79, 1991.

Goodpaster, Gary, *Reflections on Corruption in Indonesia, in* Corruption in Asia: Rethinking the Governance Paradigm 87, 87 (Tim Lindsey & Howard Dick, eds., 2002).

Gray, R.H., D.L. Owen & K.T. Maunders, *Corporate Social Reporting: Accounting and accountability* (Hemel Hempstead: Prentice Hall, 1987).

Habisch, Andre; Jan Jonker, Martha Wegner, R. Schmidpeter (eds.) (2005), *Corporate Social Responsibility across Europe.* Heidelberg: Springer.

Hennock, Mary, *China's graft: Tough talk, old message,* BBC News Online, Sept. 24, 2004.

Hu Ping, *On Corruption with "Chinese Characteristics",* Association for Asian Research, Sept. 30, 2002.

Huntington, Samuel P., *Political Order in Changing Societies,* 69, 1-968.

Kaufman, Daniel, Corruption: The Facts, 107, *Foreign Policy,* 114, 115, 1997.

Kennedy, David, The International Anti-Corruption Campaign, 14, *Conn. J. Int. L.* 455, 455, 1999.

Kuncoro, Mudrajad, *Bribes, Regulatory Constraints, and Boosting Indonesian Exports,* Jakarta Post (Indonesia), Dec. 5, 2004.

Lederman, Loayza & Reis Scares, *Accountability and Corruption: Political Institutions Matter,* World Bank Working Paper No. 2708, 2001.

Levinson, Jared, Indonesia's Odyssey: A Nation's Long, Perilous Journey to the Rule of Law and Democracy, 18 Ariz. J., *Int. & Comp. L.* 103, 112 (2001).

Lindsey, Tim, History Always Repeats? Corruption, Culture and "Asian Values," in *Corruption in Asia: Rethinking The Governance Paradigm,* 1, 1 (Tim Lindsey & Howard Dick, eds., 2002).

Lindsey, Tim, Indonesia: Devaluing Asian Values, Rewriting Rule of Law, in *Asian Discourses of Rule of Law,* 286, 286 (Randall Peerenboom, ed., 2004).

Maoro, Paolo, The Effects of Corruption on Growth, Investment, and Government Expenditure: A Cross-Country Analysis, in

Corruption and the Global Economy, 83, 91 (Kimberly Ann Elliott, ed., 1997).

Mauro, Paolo, Corruption and Growth, Vol. 110, No. 3, *Q. J. Econ.*, 681 (1995).

Meisel, Nicolas, *Governance Culture and Development* (Paris: OECD Publishing, 2004).

Moore, Matthew, Investors Desert Indonesia as Root of Corruption Sets *in, Sydney Morning Herald* (Australia), Jan. 17, 2003.

Orlitzky, Marc, Frank L. Schmidt. Sara L. Rynes (2003). "Corporate Social and Financial Performance: A 24 (3): 403-41, London: SAGE Publications.

Peerenboom, Randall, Seek Truth from Facts: An Empirical Study of Enforcement of Arbitral Awards in the PRC, 49 *Am. J. Comp. L.* 249, 309 (2001).

Roy, Edward Van, *On the Theory of Corruption,* Vol. 19 No. 1, *Econ. Dev. & Cultural Change,* 86, 89 (1970).

Sasdi, Ardimas, *Govt Must Not Waver in its Battle Against Corruption,* Jakarta Post (Indonesia), March 16, 2005.

Shieifer, Andrei & Robert W. Vishny, Corruption, Vol. 108, No. 3, *Q. J. Econ.* 599, 610 (1993).

Werner, Simcha B., New Directions in the Study of Administrative Corruption, Vol. 43, No. 2, *Public Administration Research,* 146, 147, 1983.

Widoyoko, J. Danang, Awaiting the results of SBY antigraft campaign, *Jakarta Post* (Indonesia), Oct. 20, 2005.

World Bank, Corruption and Economic Development, Helping Countries Combat Corruption: The Role of the World Bank 8, 1997.

Yao, Shuntian, Privilege and Corruption: The Problems of China's Socialist Market Economy–New Perspectives on Transition Economics: Asia, Vol. 61, No. 1, *Am. Jl. of Econ. & Soc.* 279 (Jan. 2002).

Index

A

B

C

D

E

Y

Z

***